THE *SECOND* MAN

OTHER BOOKS BY MICHAEL DORMAN

We Shall Overcome
The Secret Service Story

THE *SECOND* MAN

❧❀❧

The Changing Role of the
Vice Presidency

❧❀❧

BY

MICHAEL DORMAN

DELACORTE PRESS · *NEW YORK*

For
Raye M. O'Brien and the late Darrin O'Brien,
two of my family's distinguished delegates
from the state that sent
Thomas Jefferson and John Tyler
to the Vice Presidency.

Contents

◈◈◈

Acknowledgments

THIS book was written at the suggestion of Miss Lee Hoffman. The author is indebted to her for her perception and for her practical suggestions on researching and writing the book.

Special thanks are due also to George M. Nicholson, Ross Claiborne, Jane Greenspan, and Dorothy Markinko for faith and counsel.

A number of public figures were kind enough to discuss the vice presidency with me—on and off the record—or to put me in touch with others who could provide valuable information. It would be impossible to list them all, and some asked specifically not to be identified. But I would like particularly to express my appreciation to Vice President Hubert H. Humphrey, the late Ambassador Adlai E. Stevenson, James A. Farley, Leonard W. Hall, and James C. Hagerty.

As always, I am indebted to my wife, Jeanne, and daughters, Pamela and Patricia, for cheerfully putting up with the rigors of life in a writer's household.

It goes without saying that this could not have been written without reference to numerous historical works. A list of those reference books that were most helpful is provided at the end of this book.

THE *SECOND* MAN

CHAPTER ONE

⋅⋙⋗⋅

A New Role

THE United States Senate adjourned shortly before 5 P.M.
on April 12, 1945.

It was a lazy spring day in Washington. President Franklin
Delano Roosevelt, who had led the nation out of the Depression and was now leading it through World War II, had been
vacationing in Warm Springs, Georgia, since March 30. The
Vice President, Harry S Truman, after presiding over the
Senate session, drifted into the office of House Speaker Sam
Rayburn of Texas. He and Rayburn had planned to have a
casual drink while discussing pending legislation and the domestic and world situations.

In Truman's eighty-two days as Vice President he had
played only a minor role in the Roosevelt administration. He
had attended the President's few Cabinet meetings, but his
advice had generally neither been sought nor offered. Aside
from the Cabinet meetings, Truman had conferred with
Roosevelt only twice since taking the oath of office.

Now, at 5:05 P.M. on April 12, a message awaited Truman
as he entered Rayburn's office.

"Steve Early just called and wants you to phone the White
House right away," Rayburn told him.

Truman immediately telephoned the White House and
asked for Early, the President's press secretary.

"Please come right over," Early said in a tense voice. "And
come in through the main Pennsylvania Avenue entrance."

It was 5:25 when Truman reached the White House. He
was immediately ushered into an elevator and taken to the

second-floor study of Mrs. Eleanor Roosevelt, the President's wife.

With Mrs. Roosevelt were Steve Early and two of the Roosevelt children—John, an Army colonel, and Mrs. Anna Roosevelt Boettiger. Mrs. Roosevelt, with her usual calm and dignity, stepped forward and put an arm gently around Truman's shoulder.

"Harry," she said softly, "the President is dead."

Truman was so shocked that he could not speak at first. Roosevelt plainly had been in failing health for months, but he had felt that a few weeks in Warm Springs would restore his health. However, while posing for a water-color portrait by artist Elizabeth Shoumatoff at his "Little White House," the President had suddenly exclaimed: "I have a terrific headache." Those were the last words of the man who was believed by some to be the greatest President of the twentieth century —and by others to be a political tyrant. He had suffered a massive cerebral hemorrhage. Two hours and thirty-five minutes after slumping into unconsciousness, he had breathed his last.

Upon hearing the news, Truman was close to tears. He felt totally unprepared for the tasks that lay ahead.

Truman had entered Mrs. Roosevelt's study as a little-known Vice President—a short, bespectacled former haberdasher whose career had been marked by a close association with the notorious Kansas City political machine of boss Tom Pendergast. He would leave the room as the thirty-third President of the United States.

At last finding his tongue, he asked Mrs. Roosevelt compassionately: "Is there anything I can do for you?"

Mrs. Roosevelt, whose own compassion was matched by her understanding of the tremendous burdens of the presidency, replied: "Is there anything *we* can do for *you?* For you are the one in trouble now."

Truly, Truman was in trouble. He felt—and justifiably so— that no vice president is ever adequately prepared for the presidency. It is an office that makes or breaks a man, unlike any other in the nation or, perhaps, in the world. Now, however, Truman rose to the occasion. He immediately assumed control and took pains to establish clearly that he was the President in fact as well as in name.

As the leaders of the government flocked to the White House—all showing equal anguish and determination—Truman arranged for Chief Justice of the United States Harlan Fiske Stone to administer the oath of office. Truman's wife, Bess, and daughter, Margaret, joined him after calling on Mrs. Roosevelt. With members of the Cabinet and leaders of Congress clustered around them in the Cabinet Room, Truman picked up a Bible, raised his right hand and followed Chief Justice Stone through the oath of office provided in the Constitution:

"I, Harry S Truman, do solemnly swear that I will faithfully execute the office of President of the United States, and will to the best of my ability preserve, protect and defend the Constitution of the United States."

It was 7:09 P.M., and the ceremony had lasted only a few moments.

Immediately afterwards, everyone but members of the Cabinet withdrew from the room. Except for Postmaster General Frank C. Walker, who was ill, the entire Cabinet was present for its first meeting under the new President.

As the meeting began, Steve Early entered to present Truman with his first major decision as President. The press wanted to know whether an international conference proposed for April 25 in San Francisco—a conference to plan the organization of the United Nations—would be conducted on schedule. Without hesitation Truman instructed Early to tell the press that he intended to go through with Roosevelt's plan. The conference would proceed on schedule.

After Early's departure, Truman told the Cabinet members that he hoped all of them would remain in office at least for the transitional period. He said he planned to carry forward

President Roosevelt's programs both at home and abroad. But he made it absolutely clear—if any doubt remained—that he considered himself President in his own right.

The new President urged his Cabinet members to offer their advice freely. He said that they could differ with him if they chose but that he expected their support once he had made a final policy decision. It was inevitable that some of the Cabinet members would be replaced, Truman felt. However, he needed all of them during the critical period of transition.

The Cabinet shifts came more quickly than had been expected. By mid-July, all but four of the ten Roosevelt Cabinet members would be gone.

When the meeting was over, all the Cabinet members except one filed from the room. The one who remained was the Secretary of War, Henry L. Stimson, a man highly esteemed for his record in directing the military effort that had brought the United States back from the brink of despair following the Japanese surprise attack on Pearl Harbor.

Stimson told the new President he wanted to discuss a matter of the greatest urgency. It concerned a project that until then had been kept completely secret even from Truman, one that would lead ultimately to the explosion of the world's first atomic bomb.

The project was so secret, in fact, that Stimson did not immediately tell Truman anything such as an A-bomb was being developed. He said merely that the project concerned an explosive of almost unbelievable destructive power.

This conversation, however, was to reshape the conception of the vice presidency. For Truman was shocked that he, as the second-ranking official in the government, had been kept totally unaware of one of the most important developments in the history of mankind—while lesser officials had known about it.

Almost immediately he formed the opinion that a vice president, from that time on, should play a greater role in the operations of the executive branch of the government. When he was elected to his own four-year term as President in 1948, he saw to it that his Vice President did become a new force in American political life.

And the trend begun by Truman was continued—even accelerated—by his successors in the White House and in the vice president's chair. Thus, today, we find the vice president of the United States holding a position that would have been unthinkable to the framers of the Constitution.

CHAPTER TWO

The Beginnings

To APPRECIATE the increased importance placed on the vice presidency in recent years, it is essential to understand the low esteem in which the office formerly was held.

For many years the vice presidency was the subject of scorn and ridicule. And among those who were most bitter in downgrading the office were some of the vice presidents themselves.

It was the first Vice President, John Adams, who made one of the most frequently quoted comments on the subject: "I am Vice President. In this, I am nothing." Not quoted so often is a sentence Adams added to his remarks—a sentence that proved prophetic: "But I may be everything."

Thomas Riley Marshall, Vice President under President Woodrow Wilson, made a number of pungent comments about the vice presidency. On one occasion he said: "Once there were two brothers. One ran away to sea; the other was elected Vice President. And nothing was ever heard of either of them again."

On another occasion Marshall remarked that the vice president is "like a man in a cataleptic fit; he cannot speak; he cannot move; he suffers no pain; he is perfectly conscious of all that goes on, but has no part in it."

John Nance Garner, the Vice President during Franklin D. Roosevelt's first two terms, once advised his fellow Texan, Lyndon B. Johnson: "The vice presidency isn't worth a pitcher of warm spit."

But men who held the office were not the only ones to demean the vice presidency. Benjamin Franklin said the vice president should always be addressed as "Your Superfluous Excellency." And author Finley Peter Dunne, speaking in dialect through his character "Mr. Dooley," commented: "Th' prisidincy is th' highest office in th' gift iv th' people. Th' vice prisidincy is th' next highest and th' lowest. It isn't a crime exactly. Ye can't be sint to jail f'r it, but it's kind iv a disgrace. It's like writin' anonyous letters."

Perhaps the most devastating description of a vice president ever offered was the one provided in the satirical Broadway musical *Of Thee I Sing*. The play featured Victor Moore in the role of a fictitious Vice President named Alexander Throttlebottom. Nobody in the play could ever seem to remember Throttlebottom's name. He was at first hesitant about accepting the vice-presidential nomination for fear that his mother would hear about it. Throttlebottom spent his time as Vice President feeding pigeons in a park and trying to find two persons who would serve as references for him so that he could get a library card.

Curiously enough, in view of the later disrespect shown the office, the vice presidency was originally designed to be occupied by extremely capable men. Creation of the position was one of the great afterthoughts of the Constitutional Convention of 1787.

During the convention a dispute arose over whether the President of the United States should be chosen by popular election or legislative election. A committee whose leading members were Rufus King and Gouverneur Morris, both of New York, proposed creation of the vice presidency as part of a package that provided the Electoral College compromise to settle the dispute over the method of electing the president. Bitter debate surrounded the proposal. Many delegates to the convention argued that the proposed vice president's role as presiding officer of the Senate would violate the doctrine of separation of powers between the executive and legislative branches of government and would lead ultimately to a parliamentary system.

The opposition to the creation of the vice presidency was led by a delegate from Massachusetts, Elbridge Gerry. He argued that the office was unnecessary and that the violation of the separation of powers would prove an additional burden. Gerry eventually became one of three delegates who refused to sign the document. His opposition to the role of the vice president as presiding officer of the Senate may have been the crucial issue in his rejection of the Constitution. However, Gerry himself later became a Vice President.

As first conceived, the vice presidency was a weak office— but one expected to attract superior men. The Constitution did not originally provide for separate votes for president and vice president. Instead, members of the Electoral College were permitted to vote for two persons for president, "of whom one at least shall not be an inhabitant of the same state with themselves."

An elector was not permitted to indicate which of his votes was for president and which was for vice president. When all the votes were in, the person who had received the highest number of electoral votes was designated as president and the runner-up became vice president.

Under this system, it was presumed, the second most qualified man in the country would become the vice president and the heir apparent to the presidency. In the first years of the new nation, matters worked out the way the framers of the Constitution had planned. But it quickly became clear that truly able men would find it hard to accept the rigid confines of the vice presidency. For the authors of the Constitution had assigned only meager duties to the office. The vice president was empowered merely to preside over the Senate and to cast a vote in that body in case of a tie.

It was little wonder that the nation's first Vice President would complain: "My country has in its wisdom contrived for me the most insignificant office that ever the invention of man contrived or his imagination conceived."

The first Vice President was, of course, John Adams. A native of Braintree, Massachusetts, Adams was one of the leading patriots of the Revolutionary period—a member of the Continental Congress and a signer of the Declaration of Independence. Because of his firm belief in protecting the rights of unpopular defendants, he resisted great pressures and conducted a successful defense as the lawyer for a group of British soldiers accused of participating in the infamous Boston Massacre.

Despite criticism of his role in the trial, Adams became a popular figure throughout the original thirteen states. He performed a number of sensitive diplomatic missions on behalf of the revolutionary government.

In 1789 the new nation conducted its first election for president and vice president. It was widely assumed that General George Washington would be elected President. Adams was generally considered the Federalist candidate for Vice President.

But another Federalist, Alexander Hamilton, contrived to prevent Adams from winning an impressive total of electoral votes. Hamilton hoped to be elected President after Washington had completed his term in office. By keeping Adams' electoral vote as low as possible, he felt he could make it appear that Adams lacked general popularity. In this way he hoped to reduce the chances of Adams' later election as a successor to Washington. Hamilton urged a number of members of the Electoral College not to vote for Adams, arguing that it would be inappropriate for Adams' vote to rival the total given Washington.

As a result, Washington received one vote from each of the sixty-nine members of the Electoral College. Only thirty-four of the electors—less than half—gave their second votes to Adams. The remaining votes were divided among ten other candidates.

Thus, although elected Vice President, Adams was so embarrassed that he wrote to a friend:

> "Is not my election to this office, in the scurvy manner in which it was done, a curse rather than a blessing? Is this justice? Is there common sense or decency in this business? Is it not an indelible stain on our country, countrymen and Constitution? I assure you I think it so, and nothing but an apprehension of great mischief, and final failure of the government from my refusal, prevented me from spurning it."

Nonetheless, Adams performed diligently as Vice President. Although Hamilton served as Washington's Secretary of the Treasury and became the chief spokesman for the Federalist position, Adams remained loyal to the Federalists. In presiding over the Senate, he initially tended to lecture the members and to join in their debates. But the senators did not appreciate these efforts, and the entire Pennsylvania congressional delegation once went as far as to suggest acidly that "it might be as well to vest the whole senatorial power in the president of the Senate." Thus, in later years, Adams played a more passive role. He did, however, cast twenty-nine tie-breaking votes—setting a record never matched by any of the vice presidents who followed. One of these votes established the precedent upholding the president's right to remove an appointee without obtaining the consent of the Senate.

Adams was also criticized early in his term for devoting too much attention to the niceties of governmental etiquette. Some detractors even accused him—probably unfairly—of representing the very monarchist tradition that the revolutionists had just fought a war to escape. This opinion was spurred by Adams' insistence on having the Senate debate for hours the matter of proper ways to address the president and vice president. Should the president be referred to as "His Majesty," or "His Highness," or "His Elective Highness," or by some other elegant term? A number of senators considered the debate both a waste of time and an indication of Adams' supposed monarchist leaning. And when Adams raised the further question of how he himself should be addressed, several senators commented privately—with reference to his rather stout build—that he should be called "His Rotundity."

Adams was aware of these sarcastic remarks. He was also aware that he had a reputation—which he regarded as unfortunate but accurate—for being an extremely vain man. He tried to curb this vanity and succeeded well enough to prevent the trait from interfering markedly with his ability to help push Washington's programs through the Senate.

Washington, who had promised his Vice President "perfect sincerity . . . and full confidence," kept his word. When he was reelected in 1792, Adams was also elected to a second term.

Washington's Secretary of State from 1789 until 1793 was Thomas Jefferson, the brilliant lawyer who had been chairman of the committee that drafted the Declaration of Independence. Jefferson had also served as governor of Virginia, as a member of Congress and as minister to France.

When national political parties began to emerge during Washington's Presidency, Jefferson became the leader of the Anti-Federalists. His party was known by a number of names. At times it was called the Anti-Federalist Party, at other times the Jeffersonian Democratic Party. Later its members in the South called themselves Republicans, while those in the North called themselves Democrats. Many used the hyphenated name Democratic-Republicans. Whatever its name, this party was the forerunner of what we know today as the Democratic Party. The Democratic-Republicans advocated "equilibrium" between the federal government and the states. The rival Federalist Party, with Hamilton as a sort of early-day political boss, supported a strong central government as a check against an "excess of democracy."

In September, 1796, Washington announced that he would not seek a third term. Adams was the natural choice of the Federalists to run for the presidency. The Federalist candidate for Vice President was Thomas Pinckney, a wealthy South

Carolinian best known for negotiating a treaty with Spain that opened the Mississippi River to American navigation.

The Democratic-Republicans supported Jefferson for President and Aaron Burr, a New York lawyer who had served with honor in the Revolutionary army, for Vice President. Foreign affairs played an important part in the election campaign. The French government, bitter at the Federalists over the Jay Treaty (a commercial treaty between the United States and England), poured money and propaganda into the U. S. on behalf of Jefferson.

The Federalist members of the Electoral College held a majority—seemingly assuring the Adams-Pinckney ticket of election. But, once again, Alexander Hamilton got involved in some complicated behind-the-scenes machinations. And this time his plans went awry.

Taking note of the constitutional gap that barred electors from specifying which of their two votes was for president and which was for vice president, Hamilton set about trying to frustrate the public will. He considered Adams too independent to take orders but felt he could control Pinckney. So he concocted a plot to elect Pinckney—rather than Adams—President.

Hamilton asked South Carolina's electors to vote for Pinckney but to cast their second votes for someone other than Adams. At the same time he urged electors in the North to cast their votes for both Adams and Pinckney. The result, if successful, would have been to make Pinckney President and Adams Vice President.

But Federalists loyal to Adams learned of Hamilton's scheme and took steps to counteract it. They arranged for a number of New England electors to vote for Adams and to throw away their second votes on some other candidate.

As a result, Adams won the presidency with 71 electoral votes. But Pinckney fell short of the vice presidency with only 59. The second-highest number of electoral votes was won by the Democratic-Republican candidate for President, Jefferson, with 68. (Burr got thirty electoral votes.) Therefore, Jefferson became Vice President. The nation was confronted with a President from one party and a Vice President from another.

There were personal and philosophical—as well as political —differences between the President and Vice President. Adams had been humiliated by receiving only three electoral votes more than his opponent. His control of the government was shaky at best.

Adams considered Jefferson's belief in the goodness of human nature to be juvenile. He felt that men were creatures of passion and that it was up to the government to keep them from exploiting each other and creating upheaval in the social order. Adams believed that any legislative body would contain members with defects of character, so he was determined to have the executive branch exert effective checks and balances on the Congress. Only in this way, he insisted, could reason triumph over passion and could the public interest be served.

Moreover, Adams lacked Jefferson's way with people. He was suspicious of those around him and almost totally lacking in tact. He had a sharp temper and a biting tongue. Although he retained members of Washington's Cabinet, they soon became disenchanted with him. They and other Federalists began looking to Hamilton rather than Adams for instructions.

Adams and Jefferson also differed over foreign policy. Following the French Revolution, France went to war with England. Opinion in the United States was divided over the European war, with many Americans favoring each side. Adams and most Federalists were pro-English. Jefferson was pro-French.

Under terms of the Jay Treaty, a commercial treaty signed with England in 1795, the British were permitted to seize American provision ships bound for France on the condition that they pay for the cargoes. The French objected strenuously to having their chief source of supply endangered. In retaliation the French recalled their minister to the United

States and announced that all goods destined for England would be considered war contraband.

U. S.-French relations continued to deteriorate, and Congress began to prepare for war. The army was increased—with Washington and Hamilton, among others, appointed generals —and a Navy Department was organized. For the next two and a half years the United States and France engaged in an undeclared naval war. Each country seized a number of merchant ships belonging to the other. Finally, a pact known as the Convention of 1800 put a halt to the hostilities. (Adams considered the Convention of 1800 so important that he had mention of it made on his tombstone.) Before the Convention was signed, however, Adams used the danger of war to push through Congress the controversial Alien and Sedition Acts.

Adams and other Federalists had been looking for an opportunity to silence newspapers that supported Jefferson's Democratic-Republicans. Some of the papers, edited by French citizens, had been especially bitter in their criticism of the Federalists, and the Federalists used the Alien and Sedition Acts to force these papers out of business.

The Alien Law gave the president authority to banish foreigners from the country. The Sedition Law made it a crime to try to stir up discontent against the government or to libel the president, a member of Congress or a Supreme Court justice. (It did not, however, mention the vice president— thus presumably permitting newspapers to libel Jefferson with impunity.) The Alien Law was never put to use, but a number of foreigners fled the country for fear of action against them. The Sedition Law was used to stifle any criticism of the president, no matter how inconsequential. Under its provisions, the Federalists arrested twenty-five persons—including the editors of the four most influential pro-Jefferson papers in the country.

Jefferson and the Democratic-Republicans argued that the Alien and Sedition Acts were unconstitutional. The Federalists defended the laws but became increasingly disenchanted with Adams. The rift in the President's party was widened in the election year of 1800 when Adams forced Hamilton's friends in the Cabinet to resign.

The election of 1800 brought about an important change in the law relating to election of presidents and vice presidents. As the incumbent, despite criticism from within his own party, Adams was the candidate of the Federalists. His running mate was again named Pinckney—not Thomas this time, but his brother, Charles C. Pinckney, a diplomat. The Democratic-Republican candidates once again were Jefferson and Burr.

This time, however, Hamilton was openly outspoken in his opposition to Adams. The factional battle within the Federalist Party led to Adams' defeat. But the Democratic-Republicans, tasting their first major victory, had it soured by the circumstances of the triumph. The same flaw in the Constitution that had made Jefferson the Vice President under Adams now came back to haunt Jefferson himself.

Jefferson and Burr each received the same number of electoral votes, 73, with Adams getting 65, and Pinckney 64 and John Jay 1. Since the electors had not been able to designate which of the candidates they supported for president, Jefferson and Burr were tied for the presidency. The Constitution provided for such a tie to be broken by a vote in the House of Representatives, with each of the then sixteen states entitled to cast one ballot and a majority of the states required for victory.

Once more Hamilton tried to capitalize on the situation. He seized the chance to drive a wedge between the followers of Jefferson and Burr, hoping to create chaos in the Democratic-Republican Party. Hamilton wanted to tease Burr into thinking that the Federalists would help elect him president and then to throw the election to Jefferson at the last minute.

While no admirer of Jefferson, Hamilton considered him far superior to Burr. He had long detested Burr, regarding him as a man without principles. Hamilton hoped, through his machinations, to win concessions from Jefferson—including adoption of the Hamilton fiscal program.

Thus, after trying to lure Burr into a belief that he might be elected President, Hamilton threw his weight behind Jefferson. "I trust the Federalists will not finally be so mad as to vote for Burr," he wrote. "I speak with an intimate and accurate knowledge of his character. His elevation can only promote the purposes of the desperate and profligate."

For all his meddling, Hamilton failed in several of his purposes. It was not the Democratic-Republicans but the Federalists who were chiefly split by the dispute. Many of them made a determined attempt to elect Burr to the presidency. Moreover, Hamilton's hopes for concessions from Jefferson were short-lived.

"I would not receive the government on capitulation," Jefferson said. "I would not go into it with my hands tied."

The voting in the House dragged on for a week, with neither man able to receive a majority. Meanwhile, reports filtered into Washington that civil war might erupt if Jefferson were denied the presidency. The militias in the Democratic-Republican states were said to be prepared to march on Washington if Burr was elected.

A practical, if not altogether satisfactory, solution ultimately was found. On the 36th ballot several of the Federalists abstained, feeling that was better than switching their votes to Jefferson. The abstentions was enough to allow Jefferson to be elected President and to make Burr Vice President.

Two weeks later Jefferson and Burr were inaugurated. Their inaugurations were the first conducted in Washington, where the Capitol was only half built and Pennsylvania Avenue was merely a mile-long stretch of mud. John Adams was so humiliated and angry over his defeat for reelection that he refused to accompany Jefferson to the inauguration, becoming the only outgoing President who would ever do so.

The tie vote between Jefferson and Burr, combined with the

realization that political parties (the appearance of which had not been contemplated by the framers of the Constitution) were here to stay, persuaded the country's political leaders that immediate steps were necessary to close the constitutional loophole regarding election of the president and vice president. As a result, the Twelfth Amendment to the Constitution was proposed.

The proposed amendment provided for members of the Electoral College to "name in their ballots the person voted for as President and in distinct ballots the person voted for as Vice President." Curiously enough, such a system of separate ballots for president and vice president was opposed by some of the men who had originally fought for creation of the vice presidency.

Gouverneur Morris, who had led the campaign to create the office, said of the proposed amendment that "it might be better to abolish the office of vice president and leave to legislative provision" the question of replacing a president who died or otherwise left office before the end of his term. Morris warned that approval of the Twelfth Amendment would make the vice presidency "but a bait to catch state gudgeons."

He certainly was right about the vice presidency becoming vote-bait in future nominating conventions and elections. But, nonetheless, the amendment was approved—providing for separate balloting for president and vice president in the 1804 election.

❧❦❧

CHAPTER THREE

Aaron Burr and the Troubles

THE vice presidency could have opened vast opportunities to Aaron Burr. Only forty-four at the time of his election —a handsome man with a distinguished air—he was expected by many to follow the road of Adams and Jefferson to the presidency. Burr performed his duties in presiding over the Senate in an exemplary fashion. Some said he was among the best presiding officers in the Senate's history.

But Burr's vice presidency was to be perhaps the most bizarre in the history of the office. Several factors worked against him. First, there were the circumstances of Burr's election and the President's distrust of him. Second, there was Burr's own resentment of the way he was subsequently treated by Jefferson. Third, the most important, there was an incident that forever would cloud Burr's name.

Because of his suspicion of Burr, Jefferson refused to bring the Vice President into the inner workings of the government. In addition, he ignored Burr's counsel in the handing out of patronage jobs.

Burr, stung by these rebuffs, retaliated by opposing some of Jefferson's pet programs. On one occasion, when a key Jefferson judiciary bill resulted in a tie vote in the Senate, Burr broke the tie by voting against the legislation. Such actions prompted Jefferson to describe his Vice President as "a crooked gun whose aim you could never be sure of."

Burr soon became convinced that he would be dropped from the national ticket when Jefferson ran for reelection in

1804. But his ambition was undiminished. He knew he must find some other position of power if he were to remain in the national eye. He decided to seek the governorship of New York.

Although Jefferson refused to support him, Burr went through with his plan to run for governor—even against the opposition of his own party. He ran as an independent, with the support of some Federalists.

Once again Burr's chief critic was his old adversary, Alexander Hamilton. Although he had lost some of his old power among the Federalists, Hamilton still proved an influential political force. Burr lost the election. While he still had part of his term as Vice President to serve, he was beset by troubles —political, personal and financial. He was virtually bankrupt, and creditors were threatening to seize his New York home.

During a period of despondency and self-pity, Burr learned of several inflammatory statements made about him by Hamilton. For many years Hamilton had been highly critical of Burr in letters to friends and political allies. Then, during a private dinner, Hamilton had become even more outspoken than usual. Another guest at the dinner, anxious to embarrass Burr, carefully noted Hamilton's remarks. He then wrote two letters describing Hamilton's comments about the Vice President. Both letters were published in a newspaper in Albany, New York.

Hamilton was described in the letters as having referred to Burr as untrustworthy and dangerous. Moreover, there were hints that "a still more despicable opinion"—presumably too scandalous even to be published in the newspaper—had been voiced by Hamilton.

The letters were called to Burr's attention. After his defeat in the New York gubernatorial race, he wrote a letter to Hamilton and had it delivered by a friend. Although the letter was phrased in genteel language, it carried an undeniable challenge.

Burr's letter said:

Sir,

I send for your perusal a letter signed Charles D. Cooper, which, though apparently published some time ago, has but very recently come to my knowledge. Mr. Van Ness, who does me the favour to deliver this, will point out to you that clause of the letter to which I particularly request your attention. You must perceive, sir, the necessity of a prompt and unqualified acknowledgement or denial of the use of any expression which would warrant the assertions of Mr. Cooper. I have the honour to be

Your obedient servant.

A. Burr

Hamilton immediately recognized the seriousness of the situation. In those days Burr's letter could mean only one thing —back down or face a duel. Hamilton had no desire to bring about a duel. He tried over a period of two weeks to postpone the inevitable, carrying on a steady correspondence with Burr. Hamilton sought to shrug off the statements attributed to him as mere campaign oratory, saying he hoped Burr "on more reflection" would leave the matter at that. "If not," he wrote, "I can only regret the circumstance and must abide the consequence."

The result was that the Vice President challenged Hamilton to a duel. The challenge was reluctantly accepted.

Arrangements were made for the duel to be fought the morning of July 11, 1804, on the west bank of the Hudson River at Weehawken, New Jersey. The Vice President and his second, as previously agreed, arrived on the scene first. Shortly before 7 A.M., Hamilton arrived with his second and a physician. Burr and his second, in their shirt sleeves, were already clearing away shrubbery to make room for the duel.

The rules were explained. They provided:

The parties being placed at their stations, the second who gives the word shall ask them whether they are ready. Being answered in the affirmative, he shall say "present." After this, the parties shall present and fire when they please. If one fires before the other, the opposite second shall say "one, two, three, fire." The other party shall then fire or lose his fire.

Hamilton and Burr took their places and stepped off the designated ten paces. Hamilton's second, who had been assigned to "give the word," asked if they were ready. Each said he was.

"Present," the second ordered.

Each man raised his gun. Two shots rang out.

Hamilton fell, a bullet wound in his right side.

Burr walked to Hamilton's side, made a gesture indicating he regretted having wounded his old enemy, then turned without a word and withdrew.

The physician hurried to Hamilton's side. Hamilton muttered: "This is a mortal wound, Doctor." Hamilton was carried to the boat, which immediately set off for the coast of Manhattan. In the boat Hamilton awakened briefly and told the doctor: "Pendleton (his second) knows that I did not intend to fire at him (Burr)."

The next day Hamilton died. A controversy has raged through the years over whether Hamilton actually did fire at Burr or did intend to fire at him. His gun did go off, but some of the witnesses said this happened only after Burr's shot had wounded him.

Dueling was illegal in New York and New Jersey, although the laws against it were frequently broken in both states. After prominent Federalists brought pressure for Burr's prosecution, he was indicted on murder charges in New York, where the duel had been arranged, and in New Jersey, where it had been fought. Burr fled and remained on the move for a time. But then—in an act so bold that it was hard for many of his contemporaries to believe—he returned to Washington and resumed his duties as Vice President.

Burr's arrogance moved Senator William Plumer of New Hampshire to comment that it was the first time "God grant that it be the last, that ever a man indicted for murder presided in the American Senate. We are indeed fallen on evil times. The high office of President is filled by an infidel; that of Vice President by a murderer."

Strangely enough, it was during his final few weeks as a lame-duck Vice President—with the cloud of the murder indictment hanging over him—that Aaron Burr played perhaps his most important role in public office.

President Jefferson had been carrying on a running battle with the federal courts, which were mostly in the hands of Federalist judges. In a landmark decision in the case of Marbury v. Madison, the Supreme Court had ruled in 1803 that it had the authority to declare an act of Congress unconstitutional. Jefferson felt that the states should have this power.

If he could have found an excuse, Jefferson would have liked to remove Chief Justice John Marshall from the Supreme Court. But Marshall, although incurring Jefferson's displeasure, had done nothing to warrant being ousted. On the other hand, the President felt there were legitimate grounds for impeaching Associate Justice Samuel Chase.

The Constitution provided that judges were to hold office during their "good behavior." By Jefferson's standards, the behavior of Chase had been far from good. An ardent Federalist, Chase had made intemperate remarks about the Democratic-Republicans both in public and in private. While instructing a grand jury in Baltimore, he had delivered a lengthy harangue on what he considered the evils of democracy in general and the Democratic-Republicans in particular. Chase had told the jury that giving the vote to the common man would "rapidly destroy all protection to property."

At Jefferson's urging, Congressman John Randolph of Roanoke, Virginia, engineered a drive in the House to impeach Chase. The House ultimately voted for impeachment. This, under the Constitution, did not remove Chase from the Court. It merely set the stage for his trial in the Senate.

And who would preside at the trial? None other than the Vice President of the United States, Aaron Burr.

Jefferson, who had snubbed his Vice President since their inauguration, now sought to curry favor with Burr. He realized that the presiding officer of the Senate could play a major role in determining the outcome of the impeachment trial.

The President invited Burr to pay a social visit. He saw to it that the Vice President's stepson was appointed to a federal court bench in New Orleans and that Burr's brother-in-law was named Secretary of the Louisiana Territory. Burr was not impressed.

He presided over the impeachment trial with such fairness and skill that even some of his worst enemies were moved to praise his performance. Chase was found innocent.

Burr made his last appearance before the Senate in a closed session on March 2, 1805. It was a highly emotional event. Burr delivered a moving farewell address in which he apologized for any embarrassment the slaying of Hamilton might have brought the senators. He appealed to them to maintain always the dignity of the Senate—the very dignity that the duel had called into question.

"This house, I need not remind you, is a sanctuary—a citadel of law, of order and of liberty," Burr said. "And here will resistance be made to the storms of political frenzy and the silent acts of corruption."

Despite his flash of statesmanship in the waning days of his vice-presidential term, Burr soon reverted to previous form. He turned up in the western wilderness with a band of adventurers and embarked on a series of questionable projects. One of his schemes purportedly involved a plot to invade Mexico. Another, in which he was said to have made secret contact with Napoleon, supposedly involved a planned attack on Boston.

Word leaked out, however, and Burr was captured. He was taken to Richmond, Virginia, for a trial before Chief Justice Marshall on treason charges. Jefferson confidently told Congress that there was "no doubt" of his guilt.

But there were holes in the government's case. For one thing, Burr's chief accuser, Army General James Wilkinson, did not come to court with clean hands himself.

Wilkinson had long been secretly in the pay of the Spanish government. In addition, he had apparently violated the law by shipping Burr and two other alleged conspirators back to Virginia in defiance of civil-court orders.

Burr's trial was filled with high drama and legal significance. At Burr's insistence, Chief Justice Marshall issued a subpoena for Jefferson to appear in court with certain documents considered necessary for the defense.

Jefferson responded that the executive branch of the government would be made subordinate to the judiciary if the president "were subject to the demands of the latter and to imprisonment for disobedience, if the several courts could bandy him from pillar to post and withdraw him from his constitutional duties."

Burr demanded that Jefferson be held in contempt of court, but Marshall dropped the whole matter. Ever since, there has been no serious question about presidential immunity from witness duty.

In the end, Burr was found innocent on technical grounds —but his name was never really cleared. He later went into a self-imposed exile in Europe, then returned to New York and practiced law. He died in 1836 at the age of eighty.

Aaron Burr's vice-presidential career had a profound effect on the history of the office. Not only did his tie election with Jefferson bring about passage of the Twelfth Amendment; his behavior after the election may well have helped prompt political leaders to change their concept of the kind of man who should occupy the vice presidency. At any rate, there was a sharp decline in the caliber of men considered logical choices for the vice presidency. As Gouverneur Morris had predicted, the vice-presidential office became vote-bait.

It was used primarily to balance the ticket—both geographically and philosophically (later even religiously). A presidential candidate from the East would be balanced by a vice-presidential candidate from the West. A liberal would be balanced with a conservative. And, in some cases, the vice-presidential nomination would be handed out as a sop to a candidate from a state with a large number of electoral votes —in the hope of insuring that state's votes during the election.

Burr's successor was typical of the breed of politicians who would occupy the office for close to a century. When Jefferson decided to run for a second term in 1804, Governor George Clinton of New York was selected as his running mate.

In his time Clinton had been an outstanding public servant. The first governor of New York, he had been elected to that office six times in a row. He had also been an unsuccessful candidate for Vice President in 1788 and 1792. But by the time he was elected Vice President, he had grown old, ill, cranky and ineffectual. Northern Democratic-Republicans had persuaded him to become Jefferson's running mate in order to prevent a "Virginia dynasty" from capturing long-term control of the White House. Their theory was that, after Jefferson's second term, Clinton would be the party's presidential nominee in 1808. Members of the Virginia wing of the party had no objections to Clinton's vice-presidential nomination. They felt just such a Northerner was needed to balance the ticket. And they recognized that Clinton, who would be sixty-nine years of age by the time of the 1808 election, would be considered too old for the presidential nomination.

The fact was that Clinton was already too old to perform his duties satisfactorily when elected Vice President. He committed absurd errors in presiding over the Senate—such as miscounting members' votes and appointing several committees to perform identical functions. Senator John Quincy Adams of Massachusetts, son of the first Vice President, described Clinton as "totally ignorant of the most common forms of proceeding" in the Senate. "As the only duty of a Vice President . . . is to preside in the Senate, it ought to be considered what his qualifications for that office are at his election," Adams said. "In this respect, a worse choice than Mr. Clinton could scarcely have been made."

Clinton eventually spent increasing amounts of time away from the Senate. He whiled away much of his time at his boarding house. Nonetheless, when Jefferson decided in 1808 not to seek a third term, Clinton made it clear that he would like to step up to the Presidency. His hopes were dashed. The Democratic-Republicans considered him too old and, though they did not say so publicly, too much of a bumbler for the top office in the land. The presidential nomination went to James Madison. As a consolation prize, Clinton was nominated once again for Vice President.

Madison and Clinton were both elected but became bitter enemies. Clinton started his second term by refusing to attend Madison's inauguration, then went on to criticize many of the President's policies. He died in office in 1812 at the age of seventy-two. For the first time—but far from the last—the nation was left without a vice president.

The office did not remain vacant long, since 1812 was an election year. Madison was reelected. Because he was a Virginian, his nomination was balanced once again with the selection of a northerner for Vice President. The northerner was another governor, Elbridge Gerry of Massachusetts. Gerry, it will be recalled, had refused to sign the Constitution in part because he felt the provision that the vice president would preside over the Senate posed a threat to the legislative branch.

Although he had served with distinction as governor, Gerry became best known for his invention of a political device that made his name immortal. Gerry's invention was the manipulation of election-district lines to favor the party in power. He drew up a legislative district shaped like a salamander, so that Democratic-Republican votes in one Massachusetts city could more than outweigh the Federalist pluralities in numerous smaller towns. In honor (if that can be called the word) of both Gerry and the salamander this questionable practice later came to be called the gerrymander, a word coined from Gerry's name and the salamander-shaped district he originated. It became widespread and is still practiced today.

Gerry's vice presidency was brief and lackluster. Within three months of the inauguration Madison became seriously ill with a liver ailment. It was thought for a time that he might even die. The prospect of seeing Gerry elevated to the presidency filled many observers of the national scene with dread. Their attitude was summed up by France's minister to Washington, Louis Serieur. "The thought of Madison's possible loss strikes everybody with consternation. His death would be a veritable national calamity. The President who would succeed him for three and a half years is a respectable old man, but weak and worn-out."

These fears proved unfounded. Madison recovered. It was Gerry who did not live to serve out his term. Less than two years after his election, he collapsed in his coach while riding to the Senate and died at the age of seventy. Madison thus became the only President in the nation's history to see two of his Vice Presidents die in office. The vacancy left by Gerry's death took on added significance because the country was engaged in the War of 1812 at the time. Madison played a personal role in the defense of Washington against the British and several times risked death or capture. In the absence of a vice president, if Madison had been killed or captured, his duties would have been assumed by Senate President Pro Tem John Gaillard of South Carolina.

Fortunately, though he had some close shaves, Madison remained out of harm's way. In 1816 he continued the tradition of refusing to seek a third term. The Democratic-Republicans nominated as his successor James Monroe, who had studied law with Jefferson and later served as governor of Virginia, as a Senator and as Madison's Secretary of State and Secretary of War.

Having seen two successive vice presidents die in office, the Democratic-Republicans decided this time to choose a younger man. Again the nominee was a governor from New York, Daniel D. Tompkins. Although only forty-two when elected Vice President, Tompkins had already served as a member of the New York Legislature, as a Congressman and as a judge of the New York State Supreme Court before becoming governor.

During the War of 1812, Tompkins had been given an important military assignment covering parts of New York and New Jersey. To pay the twenty thousand men under his command, he had borrowed heavily against his personal credit and withdrawn large sums from the New York State Treasury. Unfortunately he had failed to keep track of where the money had gone.

After his election as Vice President, Tompkins was called upon to produce records of the numerous transactions in which he had been involved. He was unable to do so. As a result, although he served eight years as Vice President, he was away from Washington for long periods—trying to clear the cloud from his name. He never fully succeeded. While the matter was in dispute, he was not even paid his $5,000 yearly salary as Vice President. Eventually, Congress agreed to pay Tompkins $95,000 of the $660,000 he claimed he had spent from his own funds to support the war effort. But even after Congress approved the settlement, Tompkins' reputation remained in question.

A broken man, Tompkins died only three months after leaving the Vice Presidency. Elected largely because of his youth, he did not live to see his fifty-first birthday.

There were those who feared some sort of jinx had been placed on the vice presidency. These fears would be compounded by events that lay just over the horizon.

❦

CHAPTER FOUR

The Days of Coalition

D URING James Monroe's second term as President, the Democratic-Republican Party split into a number of factions. From the ruins emerged the Democratic Party that has survived to the present day.

The first leader of the new party was Andrew Jackson, a roughhewn man who spent much of his early life carousing and gambling, then became a national military hero. Jackson's hero status stemmed from his service as commanding general of the troops who defeated the British in the Battle of New Orleans. Though the battle was fought well after the Treaty of Ghent had officially ended the War of 1812, many Americans mistakenly considered him "the general who won the war." A native of South Carolina, Jackson had moved to Tennessee as a young man, served as a member of the state Supreme Court and as a member of Congress.

In 1824 Jackson became a surprise contender for the Presidency. But three other former members of the old Democratic-Republican Party—all of whom had served in Monroe's Cabinet—also were considered major contenders. They were John Quincy Adams, William H. Crawford of Georgia and John C. Calhoun of South Carolina. Also in the running was Henry Clay of Kentucky, the Speaker of the House.

From 1800 to 1824 a coalition between the Democratic-Republicans of New York and those of Virginia had been the most influential force in American politics. By custom, Virginia had been given the privilege of naming the presidential nominee and New York had been given the vice-presidential choice. But in 1824 this tidy arrangement fell apart. Rising sectionalism brought forth too many potential nominees for such a system to remain practical. It was only natural in these circumstances that much bargaining should develop among the potential nominees and their backers. Calhoun, who had served as Monroe's Secretary of War, was particularly active in the horse trading. Calhoun wanted to be President but sensed that the two leading contenders would be Jackson and Adams. In secret negotiations, Calhoun promised support to both men in return for their backing him as the vice-presidential candidate.

A deadlock developed in the Electoral College. Jackson, who led the field in the popular vote by 50,000 ballots, received 99 electoral votes. Adams got 84, Crawford 41 and Clay 37. Since no one had received a majority of the electoral votes, the House was left to decide among the top three candidates.

Clay, who had finished fourth and was thus ineligible for consideration in the House, threw his support to Adams. This touched off bitter charges of a "corrupt bargain" under which Adams purportedly had offered Clay the post of Secretary of State in return for his backing. The charges were neither proved nor disproved. But Clay's support was enough to give Adams the Presidency in the House balloting. And, upon becoming President, Adams did appoint Clay Secretary of State.

Calhoun, thwarted in his desire for the presidency, took second best. As Vice President, however, he presided over a Senate that included some of the most distinguished men ever to grace American political life. No fewer than four future Presidents—Jackson, Martin Van Buren, William Henry Harrison and John Tyler—were among them.

It soon became apparent to Calhoun that Jackson would be elected easily to the nation's top office in 1828. He quickly put himself in Jackson's corner. Hard feelings developed between Adams and his Vice President, but Calhoun did nothing to smooth the relationship. In fact, as presiding officer of the

Senate he sat silently and permitted Senators to deliver frequent, lengthy and vitriolic speeches against Adams.

The Jackson forces, while not particularly fond of Calhoun, recognized that he was the only logical threat to Jackson's presidential ambitions. He commanded support from all sections of the country. To neutralize the threat, Jackson supporters offered Calhoun another term as Vice President. They persuaded him that Jackson was ill, might die after serving only a short period as President, and was pledged not to seek a second term. Calhoun, envisioning himself as President by default, agreed to run with Jackson.

Adams, who should have seen the handwriting on the wall during the 1826 Congressional election when Jackson backers won control of the House, nonetheless ran for reelection. The result was a Jackson landslide. Jackson carried not only all of the South and West but also Pennsylvania and most of New York.

Calhoun settled back into his vice-presidential routine—seemingly content to let nature take its course. He was sure he would soon be President, either through Jackson's death or through election as Jackson's successor.

But fate had other plans. Jackson, far from dying, made a remarkable recovery from the illness that had previously plagued him. Like the frontiersman he was, he carried out his presidential duties with vigor and dispatch.

Those close to Jackson recognized that Calhoun had returned to the vice presidency only to advance his own interests, not to serve the President. Calhoun, for his part, decided that if he could not be President yet he would at least exert greater influence on the government than had previous vice presidents. He sought this influence through control of members of Jackson's Cabinet.

The Attorney General, the Secretary of the Treasury and the Secretary of the Navy were all in his camp. (The Postmaster General was not considered a significant force in the government.) But the remaining two Cabinet members, Secretary of State Martin Van Buren and Secretary of War John Eaton, were hardly Calhoun men.

Strangely enough, with all the pressing official matters looming for the new administration, it was a personal matter involving a woman that was to bring the power struggle within the Cabinet to a head. And it was this matter that was to provoke particularly bitter feelings between Jackson and his Vice President.

The woman involved was Peggy Timberlake Eaton, wife of the Secretary of War. Mrs. Eaton, a widow before her marriage to the Secretary, had been involved in a personal scandal. Eaton himself was a widower, whose first wife had been Jackson's ward.

When Jackson made clear his intention of appointing Eaton to the Cabinet, a storm of protest arose in Washington. Calhoun went to Jackson and warned that the public would not accept the appointment because of the supposed scandal involving Mrs. Eaton. But Jackson was adamant. He gathered that it was the society matrons of Washington who objected to Mrs. Eaton. Still, Calhoun persisted.

Jackson raged at him: "Do you suppose that I have been sent here by the people to consult the ladies of Washington as to the proper persons to compose my Cabinet?"

Despite the objections of Calhoun and others, Eaton was appointed. His wife tried to carry out her role as a Washington hostess just as if no breath of scandal had ever touched her. But her troubles continued to mount. She was young, attractive and captivating. Men found her charming. Women, as might have been expected, resented her all the more because of her popularity among the men.

In keeping with the prevailing custom, Mrs. Eaton paid a courtesy call on Mrs. Calhoun. It was a disaster. The Vice President's wife treated Mrs. Eaton badly and told her husband that she would not repay the visit. The wives of Cabinet members did likewise.

Jackson understood full well the torment facing the Eatons, for his own marriage had clouded his political career. He had unknowingly married his wife, Rachel, before her divorce from her first husband had become final. Jackson had felt compelled to fight duels to defend his wife's honor, and he had hoped to win some measure of vindication for her by making her First Lady. But, just before his inauguration, she had died.

Thus, Jackson associated the ostracism forced upon the Eatons with his own personal travail. He tried desperately to bring it to an end, pleading with the Vice President to persuade his wife to visit Mrs. Eaton. But Calhoun refused.

Secretary of State Van Buren, alone among the Cabinet members, lavished attention and respect on Mrs. Eaton. Since Mrs. Eaton had insisted on attending all the major social events in Washington—only to be snubbed repeatedly by other women—Van Buren's kindness was all the more noticeable and appreciated by both the President and the Secretary of War. Van Buren also took private measures to try to bring about some semblance of acceptance for Mrs. Eaton, but was rebuffed.

The Jackson programs for the country were temporarily blocked by the furor over the Eatons. In the end, it was Van Buren who took the steps necessary to free the President from the shackles placed on his administration by the Eaton situation. He offered to resign.

Jackson was shocked. "Never," he told his Secretary of State. "Even you know little of Andrew Jackson if you suppose him capable of consenting to such a humiliation of his friend by his enemies."

But Van Buren insisted. Eaton, who was also present, burst in to say: "This is wrong. I'm the one who ought to resign."

Eaton evidently expected Jackson to refuse to accept his resignation. But Jackson did not. Seeing a way out of the dilemma that had long confronted him—how to get rid of the Eaton problem without being cruel—he agreed to accept the resignations of both Van Buren and Eaton. This also gave him an excuse to force the pro-Calhoun Cabinet members to resign.

Starting afresh with a new Cabinet, Jackson put together a record of solid achievements. The national debt was eliminated. American prestige in foreign affairs was increased. Improvements were made in the long-troublesome tariff situation. And the Bank of the United States, which Jackson had fought as a symbol of eastern domination of other parts of the country, was liquidated.

Meanwhile, Martin Van Buren was given a recess appointment as Minister to England. In accepting his resignation as Secretary of State, the President had not forsaken him but, if anything, formed an even higher regard for him. Van Buren would soon be rewarded for his chivalry in the Eaton affair and his loyalty to Jackson.

But first Jackson would be forced to deal with his cantankerous Vice President. The nation was passing through a period when Calhoun's native Southland was becoming increasingly alienated from the remainder of the country. The issue of slavery—an institution on which the South claimed its economy depended—was becoming a growing source of irritation. Even more important, the South felt that its economy was being discriminated against. The high tariffs pushed through Congress by Northerners during the years just prior to Jackson's administration had brought reciprocal duties from European nations. Since the South needed to export cotton, tobacco and other crops to Europe in order to survive economically, these tariffs posed a great hardship.

In response to pleas from fellow southerners for a means of getting around the tariff system, Calhoun came up with a controversial doctrine called nullification. During the very year of his election to the Vice Presidency in the Jackson Administration, Calhoun had secretly written "The South Carolina Exposition and Protest"—a document that had become the Bible of the advocates of nullification.

The document argued that the United States "is not a union of the people, but a league or compact between sovereign states, any of which has the right to judge when the compact is broken and to pronounce any law null and void which violates its conditions." In short, if a southern state or any other state did not like a law such as a tariff act, it could simply declare that the law had no effect.

Some other southerners advocated even more drastic action —complete secession of the South from the Union. Calhoun held, for the time being, to the more moderate concept of nullification.

A major subject for speculation became what position Jackson, a southerner himself, would assume on the nullification issue. The stage was set for a showdown over the question between Jackson and his Vice President at a Jefferson Day dinner in Washington in April, 1830.

An electric atmosphere filled the air as more than one hundred political leaders filed into the Indian Queen Hotel for the banquet. The nullification advocates had distributed in advance two dozen printed toasts that were to be spoken later in the evening—all contrived to emphasize their disputed doctrine.

But Jackson had a toast of his own to propose, one of many that would follow the two dozen offered by the nullification spokesmen. The President sat at one end of the head table and the Vice President at the other. From time to time each shot a withering glance at the other.

Finally, the prepared toasts had all been delivered. It was Jackson's turn. A hush fell over the banquet hall as the President rose. He lifted his glass, surveyed the room, then unleashed his bombshell.

"Our Union—it must be preserved," he thundered.

The audience was shocked. It was not that Jackson had spoken words of a revolutionary nature. It was, rather, that the circumstances made it clear he was breaking openly with his

Vice President. One observer commented that "an order to arrest Calhoun where he sat could not have come with more blinding, staggering force."

Now all eyes centered on Calhoun. Would he drink the toast?

The Vice President rose with the others. His hand shook, spilling some of the wine from his glass. There were gasps as some present jumped to the conclusion that the Vice President would spill out all the wine. But the conclusions was erroneous. Calhoun drank the toast.

Next it was his turn to propose a toast of his own.

"The Union—next to our liberty the most dear," Calhoun said. "May we all remember that it can only be preserved by respecting the rights of the states and distributing equally the benefit and burden of the Union."

The open break between the President and Vice President was the signal for Calhoun's enemies to pull out all the stops in attempts to destroy his political effectiveness. Martin Van Buren's supporters were in the forefront of this campaign. They brought to the President's attention critical statements made long ago by Calhoun about Jackson during his invasion of Spanish-owned Florida during the Seminole War of 1818. Jackson had always understood that Calhoun supported the action. Now he was told that Calhoun, then Monroe's Secretary of War, had actually advocated his arrest.

Jackson wrote to the Vice President, insisting on an explanation. Calhoun wrote a lengthy reply, admitting that what Jackson had been told was true. But he stressed: "I neither questioned your patriotism nor your motives."

Jackson was hardly satisfied by this response. He wrote Calhoun: "I had a right to believe that you were my friend and, until now, never expected to have occasion to say of you, 'Et tu, Brute.' "

The controversy raged for months, with publication of the correspondence only serving to point up further the irreparable break between the President and Vice President. When

Jackson announced in 1831 that he would seek a second term, contrary to assurances originally given Calhoun, it was taken for granted that Calhoun would be dropped from the ticket. Speculation on his successor naturally turned to Van Buren.

A short, curly-haired man with red sideburns, Van Buren was an accomplished politician. Some called him "the Little Magician" because of his skill at political in-fighting. He had served as New York's governor before entering Jackson's Cabinet.

But Calhoun and his supporters, knowing full well that Van Buren's friends had widened the gap between them and Jackson, were bent on revenge. They got their chance following Van Buren's appointment as Minister to England. Since the Senate had not been in session at the time of the appointment, Van Buren had been sent to England without the benefit of Senate confirmation.

Six months after he had taken up his duties in London, Van Buren's enemies in the Senate—including a number who were not Calhoun supporters—determined that they had enough votes to reject his appointment. But they were not satisfied merely with bringing about his recall; they wanted to disgrace him in the process.

The Van Buren opponents decided to conduct a full-scale "trial" in the Senate. Four main charges were leveled at Van Buren—that he had brought about the rupture between the President and the Vice President; that he had caused the resignations of fellow Cabinet members in order to advance his own career; that he had created the spoils system of patronage; and that he had, as Secretary of State, bungled the negotiation of a trade treaty with England.

The "trial" was a disgrace. Although there were more than enough votes to assure the rejection of the appointment, a number of Van Buren foes abstained from voting in order to bring about a tie. This gave Calhoun the opportunity to cast the decisive vote.

The Vice President could not restrain his glee as he shouted

"No" from the presiding officer's chair. While cheers resounded through the chamber, Calhoun remarked: "It will kill him."

But Senator Thomas Hart Benton of Missouri told a fellow Senator: "You have broken a minister and elected a Vice President."

Jackson was infuriated by the Senate action. Until that time he had merely leaned toward Van Buren as his vice-presidential candidate. Now he was unalterably committed to the nomination of "the Little Magician."

The 1832 election was significant for a number of reasons. Most notable of them was the fact that, for the first time, the candidates were chosen at national nominating conventions. In the past the candidates had been selected in congressional caucuses.

Jackson's renomination was a foregone conclusion. But his party called a convention to choose its vice-presidential candidate.

Determined to make clear the party's support of Van Buren, Jackson and his backers set an important precedent during this convention. They adopted a so-called "two-thirds rule"—providing that the nominee must gain the votes of at least two-thirds of the delegates.

It was felt that Van Buren's nomination by such a margin would establish him as a commanding candidate. Against only token opposition, he encountered no trouble in winning the nomination. But the two-thirds rule was to haunt the Democrats for many conventions to come—preventing a number of capable men from being nominated. It was not until after the Democratic National Convention of 1932, when Franklin D. Roosevelt almost was denied the presidential nomination, that the two-thirds rule was abandoned. From that time forward a majority of delegate votes was sufficient to achieve nomination.

The National Republicans also nominated their ticket for 1832 at a convention. In fact their convention took place before the Democrats' meeting. The National Republicans were advocates of a protective tariff, a national bank and other conservative measures. At their first convention they unanimously nominated Henry Clay for President on the first ballot.

Again Jackson won in a landslide. His popular vote led Clay's by nearly 160,000. The Electoral College gave him 219 votes, with only 49 for Clay.

Calhoun was subjected to one humiliation after another in the waning months of his vice-presidential term. A number of Senators made cutting, if veiled, attacks on him from the floor. When he tried once to respond, he was rebuked on the ground that the vice president had no right to address the Senate except on procedural matters.

During the largely absentee vice presidency of Daniel Tompkins, the Senate had been presided over by President Pro Tem John Gaillard. Gaillard had been so effective that the Senate, for the first time, had given "the presiding officer of this house" the important power to name the members of the chamber's committees. When Calhoun became Vice President, this power presumably would have passed to him. But the Senate withheld the appointive power from Calhoun.

After having his fill of such indignities, Calhoun resigned as Vice President in December, 1832. He thus became the only Vice President in history to leave office in such a way. The dignity of the vice presidency had reached one of its all-time-low watermarks.

But if Calhoun had been bypassed in Washington, he was still a hero in South Carolina. He returned to his home state and resumed the battle to put his theory of nullification into practice. In late 1832 a special convention authorized by the South Carolina legislature adopted an ordinance purporting to nullify two federal tariff acts. The ordinance, which Calhoun took a hand in drafting, threatened that South Carolina would secede from the Union if the Federal Government tried to use force to uphold the tariff laws.

The ordinance said:

We will not submit to the application of force, on the part of the Federal Government, to reduce this state to obedience. The people of this state will thenceforth hold themselves absolved from all further obligation to maintain or preserve their political connection with the people of other states, and will forthwith proceed to organize a separate government. . . .

President Jackson had no intention of seeing the Union crumble under the threat posed by Calhoun and other South Carolinians. Buoyed by the proportions of his reelection victory, Jackson increased the military garrisons in South Carolina and made it clear that he was prepared to send an additional 40,000 troops into the state. He issued a firm proclamation to the people of South Carolina:

I consider the power to anul a law of the United States, assumed by one state, incompatible with the existence of the Union, contradicted expressly by the letter of the Constitution, unauthorized by its spirit, inconsistent with every principle on which it was founded, and destructive of the great object for which it was formed.

In the meantime Calhoun had made arrangements to return to the Senate. This time, however, there would be no question about his right to speak. For he was returning as a duly elected Senator from South Carolina.

Daniel Webster engaged in a historic debate with Calhoun over the nullification issue. In the end Jackson's supporters passed legislation authorizing the President to use force, if necessary, to collect revenues in South Carolina.

But the statesmanship of a number of public officials—among them Calhoun—averted a showdown. Henry Clay introduced a compromise tariff bill aimed at gradually reducing the rates that South Carolina found oppressive. Calhoun helped push the compromise through the Senate. Jackson signed into law both the tariff bill and the "force bill" designed to halt South Carolina's possible secession. South Carolina responded by repealing its ordinance "nullifying" the old tariff acts, then took the face-saving action of passing another ordinance purporting to nullify the "force bill."

During all this turmoil Martin Van Buren carried out his duties as Vice President in routine, undistinguished fashion. But he advoided making some of the mistakes committed by his predecessors. When the time came for Jackson to retire, Van Buren had long since been hand-picked as his successor. He was to become the last man ever elected directly to the presidency from the vice presidency (at least at this writing).

In the election of 1836 Van Buren's running mate was Richard Mentor Johnson, a Kentuckian whose chief claim to fame was that he was reputed to have killed the Indian warrior Tecumseh during a battle in 1813.

Johnson's supporters originally tried to get him nominated for President but could not overcome the Van Buren tide. However, their publicity campaign on his behalf—including a nationwide poster distribution, a five-act play concerning his military exploits and a song about "The Warrior Sage"—projected him into contention for the vice presidency. Van Buren's backers, seeking to capitalize on Johnson's popularity and feeling that his nomination would balance the ticket, offered him the running mate's spot. He gladly accepted. But Virginia delegates to the national convention, who wanted someone else nominated for vice president, refused to support Johnson—although backing Van Buren. This would later have unusual consequences.

The opposition to Van Buren and Johnson consisted of a loose-knit conglomeration of enemies of the Jackson administration, banded together under the name of the Whig Party. The name was chosen in imitation of the eighteenth century Americans and Englishmen—calling themselves Whigs—who had opposed King George III. The new Whigs contended that Jackson and his followers, among them Van Buren and Johnson, were every bit as dangerous to liberty in 1836 as George III had been in 1776.

Because it was made up of so many disparate groups, whose

main tie was opposition to Jacksonian democracy, the Whig Party was unable to agree on a single ticket to oppose Van Buren and Johnson. The party did not even conduct a national convention. In Pennsylvania the Whigs nominated and voted for William Henry Harrison for President. In Massachusetts their candidate was Daniel Webster. In other states the votes went to favorite sons who were little known on the national scene.

This fragmentation eased the way for Van Buren's victory. He received 762,978 popular votes, while all the Whig candidates combined received 736,250. Van Buren got 170 of the 294 electoral votes, while the leading Whig candidate, Harrison, received only 73. In the vice-presidential race, Johnson opened up a wide margin over his leading opponent—but it was not wide enough. The Virginia electors, although giving Van Buren their 23 electoral votes, withheld them from Johnson. He thus fell one vote short of the necessary majority. The choice of a vice president—for the only time in American history—was placed in the hands of the Senate.

The Senate elected Johnson to the office by a margin of 33 to 16 over a Whig, Francis Granger. Johnson, the first of three southerners by that name elected to the vice presidency, was even less effective in the office than some of his least illustrious predecessors. As a matter of fact, he whiled away one summer during his term as the manager of a hotel.

In 1840 the Democrats renominated Van Buren for President. But, convinced that Johnson would only lose votes for the ticket, the delegates decided to dump him. The only problem was that they could not agree on another vice-presidential candidate. So, in one of the most devastating slaps ever taken at the office, the Democrats nominated no one for vice president. The action was unprecedented. Democratic members of the Electoral College were left free to vote for any vice-presidential hopeful they chose.

It mattered little, for the Democrats were swamped by the

Whigs anyway. This was the famous "Log Cabin and Hard Cider" campaign of "Tippecanoe and Tyler, Too."

The Whig presidential candidate was William Henry Harrison of Ohio, hero of the battle with the Indians at Tippecanoe. Because Harrison had once worn a coonskin cap, lived in a log cabin and drunk hard cider, the symbols of his party became coons, cabins and cider. The vice-presidential candidate was John Tyler, a former governor, Congressman and Senator from Virginia.

It was a raucous campaign that set the tone for many campaigns to follow. The Whigs used techniques formerly associated with circus advance men, generating all sorts of hoopla and public interest.

Huge balls, supposedly representing the gathering majority for the Whigs, were rolled by men and boys from town to town and state to state. As they rolled along, the men and boys chanted:

> What has caused this great commotion, motion, motion,
> Our country through?
> It is the ball a-rolling on for
> Tippecanoe and Tyler, too—
> Tippecanoe and Tyler, too.
> And with them we'll beat little Van, Van, Van,
> Oh! Van is a used-up man!

The Democrats countered by ridiculing Tyler as a vice-presidential candidate. After all, they argued, he was no Whig —he was really a Democrat, a follower of John Calhoun, and differed with most other Democrats only in his distaste for Andrew Jackson.

But the Whigs retorted with another chant.

> We'll vote for Tyler, therefore,
> Without a why or wherefore.

Vote for him—and for Harrison—they did. And so did the electorate at large, in unprecedented numbers. The total popular vote exceeded that of 1836 by about 1,000,000. Van Buren carried only seven states with 60 electoral votes, while Harrison put together 234 electoral votes.

It was on a frigid March day in 1841 that William Henry Harrison was inaugurated as the ninth President of the United States. He stood hatless in the chill wind for almost two hours —delivering the longest inauguration speech in American history. He pledged to serve only one term.

Actually, he would serve a far shorter term than anyone dreamed. The flippant phrase "And Tyler, Too" would long be remembered. But it would soon be a case of "Tyler, Alone."

And the vice presidency would never again be quite the same.

❧❀❧

CHAPTER FIVE

Powers and Duties

WILLIAM HENRY HARRISON'S presidential term lasted precisely one month.

A chill he had taken on Inauguration Day developed into pneumonia. On April 4, he died—the first President to die in office.

Vice President Tyler was at his home in Williamsburg, Virginia. It was not until the next morning that a courier brought the news of Harrison's death. And it was not until the following day that Tyler arrived in Washington to take over the reins of government. For more than two days the nation had been without a Chief Executive. It was to be the longest such period in American history.

But, more important, there was the whole question of Tyler's rights and duties. Was he really President? Or was he merely Acting President?

The question had never arisen in the past. And the Constitution was woefully vague. The controlling passage of the Constitution—in Article II, Section 1—provided: "In case of the removal of the President from office, or of his death, resignation or inability to discharge the powers and duties of the said office, the same shall devolve on the Vice President."

The rub came over interpreting whether the word "same" referred to the word "office" or to the words "powers and duties." Tyler, who insisted that the Presidency had been automatically handed to him, argued that the word "same" modified "office." In other words, he felt the Constitution should be interpreted as meaning that "the office of President shall devolve on the Vice President."

But many members of Congress argued, instead, that only the "powers and duties" of the Presidency should be handed over to him. It was an argument that would rage for years, subside temporarily, then flare again. Many years later, study of original drafts of the Constitutional passage would convince scholars that the Founding Fathers had no intention of seeing a vice president become president under Tyler's interpretation. But by that time it would be much too late to turn back the clock.

Tyler insisted that he was President in fact, in name and in every other respect. He took the oath of office. He demanded all the privileges of the presidency—residence in the White House, presidential salary and all the rest. And, despite attempts in both houses of Congress to anchor him with the title of Acting President, his position prevailed. It has continued to prevail through the years. All evidence indicates that, no matter what the intention of the Founding Fathers, this interpretation has served the United States well. For, without it, chaos might well have developed following a number of presidential deaths.

The Whigs soon discovered that Tyler, who had been chosen (like so many other vice-presidential candidates) as a political expedient, would be no mere figurehead President. They also discovered that, as the Democrats had charged, he was not really a Whig but a renegade Democrat.

Tyler quickly set about establishing that he was in firm control of the administration. Secretary of State Daniel Webster told him that Harrison's policy had been to make decisions by a majority vote of the Cabinet—with each member, including the President, having one vote. Tyler did not believe in government by committee. He was the President, not a committee chairman. He would have the final say on matters of importance. The Cabinet did not like it but accepted his decisions at first.

Trouble, however, was not long in coming. Secretary of the Treasury Thomas Ewing helped draft legislation to grant a new charter for a national bank. The legislation was passed by Congress. But when it was presented to the President for his signature, he vetoed the measure. A compromise bill, designed to meet objections raised by Tyler, was hastily written and passed. Again it was vetoed. The Whigs were aghast; the Democrats were joyous.

Whigs in Congress promptly appointed a committee to prepare a message for the country. It declared that all relations between the party and the President were at an end. At the same time all members of the Cabinet except Webster resigned.

Tyler's term was marked by storm after storm. In four years no fewer than twenty-three Cabinet members entered and left the Administration. After going through four Secretaries of State, Tyler brought in his old friend, John Calhoun, to fill the office. But even Calhoun had little sympathy left for the President.

Although a man of great skill and charm, Tyler had come to office under circumstances that seemed preordained to lead to trouble. His choice for the vice presidency had come about in the worst possible way—through the old vote-bait method. And his political stance—neither fish nor fowl—had left him with many enemies and almost no allies.

The situation deteriorated to such an extent that Tyler was even threatened with impeachment. A Whig member of the House, John M. Botts of Tyler's home state of Virginia, filed several charges against the President and proposed a resolution appointing a committee to investigate the accusations, but the resolution was defeated by a vote of 127 to 83.

Despite all the turmoil, Tyler's administration was one of substantial accomplishments. These included the Webster-

Ashburton Treaty (resolving disputes with Britain over the northeastern frontier), the annexation of Texas, the opening up of the Orient to American trade through a treaty with China and the ending of the second Seminole War.

And if he had done nothing more than establish the precedent for a vice president's succession to the actual office of the Presidency, John Tyler's place in history would have been assured.

It should have been clear to Tyler that one term in the Presidency was all he was going to have. The Whigs certainly would not support him for reelection. He cast a longing eye back to the Democratic Party, but it had no interest in permitting the wandering son to return. He sought to run as an independent, but his supporters consisted almost entirely of federal jobholders who wanted merely to remain in office.

A major issue of 1844 was the proposed granting of statehood to Texas. Tyler favored it. But the two men considered leading contenders for the Presidency, Van Buren for the Democrats and Henry Clay for the Whigs, opposed it. Tyler hoped to capitalize on their opposition, since he was sure the majority of citizens favored the annexation of Texas.

As expected, the Whigs chose Clay to head the ticket, with Theodore Frelinghuysen of New Jersey as the vice-presidential candidate. But the Democrats did not follow the form. Once again it was not Van Buren's year. His old benefactor, Andrew Jackson, found that Van Buren could not get the nomination.

It was not until the eighth ballot at the Democratic National Convention that the name of James K. Polk—the original dark horse in the history of the American Presidency—was even mentioned. Polk, a former Speaker of the House and Governor of Tennessee, got only 44 votes on that ballot. But Jackson was behind him. By the next ballot Polk was suddenly swept into a unanimous nomination.

Significantly, Polk favored Texas statehood. Thus Tyler's chief issue had been stolen. Accordingly, he withdrew from the race and his backers lined up behind Polk.

Apparently the Democrats had not learned the lesson of the Harrison-Tyler administration. Since many of them did not favor Texas statehood, they resorted to the vote-bait technique in seeking a vice-presidential candidate. There would be something for everybody. For those who favored statehood there would be Polk at the top of the ticket. And for those who opposed statehood there would be Senator Silas Wright of New York as the vice-presidential nominee.

Or would there?

Wright was not at the Democrats' Baltimore convention. He was back at the Capitol in Washington when word of his nomination was flashed by telegraph. But he considered it absurd to run on a ticket with a man whose views differed so sharply from his own. So he refused to accept the nomination. Never before had this happened in American politics.

Other Democrats tried to persuade him to change his mind, but he was adamant. Ultimately, the Democratic convention chose an advocate of Texas statehood—George Mifflin Dallas, for whom the city in Texas was named—as a substitute vice-presidential candidate. Dallas had an illustrious record as Mayor of Philadelphia, Minister to Russia and Senator from Pennsylvania.

Clay was far better known to the electorate than Polk. In fact, the Whig slogan—used to excellent effect in the early campaigning—was: "Who the hell is Polk?"

But, as Clay was to learn, fame has its debits as well as its credits. Since Polk had been away from the national spotlight of Washington for five years, his positions on a number of controversial issues were not generally known.

The voters made their choice—Polk and Dallas.

George Dallas was considered one of the most capable, high-principled men ever to occupy the vice presidency. He was given an important role in the Administration and showed unswerving loyalty to Polk.

This loyalty was put to the test in 1846 when Senate voting ended in a tie on a bill designed to lower tariffs. The bill was favored by the President but opposed by the Vice President. From a sense of duty to Polk, Dallas set aside his own feelings and cast the tie-breaking vote in favor of the bill.

Ironically, this act of what Dallas considered honor was to bring him only dishonor back home in Pennsylvania, where high tariffs were generally favored. One Pennsylvania editor went as far as to write: "Farewell to all Vice Presidents from Pennsylvania for the future. We have had enough . . ."

Since that time—for whatever reason—Pennsylvania has not sent another man to the vice president's chair. In fact, it has not even seen one of its sons nominated for the office.

In 1848 President Polk declined renomination. Once again the Democrats went looking for a presidential candidate. Vice President Dallas was considered out of the question. Martin Van Buren was still around and wanted another chance. But the Democratic National Convention chose, instead, Lewis Cass—an able man who had served as a state legislator in Ohio, Governor of the Michigan Territory, Secretary of War, Minister to France and Senator from Michigan.

The Whigs chose a presidential candidate almost totally lacking in political skill but possessing an abundance of popular appeal. Their nominee was General Zachary Taylor, affectionately known as "Old Rough and Ready." Taylor had been a hero of the Mexican War and was to fall into a mold all too familar in American political life—an expert military man but a woefully inadequate politician who had never even voted.

The Whigs' selection of a number-two candidate was a classic example of how not to go about choosing a vice-presidential nominee. All the ticket-balancing and vote-bait techniques of past conventions were exhibited.

Since Taylor was from Louisiana, the Whigs felt obliged to balance the ticket with a Northerner. Obviously the populous state of New York offered the most vote bait. But which New Yorker should get the consolation prize?

Henry Clay, in his fifth attempt at the Presidency, had been denied the nomination. The Whigs felt compelled to make some gesture aimed at soothing the old man's feelings.

One of Clay's leading opponents from New York was Thurlow Weed, a newspaper publisher and behind-the-scenes power in Whig politics. Weed wanted one of his men, William H. Seward, elected to the Senate or the vice presidency as a stepping stone to the Presidency. And one of Weed's opponents was a virtual unknown named Millard Fillmore.

Fillmore was no particular supporter of Clay. But because of his opposition to Weed, the impression was spread at the convention that Fillmore was a Clay man. Thus, when Fillmore's name was placed in nomination for the vice presidency, it seemed a tidy answer to a multitude of problems.

Here was a candidate who served the purpose of balancing the ticket, whose purported support of Clay would be a sop to the elderly Kentuckian's followers and whose political record was so lackluster as to be inoffensive to most voters. At the time of his nomination for Vice President he was serving as state comptroller—an important office but hardly one regarded as a jumping-off point for the vice presidency.

In the end it was not the Whig team of Taylor and Fillmore but that old Democrat, Martin Van Buren, who brought about the defeat of the Democratic ticket in the 1848 election. Denied the presidential nomination by the Democrats, Van Buren became the nominee of a splinter party, the Free Soilers, on a platform that opposed extension of slavery into newly acquired U. S. territory.

The Democratic presidential candidate, Cass, won majorities in fifteen states to Taylor's fourteen. But in the key state of New York, Van Buren took enough votes away from Cass to give the majority to Taylor. New York's 36 electoral votes sewed up the election for Taylor. If Van Buren had stayed out of the race, Cass would have been elected easily, for Van Buren had also pulled votes away from him in other states.

Taylor embarked on an undistinguished Presidency. And

Fillmore seemed relegated to an insignificant role as Vice President.

The President bypassed Fillmore in distribution of patronage—instead favoring Seward and his benefactor, Weed, who had worked loyally in Taylor's campaign. Taylor also ignored his Vice President on important legislative matters. This was a mistake. For, despite other shortcomings, Fillmore had shown as a Congressman that he had a talent for managing legislation.

Slavery and its potential for destroying the Union posed the major problem facing the Taylor-Fillmore administration. Southern leaders were again talking about secession. The issue came to a head over the proposed granting of statehood to the California Territory. The discovery of gold in California in 1848 had brought about a rush of settlers. Almost immediately after his inauguration President Taylor had sent agents into the territory to urge the settlers to draw up a territorial constitution and apply for statehood.

In September 1849 a territorial convention met and drew up a constitution. Two months later this constitution, which outlawed slavery, was approved by the public.

The admission of California to the Union as a free state would have disturbed the precarious balance between slave states and free states. For that reason many members of Congress from slave states opposed the granting of statehood. Surprisingly, President Taylor—despite his southern origin and his ownership of slaves—came out strongly in favor of admitting California.

With the future of the nation hanging in the balance, Henry Clay stepped into the breach. Clay, at seventy-two, had returned to the Senate after failing to get the presidential nomination in 1848. He now began using all his vaunted talents for persuasion in an attempt to bring about a compromise.

Clay pulled together a package of proposals previously offered by members of Congress from both the North and the South. He urged California's entry into the Union as a free state, abolition of slave trade within the District of Columbia, passage of a stricter fugitive-slave law and organization of Utah and New Mexico as territories without restriction on the slavery issue.

The attempted compromise brought on another historic debate in the Senate. Vice President Fillmore sat in the presiding officer's chair, unable to do more than rule on procedural matters. Once again the President had failed to take advantage of the Vice President's legislative skill. In the behind-the-scenes maneuvering Fillmore could have played an important role. Instead, he was relegated to second-class status.

The familiar figures of Clay, Daniel Webster and John Calhoun passed across the pages of American history in the Senate debate. Webster supported Clay's compromise, casting aside his long-time opposition to the fugitive-slave laws. But Calhoun was more intransigent than ever. He rejected the compromise proposal and accused northerners of trying to provoke the South into seceding.

Attention began to center on Vice President Fillmore as the debate dragged into the summer of 1850. Head counts among the Senators indicated that the vote on the Clay compromise, when it finally came about, might well end in a tie. The long-neglected Fillmore then would have an opportunity to exert his influence at last, in casting the tie-breaking vote.

Though an opponent of slavery, Fillmore felt that some concessions on the issue might be necessary to save the Union. He considered the preservation of the Union so essential that he was willing to accept some of the less palatable provisions of the compromise.

In early July, Fillmore visited the White House and told the President that he might vote for the compromise if a tie did indeed come about. However, Fillmore soon assumed a role far more important than that of merely breaking a tie vote.

On July 4 President Taylor took part in Independence Day ceremonies in Washington. It was a miserably hot day and to refresh himself Taylor drank large quantities of water. Later he ate a great number of cherries and drank some iced milk. Within a short time the President was doubled over with excruciating stomach cramps.

Physicians diagnosed his illness at first as cholera, then noted additional symptoms indicating typhus. His condition worsened over a period of five days. The night of July 9, as Vice President Fillmore sat home alone, he was notified that Taylor had died.

Fillmore was sworn in as President on July 10 before a joint session of Congress. The precedent set by John Tyler was not questioned. It was assumed that Fillmore was President—not Acting President—and that he had all the powers of the highest office in the land.

After a decent interval to allow for mourning of the late President, the struggle over the compromise proposal resumed. Fillmore announced that he was prepared to support the compromise. The announcement had no sooner been made than Taylor's old Cabinet resigned *en masse*. Fillmore promptly named a Cabinet composed of Whigs who took a moderate position on the slavery question.

The new President's support for the compromise legislation swung some additional votes into line behind Clay's plan. In time, after more flurries of opposition, all the bills supported by Clay were approved. Fillmore signed them into law.

But the strokes of his pen also wrote an end to Fillmore's hopes of winning his own elected term as President. When the time came for the Whigs to choose their presidential candidate in 1852, Fillmore drew support chiefly from the South. His home state of New York opposed him.

After 53 ballots, Fillmore dropped out of contention. The Whigs nominated General Winfield Scott.

The Democrats nominated Franklin Pierce, a former member of the House and Senate from New Hampshire. To balance the ticket they selected a vice-presidential candidate from Alabama. But this time their choice was a man of great skill and experience—Senator William King. He had served as a Senator for thirty years, been President Pro Tem of the Senate and the chamber's presiding officer during the vice-presidential vacancy left by Fillmore's succession to the presidency.

The Whigs conducted a listless campaign—indicative of the fact that their party was about to come apart at the seams. The 1852 election would be the last in which the Whigs would field a national ticket.

Pierce and King swept to victory. Ironically King—so admirably qualified to carry out the duty of presiding over the Senate—never got the chance to do so as Vice President. He fell ill following the election and went to Cuba to recuperate. A special law was passed by Congress to permit him to take the oath as Vice President in Havana. A month after being sworn in as Vice President, he left Cuba and went to his Alabama home. He died there the day after his arrival.

Thus, for all practical purposes, the United States had no vice president from the time of Zachary Taylor's death in 1850 until Inauguration Day in 1857.

~§~

CHAPTER SIX

A Vacancy and the Civil War

THOSE who maintained that there was a hex on the vice presidency had ample evidence to support their contention during the middle of the nineteenth century.

Not only did the office remain vacant from 1850 to 1857, with the exception of the one month in which William King was nominally Vice President, but the next occupant was to end his life in disgrace.

In 1856 the Democrats refused to renominate President Pierce. They chose as a compromise candidate James Buchanan of Pennsylvania—a former member of the House and Senate who had also served as Minister to Great Britain and as President Polk's Secretary of State. Their vice-presidential candidate was Representative John Breckinridge of Kentucky, whose grandfather had been an adviser to Thomas Jefferson and an influential Senator.

The Whigs had faded from the scene. Opposition came from the new Republican Party, which nominated John Fremont for President and William Dayton for Vice President. Buchanan and Breckinridge won the election.

At the age of thirty-six, Breckinridge was the youngest man ever to serve as Vice President. When the Democratic Party split into Northern and Southern wings in 1860, Breckinridge became the presidential candidate of the Southern branch that favored continuation of slavery. The Northern wing nominated Senator Stephen A. Douglas of Illinois. Oddly enough, Douglas had not been a particular opponent of slavery. In fact, in the famous series of debates he conducted with Abraham

Lincoln during their race for the Senate in 1858, he argued for "popular sovereignty"—the right of the people in any section of the country to vote to legalize slavery on a local-option basis. Douglas defeated Lincoln in the senatorial race.

But it was a different story in 1860. Lincoln became the presidential candidate of the Republican Party. And he defeated both Douglas and Breckinridge (gaining 180 electoral votes to 72 for Breckinridge and 12 for Douglas).

After serving out the lame-duck portion of his vice-presidential term, Breckinridge left his chair as presiding officer of the Senate—but took another seat as Senator from Kentucky. He said he would try to aid those seeking a compromise to avert civil war. However, no compromise could be reached.

The Civil War finally broke out in 1861.

Breckinridge's home state declared it was neutral in the war, but the former Vice President clearly sided with the Confederacy. Nonetheless, he remained in his Senate seat during the early part of the war—voicing strident opposition to Lincoln's military program.

In late 1861, as a result of various acts designed to aid the Confederacy, Breckinridge was indicted by a federal grand jury in Kentucky on a charge of treason. Soon afterward the Senate declared him to be a traitor and banished him from the chamber.

Breckinridge fled to the South, becoming a general in the Confederate Army and later Secretary of War in the Confederate government. When the war ended in disaster for the Confederate cause, he skipped the country and lived in exile for four years. He eventually received permission from the Government to return to the United States without fear of punishment. But when he did come back, it was to live out his remaining years in disgrace.

When Lincoln had first been elected President, his Vice President had been Hannibal Hamlin, a renegade Democrat who had previously served as both Governor and Senator from Maine. Hamlin had played only a minor role in the Lincoln administration. He and the President had differed on a number of issues.

In 1864, with Lincoln seeking reelection, there seemed little advantage to the President in retaining Hamlin as his vice-presidential candidate. The political rift between the two men was only one of several reasons for Lincoln to consider dumping Hamlin from the ticket.

Since Hamlin came from Maine, a state considered safely tucked in Lincoln's column, there was no vote-bait appeal involved in his renomination. With the Civil War going badly for the Union, Lincoln was enduring sharp criticism and could use any vote-bait he could find. The model vice-presidential candidate would be a man who could lure votes from Democrats supporting the war.

Such a candidate was available in Andrew Johnson of Tennessee. Johnson, a native of North Carolina, was apprenticed at an early age to a tailor who prevented him from attending school even for one day. He later moved to Greeneville, Tennessee, and opened a tailor shop of his own. It was not until after he was married that he learned to read and write, under the tutelage of his wife.

Shortly after becoming literate, Johnson entered politics on a modest scale—as a Greeneville alderman. His political rise was meteoric. He served terms as mayor, member of the Tennessee Legislature, Congressman, Governor and Senator.

It was in the Senate that Johnson made his biggest initial impression on national politics. Originally a Democrat, he was an ardent advocate of the interests of the common man, as opposed to the wealthy slaveowners in his state. By the beginning of the Civil War, Johnson was one of the most influential members of the Senate.

And, with the outbreak of the war, he was the only southern Senator to remain on the job in Washington. It was an act of political courage that earned the respect of Lincoln and numerous others. On the Senate floor Johnson railed against his fellow Southerners for seceding—arguing that they were committing treason.

Johnson left the Democratic Party when its officials in Tennessee lined up on the side of the slaveholding aristocracy. The way for his break with the Democrats was eased by the fact that Lincoln had temporarily changed the name of the Republican Party to the Unionist Party. It suited Johnson's interests to be called a Unionist rather than a Republican.

In 1862 Lincoln asked Johnson to take on the job of returning federal authority to war-torn Tennessee. With a presidential appointment as military governor of the state, Johnson embarked on the seemingly thankless assignment. For his efforts he won the undying enmity of many Southerners. But he also earned the plaudits of countless Northerners.

It was against this background that Johnson was first considered as a running mate for Lincoln in 1864. The renaming of the Republican Party was designed to entice into the Lincoln camp disenchanted Democratic voters. And it was widely assumed that, in a further attempt to attract these voters, a Democrat would be on the ticket.

Lincoln maintained a public neutrality over the choice of the vice-presidential candidate. But his silence only heightened the belief that he wanted Hamlin off the ticket. If he intended to keep Hamlin, it was reasoned, he would have said so. There were indications that Lincoln wanted Johnson as his running mate, but any encouragement he may have offered was kept secret.

At the nominating convention Johnson took a slim lead over Hamlin and a number of other candidates on the first ballot. In short order, numerous delegates switched their allegiance and lined up behind Johnson. His nomination was assured.

The Democrats nominated for President one of the most popular of the Union Army generals, George B. McClellan. Although a skilled military man—and before that a railroad executive—McClellan had no experience in politics. He had voted for the first time in 1860. Moreover he was a most erratic man. He was obsessed with the idea of becoming a dictator and made little effort to conceal the fact. McClellan's running mate was George H. Pendleton, a Congressman from Ohio.

Despite McClellan's failings, it seemed for a time that his popularity as a general would carry him to victory. As late as August of 1864 Lincoln himself almost despaired of winning reelection. "I do not see how we can defeat McClellan," he said. McClellan had long been disdainful of Lincoln. While still serving in the Army he had said of his Commander-in-Chief: "The President is nothing more than a well-meaning baboon. He is the original gorilla. What a specimen to be at the head of our affairs."

But just before the election Union troops won a series of major battles. These served to refute the Democratic campaign argument that Lincoln was bungling the war effort. The military triumphs were enough to boost the Lincoln-Johnson ticket to victory.

The vice presidency of Andrew Johnson was launched in a most inauspicious manner. He showed up drunk for his inauguration. There were extenuating circumstances, it is true. But, nonetheless, Johnson's antics on Inauguration Day made him a laughing stock for some time.

Following his election to the vice presidency, Johnson had been stricken with typhoid fever. Because he was still recuperating, he had hoped to be spared the strain of coming to the Capitol for the inauguration. But Lincoln had insisted.

On the night before the inauguration, although still weak from his illness, Johnson attended a party in his honor. He and others at the party drank a few too many. When he arrived at the Capitol the next morning for the inauguration, the Vice-President-elect had an old-fashioned hangover. To calm himself, he belted down a few more drinks.

Thus, when the time came for outgoing Vice President

Hamlin to administer the oath of office, Johnson neglected to wait for the swearing-in before launching into his inaugural speech. And quite a speech it was.

It rambled on and on. Johnson spoke off the cuff, without even referring to notes. He began by telling the audience that he really did not have adequate credentials for the vice presidency—that he lacked the necessary wisdom and knowledge of parliamentary procedure.

Johnson downgraded not only his own qualifications but those of members of the Lincoln Cabinet. Through it all Lincoln sat staring at the floor in embarrassment. One senator covered his face with his hands. A Cabinet member, Attorney General James Speed, whispered to the man beside him: "This man is certainly deranged."

At long last Johnson completed his speech. He belatedly took the oath of office, gave the Bible a sloppy, noisy kiss and sat down.

He was followed to the rostrum by Lincoln, who delivered an address that was as distinguished as Johnson's was intemperate. Lincoln said:

> Fondly do we hope—fervently do we pray—that this mighty scourge of war may speedily pass away. With malice toward none; with charity for all; with firmness in the right, as God gives us to see the right, let us strive on to finish the work we are in; to bind up the nation's wounds; to care for him who shall have borne the battle, and for his widow, and his orphan —to do all which may achieve and cherish a just and lasting peace among ourselves, and with all nations.

As moving as was Lincoln's speech, it was all but ignored at first in the furor over the Vice President's antics. Some senators even considered asking for his resignation. They thought better of the idea—but, as a result of the inaugural fiasco, the Senate passed a resolution barring liquor from its wing of the Capitol building.

The episode was immortalized in verse by one of Johnson's

critics. He composed a ditty that was to haunt Johnson for the rest of his days:

> Oh, was it not a glorious sight,
> To see the crowd of black and white,
> As well as Andy Johnson tight
> At the inauguration.

Lincoln maintained his sense of proportion over the incident. A few days after the inauguration he told a member of the Cabinet: "I have known Andy Johnson for many years. He made a bad slip the other day, but you need not be scared. Andy ain't a drunkard." Lincoln's assessment was entirely accurate. While obviously not a teetotaler, Johnson drank less than most of his contemporaries.

The inauguration took place on March 4, 1865. On April 9 the Civil War ended with the surrender of Confederate General Robert E. Lee at Appomattox, Virginia. But that did not mean that all violent resistance to the Lincoln administration was over.

In a Washington boardinghouse on H Street, between Sixth and Seventh, there lurked a band of conspirators bent on avenging the defeat of the Confederacy. This band, led by John Wilkes Booth, an actor and fanatic advocate of the Confederate cause, planned the assassination of Lincoln and the leading members of his administration.

Booth himself took on the assignment of murdering the President. A Virginia carriage-maker named George A. Atzerodt was designated to assassinate Vice President Johnson. A disabled veteran of the Confederate Army named Lewis Paine was to kill Secretary of State William H. Seward.

While there were other members of the conspiratorial group with assignments of their own, these three men carried the major burdens. Booth was confident of his own ability and courage. He was likewise convinced that Paine would be a tower of strength. But he feared—and with good cause—that

Atzerodt, a drunkard, a weakling and a coward, might prove to be the weakest link in the conspiracy.

According to the plan, Booth was to shoot Lincoln while the President was attending a play the night of April 14 at Ford's Theater. Meanwhile, Paine was to get into Secretary Seward's home and murder him. Atzerodt was to check into a hotel room directly above the one occupied by Vice President Johnson. At 10:15 P.M. he was to rap on Johnson's door. When the Vice President opened the door, Atzerodt was to shoot him.

Booth, fearing that Atzerodt might waver, decided to call on him at the hotel on the afternoon of the planned assassinations. He intended to give Atzerodt a pep talk. But Atzerodt was not in his room. Booth did not know it at the time, but his fellow conspirator actually was out drinking.

At this point Booth took a bold step. He asked the room clerk whether the Vice President was in his room. When the clerk said that Johnson was out, Booth asked for a card on which to write a message for the Vice President.

On the card Booth wrote: "Didn't wish to disturb you. Are you at home? (signed) J. Wilkes Booth."

This strange message later was to pose a riddle for historians —but, even more important, it was to bring down on Andrew Johnson the wrath of many Americans who came to believe he had been involved in the plot.

That night Booth and Paine went through with their assignments. Booth entered the presidential box at the theater, tiptoed to within a few feet of the President and shot him in the back of the head with a tiny derringer pistol. He then stabbed another occupant of the box with a dagger, shouted "The South is avenged," and leaped to the stage. In the confusion he escaped—only to be hunted down later.

Meanwhile, Paine went to Secretary Seward's home, entered on the pretext of delivering a package, battled his way into Seward's room and savagely stabbed him several times. He also stabbed four other men in the house before fleeing.

George Atzerodt, however, not only did not shoot Vice President Johnson; he never even tried. Instead, he spent the evening wandering the streets and drinking at the bar of the Vice President's hotel.

About 10:30 P.M. there was a frantic pounding on the door of Johnson's hotel room. The Vice President, who was nearly alseep, was a long time answering the door. When he finally pulled it open, he was surprised to see his friend, Former Governor Leonard J. Farwell of Wisconsin, standing outside.

Farwell had just come from Ford's Theater. He whispered to the Vice President: "Someone has shot and murdered the President."

Actually, Farwell was wrong. Lincoln was still alive and would linger until 7:22 the next morning.

Johnson could not believe the news at first. But when Farwell convinced him he was telling the truth, the two men threw their arms around each other in anguish, as if each would fall without the other's support.

Soon Johnson's hotel lobby was swarming with stunned citizens. Guards were posted inside and outside his room. The Vice President sent Farwell back to the theater to learn Lincoln's condition. When he returned, Farwell brought with him Major James R. O'Beirne, provost marshal of the District of Columbia. He also brought news that Lincoln was dying and that Seward had been stabbed.

Johnson wanted to go to Lincoln's side, but O'Beirne begged him to stay in the hotel room—saying it was obvious there was a plot to assassinate all the leading members of the government.

The Vice President, however, was adamant. He insisted that his place was with the President. He plunged through the crowd in the hotel lobby and walked the four blocks to a home across from the theater, where Lincoln had been carried after the shooting.

Admitted to the room where the President lay dying, Johnson stood among the physicians and dignitaries, staring solemnly at Lincoln's face. The doctors told him the President's condition was hopeless. It was only a matter of hours before he would die. With feelings of helplessness and despair, Johnson walked back to his hotel.

The next morning, after receiving word that the President had died, Johnson took the oath as President in his hotel. Thus the man who only six weeks earlier had been the laughingstock of Washington—the butt of jokes about his drunken performance on Inauguration Day—now was the seventeenth President of the United States.

The tragic circumstances under which Johnson entered the Presidency brought him a certain amount of sympathy at first.

There were many Americans, including a number of radical members of Congress, who looked upon the assassination as a sort of blessing. Although they mourned Lincoln, they had feared while he was alive that he would take too soft an attitude in dealing with the defeated southern states. Johnson, even though a southerner, had been outspoken before Lincoln's death about the necessity for severe action against the leaders of the Confederacy. As Vice President, Johnson had called for the hanging of Confederate President Jefferson Davis and certain other southern officials.

However, it was not long before Johnson changed his mind about how to deal with the South and before the radicals grew disenchanted with him. Abandoning the harsh attitude he had taken before Lincoln's death, he soon began to put into effect the very policies his predecessor had planned for the South. Under a program he called Restoration, Johnson issued a proclamation of pardon and amnesty that freed most southerners from the threat of prosecution for acts committed on behalf of the Confederacy. He also moved to bring the Confederate states back into the Union and to assure that their state governments were under the direction of responsible men.

The radicals in Congress rebelled at Johnson's Restoration program. They refused to seat congressional delegations sent to Washington by southern states and threw other obstacles in the path of the Johnson plan to rehabilitate the South.

The rift deepened as the congressional elections of 1866 approached. Johnson had vetoed a number of bills proposed by the radicals, and they had overridden his vetoes on others. The President's enemies were determined to accumulate two-thirds majorities in both houses of Congress, so they would be sure of having enough votes to defeat any future vetoes.

The President decided to fight the radicals by going to the people. He made a campaign tour of numerous cities, but the tour was far from successful. In many cities Johnson permitted himself to be drawn into word battles with street hecklers. He came off second-best.

The congressional elections were disastrous for Johnson. His enemies succeeded in winning their desired two-thirds margins in the House and Senate. Having done so, they killed the President's program for the South and established an oppressive military rule there.

Emboldened by their triumphs at the polls and in the halls of Congress, the radicals launched the first of two attempts to subject President Johnson to the ultimate humiliation—impeachment.

In January of 1867, Republican Representative James Ashley of Ohio took the floor of the House to accuse the President of "acts which, in contemplation of the Consitition, are high crimes and misdemeanors for which, in my judgment, he ought to be impeached." The supposed crimes included Johnson's purported participation in the plot to assassinate Lincoln and his advocacy of a "soft" approach for dealing with the South. The House Judiciary Committee was assigned to make an investigation.

Ashley's initial charges were rather vague. But, later the same month, much more specific and inflammatory accusations were hurled at Johnson on the floor of the House.

On January 24 Republican Representative Benjamin Loan of Missouri charged that southern leaders had decided to assassinate Lincoln because next in line for the Presidency "stood one who by birth, education and association was a southern man, a lifelong pro-slavery Democrat . . . influenced by all the grossest instincts of his nature, without moral culture or moral restraint, with a towering ambition."

Loan claimed that the Southern leaders "were quick to understand the advantages offered them by such a person occupying the second office in the government." He told the House:

> They readily comprehended the means necessary to reach and use such a subject. But one frail life stood between him and the chief magistracy of the republic. An assassin's bullet wielded and directed by rebel hand and paid for by rebel gold made Andrew Johnson President. The price that he was to pay for his promotion was treachery to the Republicans and fidelity to the party of treason and rebellion.

Loan said evidence was available and would soon be made public. However, the investigation by the House Judiciary Committee produced virtually no responsible evidence against Johnson—merely more wild accusations.

Later testimony revealed that several Congressmen had tried to build a phony case against Johnson by bribing witnesses. In the end, the House voted by an almost two-to-one margin to defeat the impeachment resolution offered by Ashley. Many of the radicals—despite their desire to oust Johnson—could not bring themselves to vote for impeachment in view of the almost total absence of evidence.

During 1867 the radicals pushed through Congress a law called the Tenure of Office Act. The law forbade the President to remove from office without the Senate's consent any official who had required Senate confirmation at the time of his appointment.

Johnson refused to abide by the law. Members of the Lincoln Cabinet had remained in office and most of them had loyally served the new President. However, Secretary of War Edwin M. Stanton was an exception. He had worked hand in glove with Johnson's radical enemies in Congress and had become an intolerable nuisance to the President.

Finally, Johnson asked for Stanton's resignation. But the Secretary of War refused to comply. Johnson fired him—without getting permission from the Senate.

The President ordered General Ulysses S. Grant to bar Stanton from occupying his office. Grant disobeyed the order. Stanton not only occupied the office for a time but even barricaded himself inside. The resulting quarrel earned Grant the approval of the congressional radicals and helped propel him into a political career.

For Johnson, it was the beginning of another threat of impeachment.

The radicals promptly drew up eleven articles of impeachment against Johnson, based on his violation of the Tenure of Office Act. In February 1868 the House approved by a vote of 126 to 47 a resolution providing "that Andrew Johnson, President of the United States, be impeached of high crimes and misdemeanors in office." Even while voting for the impeachment, some of the radicals admitted that the Tenure of Office Act had never been intended to apply to Lincoln's appointees in Johnson's Cabinet.

The charges drawn in the House were sent to the Senate, which was to serve as a court to decide whether the President should, in fact, be impeached. The trial turned into a shambles. The old, discredited accusations that Johnson had been involved in Lincoln's assassination were dredged up for still one more airing. Johnson was described before the Senate as "the elect of an assassin" —a man who had succeeded to the Presidency by "murder most foul."

Johnson did not appear before the Senate during the trial but was represented by extremely capable lawyers. When stripped of their high flown language, the articles of impeachment accused Johnson of little more than carrying out his rightful duties as Commander in Chief and making speeches offensive to congressmen.

The climactic Senate vote came on May 16, 1868. There were then fifty-four senators. Every one of them was present for the vote—even one who had to be brought in on a stretcher. Senate President Pro Tem Benjamin Wade, an Ohio Republican who was next in line to become President if Johnson were impeached, insisted on casting a vote in spite of the fact that he obviously had a self-interested stake in the outcome. Wade was so certain that Johnson would be impeached—and that he himself would become President—that he had already chosen a Cabinet.

Wade voted to impeach Johnson. So did thirty-four other senators. But nineteen senators, a dozen Democrats and seven Republicans, voted against impeachment.

That left the radicals one vote short of the two-thirds necessary for impeachment. Thus, by the slender margin of one vote, the integrity of the American Presidency was upheld.

However, Johnson's prestige had been so badly shaken by the constant assaults that he was unable to govern very effectively during the remainder of his presidential term. His Presidency ended ignominiously—just as his vice presidency had begun. Those who felt there was a jinx on the vice presidency, and on all men who occupied the office, now had still more fuel for their fires.

CHAPTER SEVEN

◆§§◆

Reconstruction and Assassination

IF ANYONE believed that the vice presidency would become a less-controversial office in the years immediately following the Andrew Johnson furor, he was badly mistaken. The two men who followed Johnson into the office were both tarred by scandal—one as he was about to leave the vice presidency and the other as he was about to enter it.

Johnson was followed to the Presidency by the general who had defied him in the struggle to oust Secretary of War Stanton. Those who contend that military men generally make poor presidents invariably point to Ulysses S. Grant as an example. Although Grant was a hero of the Civil War, he proved to be one of the most inept Presidents in American history. Some of his critics even called him "Useless S. Grant."

One of the many ironies of Grant's election to the Presidency lay in the fact that his opponent was one of the most capable, idealistic men ever to grace the political scene. His name was Horatio Seymour and, though he is little known today, he was a legend in his time.

Seymour, who had served with distinction as Governor of New York, was one of the most reluctant candidates ever offered for the Presidency. No fewer than five times did Seymour refuse the Democratic presidential nomination. Yet the Democratic convention swiftly cast aside his objections and nominated him for President, with journalist F. P. Blair as his running mate.

Seymour thus became the only candidate actually forced to run for the Presidency. Despite his prior reluctance, he waged a vigorous campaign. He polled 2,703,249 votes, but Grant polled 3,012,833. However, Seymour would have come much closer—and some say might even have defeated Grant—if many of his supporters had not been forbidden to vote under the Reconstruction policies then in effect.

Elected Vice President under Grant was Schuyler Colfax of Indiana, who had been Speaker of the House. An extremely diligent worker, he had won the reputation of being one of the most effective Speakers in history.

Colfax possessed an uncanny knack for making friends and ingratiating himself with persons both in and out of politics. He always seemed to have a slight smile on his lips—which led people to call him "Smiler" Colfax. At the 1868 Republican convention Colfax was one of those considered for the presidential nomination. After the nomination went to Grant, Colfax was chosen as his running mate. Since he was much more experienced in politics than Grant, Colfax did the major share of the campaigning.

Colfax had not been Vice President long before Grant began to suspect him of scheming to win election as President. In the fall of 1870 the Vice President announced that he would retire after his first term. Although Colfax denied it, Grant was convinced the Vice President's announced retirement plans were phony—designed to bring about his draft for the Presidency.

Despite his denials, there is some evidence that Colfax hoped Grant might be persuaded to retire, himself, after one term. Any such hopes he may have harbored were soon dashed. Grant decided not only to seek reelection but to turn the tables by dumping Colfax from the ticket. Colfax hastily let it be known that he would accept a second term if drafted. No draft—only a chilly reception—greeted his decision. Grant's vice-presidential candidate in 1872 was Henry Wilson of Massachusetts, a poor boy who had risen from a cobbler to a shoe manufacturer to an editor to a Senator.

The Democrats nominated influential newspaper editor

Horace Greeley for the presidency—the man who made "Go West, Young Man" a phrase known throughout the world. They looked to the Midwest for their vice-presidential candidate—Governor B. Gratz Brown of Missouri.

Brown's heavy drinking during the campaign brought him the nickname "Boozy Gratz" Brown. During a speech in the East at Yale University, he made the classic error of ridiculing everything the East represented. He compounded the felony by getting smashingly drunk. His election as Vice President undoubtedly would have brought dishonor to the office. The country would be spared that fate. Grant and Wilson were clearly headed to victory.

However, both Colfax and Wilson brought their own dishonor to the vice presidency—not the dishonor of intemperance but the dishonor of greed. At the height of the presidential campaign both were involved in a scandal that touched many other men prominent in politics.

The scandal had its roots as far back as 1861. A Californian named Collis P. Huntington spent that winter in Washington, lobbying on behalf of a Pacific railroad bill. He carried $200,-000 to Washington and spent it where it would do the most good.

With the aid of bribes, Huntington brought about passage of a bill providing for a government loan to the builders of the prospective railroad in the form of $55,000,000 worth of government bonds. In addition, the government promised to give the builders 10 square miles of public land for every mile of track laid for the railroad.

Two years later another railroad lobbyist named Thomas C. Durant spent twice as much money as had Huntington—and came back with double the concessions from the government.

All told, the railroads represented by Huntington and Durant—the Central Pacific and the Union Pacific—received from the government 23,000,000 acres of land estimated to be worth between $50,000,000 and $100,000,000. The two railroads had joined forces, with the Central Pacific scheduled to build the road running east from California and the Union Pacific building west from Omaha, Nebraska.

To accomplish their purpose they set up a dummy corporation in Pennsylvania named the Credit Mobilier of America. One of the promoters involved in the scheme from the beginning was Oakes Ames, a member of Congress. All the money supplied by the government was paid to the Credit Mobilier. The railroad assigned contracts to the Credit Mobilier for the construction work.

Later evidence disclosed that the Credit Mobilier had charged the government $173,000,000 for work that had actually cost $83,000,000. The $90,000,000 balance—the fruits of one of the most monumental frauds in history—were to be split among the railroad stockholders.

But the stockholders began feuding over how to divide the loot. Rumors of a vast scandal blossomed, and there were hints a congressional investigation would be launched.

Congressman Ames, fearing exposure and disgrace, set out to head off the investigation. He distributed several thousand shares of Credit Mobilier stock among fellow members of Congress. The congressmen were permitted to buy the stock at ridiculously low prices and, if unable to pay for the shares, were allowed to make the payments out of the huge dividends then being paid. In 1868 alone each share paid $341 in dividends. The total profits distributed in legislative circles were estimated at more than $33,000,000.

Then, during the fall of 1872, the whole sordid story came to light. The New York Sun dug up the names of the officials who had shared in the profits and published the entire list. At the head of the list was Vice President Colfax. Right behind him was the vice-presidential candidate, Senator Wilson. Also included were House Speaker James G. Blaine and an Ohio Congressman destined for higher office, James A. Garfield.

Belatedly, the House of Representatives decided to go through with an investigation. Colfax came off rather badly. Congressman Ames told the congressional investigating committee that Colfax had paid for some stock, although it had never been listed in his name. Colfax testified voluntarily. He denied buying any stock or even being offered any.

The Vice President also denied using any influence—either in his vice presidency or while Speaker of the House—to aid legislation favoring the Credit Mobilier. Almost in passing he made the astounding statement that, anyway, he saw nothing wrong with the railroad promoters creating a dummy corporation to permit them to do business with themselves—at the government's expense.

In an attempt to clear up the conflict between the testimony of Colfax and Ames, the congressional investigators ordered Ames back to the witness chair. This time he provided a fuller account of his transactions with the Vice President. He told of paying Colfax $1,200 in dividends from the Credit Mobilier stock in June, 1868. The Vice President's bank records showed a $1,200 deposit during that month.

Colfax also returned to the witness chair. He again denied having any such dealings with Ames. As for the $1,200 deposit, he had an explanation for that. It seems that he was opening his mail one morning when a $1,000 bill fairly leaped into his hand from an envelope. And who had sent the money? A man now dead, Colfax said. The man was a New Yorker named George F. Nesbitt, who had supposedly intended the money to be used as a contribution toward Colfax's campaign for Vice President.

The idea of someone sending a $1,000 bill through the mail was improbable enough. Added to the fact that Colfax's supposed financial angel was now dead—and to the fact that the Vice President's account still left $200 unexplained—it was only natural that the story should be suspect.

Impeachment of Colfax was considered. But, partly since his term was almost over and partly since his suspect actions had taken place before he became Vice President, no such action was taken. The investigating committee let him off the hook without either clearing or accusing him. In fact, the only official censured by the committee was Ames.

But the press and public were not nearly so lenient. The influential magazine, *The Nation*, summed up the investigation's results this way: "A total loss, one senator; badly damaged and not serviceable to future political use, two Vice Presidents, and eight congressmen. The condition of Ames's reputation, language is inadequate to describe."

It developed that Senator Wilson had accepted twenty shares of Credit Mobilier stock, paying cash for them. Upon reflection, he had decided to return the stock and get his money back. He had done so before the newspaper article revealing the scandal had been published.

Wilson survived the scandal to be elected Vice President with Grant. But, after serving less than three years of his term, he was paralyzed by a stroke while presiding over the Senate. He later became the fourth Vice President to die before completing his term.

Some of Grant's most strident opposition came not from Democrats but from dissident Republicans. The split in the Republican ranks—plus general disaffection with the scandals of the Grant regime—almost cost the Republicans the next presidential election. In fact, there is considerable evidence that the Republicans actually lost the election, only to "steal" it from the Democrats.

In 1876 the Republicans nominated three-time Ohio Governor Rutherford B. Hayes for President. Their vice-presidential candidate was William A. Wheeler, a Congressman from upstate New York.

The Democratic presidential candidate was New York Governor Samuel J. Tilden, a brilliant political tactician who had first won fame for prosecuting corrupt members of his own party—those in the infamous Tweed Ring in New York City. His running mate was Governor Thomas A. Hendricks of Indiana, making the first of his two races for the vice presidency.

Two days after the election the popular vote stood at 4,285,992 for Tilden and 4,033,768 for Hayes. Tilden also led in the electoral vote with 184 votes to 166 for Hayes. But the electoral votes of three Southern states—South Carolina, Florida and Louisiana—were still in doubt. And if Hayes could win all three, he would be elected by an electoral majority of just one vote.

In all three doubtful states there were two factions with separate electoral boards. One faction consisted of Republican carpetbaggers and Negro voters who followed their lead. The other consisted of local whites, virtually all of them Democrats.

President Grant, in the waning days of his term, sent federal troops into the three doubtful states to enforce the carpetbaggers' vote tallies at bayonet point. The Republicans, with the military supporting them, resorted to every imaginable device to take the election away from Tilden. In Louisiana, where Tilden held a 17,000-vote majority, the Republican electoral board tossed out 13,000 of his votes. In Florida, where he held a decisive majority, the Republican board ignored the results and declared Hayes the winner. There is considerable evidence to indicate that Hayes made a deal with some Southern Democrats, promising to end Reconstruction if he were elected.

In the end, Congress passed a law creating a special commission to decide the election. The commission—composed of five members of the Senate, five members of the House and five judges—included seven Democrats, seven Republicans and one judge who was supposed to be neutral. The commission split along party lines. The "neutral" judge, after spending the entire night before his decision with a Republican Cabinet member and a Republican senator, voted in favor of Hayes.

By this strange process did Rutherford B. Hayes become President and did William A. Wheeler become Vice President. Shortly after entering the presidential office, Hayes put an end to Reconstruction—thus reinforcing the suspicion that he had made a deal with Southern Democrats. Neither Hayes nor Wheeler left much of a mark on his office. However, Hayes did begin to change the system for choosing civil servants, substituting merit for party affiliation. He was supported strongly in these efforts by his Vice President. Wheeler was a frequent visitor at the White House, sometimes joining the Hayes family for an evening of prayer and hymn singing. Relations between Hayes and Wheeler remained extremely warm throughout their term. As Hayes put it: "He (Wheeler) was one of the very few Vice Presidents who was on cordial terms —intimate and sincerely friendly—with the President. Our family all were heartily fond of him. . . . In character, he was sterling gold."

However, Hayes had many problems with other members of his party. He was so unpopular among them that he asked not to be renominated in 1880. Wheeler was never seriously considered as his successor.

The Republican convention in 1880 was one of the most bitter in the party's history. The party was split into factions known as the "Stalwarts" and the "Half-Breeds." Making an attempt to return from political oblivion was Ulysses S. Grant, who had come back from a world tour with some of the respect he had lost during his two terms as President. He wanted another chance to occupy the White House.

Grant's chief opponent for the nomination appeared to be James G. Blaine, who, despite his part in the Credit Mobilier scandal, was considered one of the most attractive political candidates of his time. He had served as Speaker of the House, as Secretary of State and as a Senator.

The split in the party was so deep that a deadlock between Grant and Blaine persisted for more than 30 ballots. On the 34th ballot, some of Blaine's "Half-Breeds" swung their votes to Congressman James A. Garfield of Ohio. Garfield protested the support. He had come to the convention not as a candidate but as floor manager of a dark-horse campaign on behalf of John Sherman. However, his protest was ruled out of order.

Although Grant's "Stalwarts" fought savagely until the end, Garfield was nominated on the 36th ballot.

In the time-honored "vote-bait" tradition, Garfield decided to permit the "Stalwarts" to name the vice-presidential candidate. The dominant figure at the convention was the political boss of New York, Senator Roscoe Conkling—a "Stalwart." He had been deprived of much of his patronage power under the civil-service reform program begun by Hayes. He made it clear that no political ally of his could be expected to take the vice-presidential nomination—at least not if he expected to retain Conkling's loyalty.

Thus, when Garfield gave the New York "Stalwarts" the right to choose the vice-presidential nominee, Conkling did not even attend the meeting at which the selection was to be made. At the meeting a surprise drive arose to give the second spot on the ticket to Chester A. Arthur.

Arthur was a rare man in those days of gamy politics—a true intellectual. He had been graduated from college, with a Phi Beta Kappa key, at the age of seventeen. He had taught school, practiced law, then entered politics.

Under Conkling's tutelage Arthur had become New York's collector of customs. The customs house was a prime source of patronage and political corruption—with bribes and blackmail against merchants the order of the day. Although Arthur himself did not participate in the thievery, he closed his eyes to the crimes of Conkling's other appointees.

During President Hayes' cleanup of the civil service, he sent investigators into the customs house. Their revelations persuaded him to oust both Arthur and his chief aide, Alonzo Cornell, who was also Republican state chairman. This led Conkling to break with Hayes. In defiance of the President, Conkling saw to it that Cornell was elected governor and that Arthur replaced him as Republican state chairman.

Thus the drive to nominate Arthur for Vice President came at a time when he was known cheifly as a Conkling patronage hack.

The New York "Stalwarts," with Conkling absent, eventually put their seal of approval on Arthur's candidacy.

Arthur then sought out Conkling to get his approval.

He mumbled that Garfield's supporters had agreed to accept him as the vice-presidential candidate. Conkling snapped that Arthur should refuse the nomination, since Garfield was certain to be defeated in the election.

However, Arthur—for once—stood up to his mentor. He said: "The office of Vice President is a greater honor than I ever dreamed of attaining. A barren nomination would be a great honor. In a calmer moment, you will look at this differently."

Conkling bristled. He told Arthur that, if he wanted his respect, he would "contemptuously" refuse the nomination.

But Arthur was adamant. "Senator Conkling, I shall accept the nomination and I shall carry with me the majority of the New York delegation," he said.

Arthur's name was placed in nomination, and he captured almost two-thirds of the delegate votes on the first ballot. Few of the delegates, it seems certain, realized the gravity of their decision. Garfield, at forty-eight, appeared young and healthy enough to complete his presidential term.

The Democrats nominated General Winfield Scott Hancock for President. Hancock had been one of the most heroic Union officers in the Civil War. He also served with distinction as an extremely fair military governor in the defeated South. The vice presidential candidate was William H. English.

During the campaign the Democrats dredged up all the old, justified Credit Mobilier charges against Garfield. In addition, they concocted some new, fictitious charges—including a forged letter that purported to show Garfield favored importation of cheap Chinese labor.

Garfield went to New York during the campaign to confer with the "Stalwarts." Conkling refused to see him but was represented by Thomas C. Platt, Conkling's candidate for the second New York Senate seat. Platt insisted that, if elected, Garfield clear all New York patronage appointments with Conkling. Garfield said he would have to give some patronage jobs to anti-Conkling New Yorkers who had supported him at the convention—but he agreed to "consult" with Conkling on appointments.

Taking Garfield at his word during the campaign, Conkling supported the national ticket. Garfield and Arthur carried New York in winning the election.

Shortly after the election Garfield and Arthur fell out over the distribution of patronage. Arthur, once elected, had mended his fences with Boss Conkling—much to Garfield's dismay. When Garfield ignored the pleas of Arthur and Conkling that high-level jobs be given to "Stalwarts," the breach widened.

The final straw came when Garfield, reneging on his promise to "consult" with Conkling, appointed an opponent of the New York political boss, William H. Robertson, to the sensitive customs-house job from which Arthur previously had been ousted.

Vice President Arthur supported Conkling in the dispute that followed. He went to see Garfield, pleading that Robertson's appointment would ruin the Republican Party in New York. But the President was firm; he would not bow before Roscoe Conkling.

This prompted Arthur to rebuke the President in public. "Garfield has not been square, nor honorable . . . with Conkling," he said. "It's a hard thing to say of a President of the United States—but it is, unfortunately, only the truth."

In a grandstand play, both Conkling and his hand-picked fellow Senator, Thomas Platt, resigned their Senate seats. They announced their intention to return to New York, win reelection and thus prove that the state believed them right in their struggle with the President.

However, it was not the public—but the New York state legislature—that would decide whether the two men returned to the Senate. In that period senators were still chosen in legislative elections—rather than popular elections. While Conkling and Platt were seeking reelection, Garfield's appointment of Robertson as customs collector was confirmed by the Senate in a near unanimous vote.

Congress shortly adjourned. Vice President Arthur, free from the duty of presiding over the Senate, hastened to Albany to lobby in the legislative back rooms on behalf of Conkling and Platt. He was subjected to merciless ridicule in the press, which characterized him as a lackey for Boss Conkling.

The struggle continued for months. Its duration forced Platt to leave the field. During the long fight he became involved in a personal scandal that became the talk of Albany. In disgrace, he announced his withdrawal from the race.

When the legislature recessed for weekends, Arthur and Conkling regularly rode the Hudson River boats down river to New York City to escape the dreariness and heat of the state capital. On Saturday, July 2, 1881, the day that Platt pulled out of the Senate race, the two political allies stepped from their boat onto a Manhattan dock to be met by the usual swarm of reporters. They expected to be asked the usual questions about the events in Albany.

To their shock, they learned from the newsmen that President Garfield had been shot in the back less than an hour earlier in the Washington railroad depot.

Garfield's assailant was an egomaniac named Charles J. Guiteau, who had been a hanger-on around Republican campaign headquarters. The Republican campaign leaders considered him a crank. But, nonetheless, he managed to wangle about a dozen interviews with Chester Arthur during the vice-presidential candidate's campaign.

When Garfield and Arthur were elected, Guiteau tried to cash in his worthless chips. He thought he deserved a responsible government job. His demands were hardly modest. He wanted nothing less than the highly prestigious post as American Consul in Paris.

Not easily rebuffed, Guiteau forced his way into the White House—in fact, into Garfield's private office—to ask what was holding up his appointment. When Garfield brushed him off he appealed to Arthur. But the Vice President was no more receptive than the President. Guiteau began to write demanding letters to Garfield.

Finally he got the message. He was not wanted. From that time on, he claimed, he began getting messages from God— telling him that Garfield must be removed from office and replaced by Arthur. And he would be the instrument of God's will, the emissary on a holy mission of assassination.

Guiteau bought a revolver, practiced firing it in the woods along the Potomac and then began stalking Garfield, waiting for the perfect opportunity to kill him. When he learned that the President was to leave the Washington railroad depot alone on the morning of July 2 to deliver a commencement address at his alma mater, Williams College, Guiteau decided that the time had come to strike.

Guiteau had no hope of escaping. In fact, he made advance arrangements with a hackman to give him a ride to a point near the city jail so that he could turn himself in after the shooting. His whole plan was centered on calling attention to himself.

At 9:20 A.M., ten minutes before train time, Garfield arrived at the railroad station with Secretary of State James G. Blaine. In those days the Secret Service—which was later assigned the duty of protecting Presidents and Vice Presidents—was responsible chiefly for suppressing counterfeiting. Thus there was no presidential guard on hand to shield Garfield from assailants and cranks.

Guiteau, standing behind a bench when the President entered the waiting room, watched Garfield walk about three-fourths of the way across the room. He then drew his revolver, approached within a few feet of the President and shot him in the back.

"My God, what is this?" Garfield gasped.

Guiteau stepped forward and fired again, but this shot merely passed harmlessly through Garfield's sleeve. The assassin then tried to reach the hack waiting to take him to the jail but was intercepted by a policeman.

"Now Arthur is President of the United States," he told the officer exultantly. "I am a stalwart of the Stalwarts."

But Guiteau was wrong. Arthur was not President of the United States—not yet.

For Garfield was alive—gravely wounded, but alive. Guiteau's first bullet had fractured two of his ribs, gone through his backbone and become lodged in his body. The President was rushed back to the White House.

Vice President Arthur, upon hearing of the shooting, rushed to Washington and visited the White House. He received a cool reception from members of Garfield's Cabinet. Although no responsible person accused Arthur of complicity in the assassination attempt, many felt that the Vice President's open break with the President had helped create a climate that made the shooting seem rational to Guiteau.

Newspapers, politicians and ordinary citizens echoed one theme: If Garfield died, a nonentity would become President and Boss Conkling would be the power behind the throne.

For the first time the nation was confronted now with the problem of interpreting the section of the Constitution providing that the powers and duties of the President "shall devolve on the Vice President" in the event of a President's disability.

It seemed clear that Garfield would never be able to carry on as President. However, for two and a half months he lingered in that nether world between life and death.

The members of Garfield's Cabinet were in agreement that he could not perform his duties. But they were afraid that, once Arthur assumed the President's responsibilities, there would be no way of returning Garfield to power if he should make some sort of miraculous recovery.

Arthur, for his part, made no move that could be interpreted as an attempt to usurp the Presidency. He returned to New York and went into seclusion.

In late August complications developed in Garfield's condition. His physicians said all hope for his recovery was gone. Because he felt most at home near the ocean, the President was taken to a house on the New Jersey shore to live out his waning days. His family and members of his administration joined him. On September 19 he died.

Charles Guiteau was tried for Garfield's murder, convicted and sentenced to death. Just before going to the gallows he read to reporters a poem he had written in his jail cell. It read in part:

> I saved my party and my land
> Glory, Hallelujah.
> But they have murdered me for it, and that is the reason
> I am going to the Lordy.

As the gallows trap door was swung, his last words were "Glory, glory, glory. . . ."

Whether Guiteau saved his party and his land is an open question. But those who had predicted Chester A. Arthur would make a shambles of the Presidency were mistaken.

From the outset Arthur made it clear that his administration would be free from domination by Roscoe Conkling. The one-time political boss, who had lost both his reelection campaign and much of his power, made only a half-hearted attempt to exert influence upon the new President. And that attempt fell on its face. Conkling came to Washington, had a long meeting with Arthur and urged him to replace the rebellious William Robertson as customs collector in New York. But Arthur refused, and Conkling returned to New York to sulk.

This incident was a forerunner of what was to be the major thrust of Arthur's early period as President. He devoted himself zealously to reform of the civil service, calling for appointments to government posts on the basis of proved ability, attempts to maintain a stable corps of government workers immune to political manipulation, promotion of capable employees to higher positions and prompt investigation of complaints of official corruption.

A law incorporating Arthur's suggestions, named the Pendleton Act in honor of a long-time champion of reform, Senator George Pendleton of Ohio, was passed by the Congress in 1883 and signed by the President. The act created a Civil Service Commission to supervise the reform program—a program which, in expanded form, today protects the interests of millions of government workers and assures consistent standards of performance in public service.

In most other respects as well Arthur was an exemplary President. During his term, numerous progressive projects—in such fields as conservation and education—were first undertaken. His administration also reformed the tax structure, revised tariff schedules and strengthened the Navy.

But Arthur's hope of breaking the jinx on "accidental" presidents, and winning his own full term in the White House, was short-lived. Political troubles had loomed for Arthur as early as 1882. In the congressional elections that year his home state of New York had gone overwhelmingly Democratic. Although much of the national electorate felt Arthur had done an admirable job as President, many of the political professionals considered his performance something of a freak. Moreover, they felt it was time to give James G. Blaine a chance at the nation's top office.

At the Republican convention Arthur remained in the running for the nomination through four ballots. But Blaine ultimately won the nomination.

The Democrats nominated Grover Cleveland, a former ward politician who had risen to the governorship of New York through such jobs as sheriff of Erie County and mayor of Buffalo. Cleveland's running mate was Thomas A. Hendricks of Indiana, who had been the unsuccessful candidate for Vice President with Tilden in 1876.

The campaign of 1884 was one of the most bitter, and dirty, in the history of presidential contests. Charges of public and personal scandal were brought against both nominees. In the end it was Cleveland's home state of New York—which he carried by the slender margin of 1,100 votes—that propelled him into the Presidency. The national popular vote went to Cleveland by 4,874,986 to 4,851,981.

Vice President Hendricks got little chance to leave a mark on his office. He was sixty-five years of age and in poor health when he entered the vice presidency. He had suffered two paralytic strokes in the previous five years. Less than a year after taking office, he became ill in Indianapolis just before returning to Washington for the opening of a new Congress. He died a short time later. Since Congress had previously ended a special session without electing either a House Speaker or a Senate President Pro Tem to serve during the adjournment period, the nation was temporarily left without a line of succession in case of the President's death or disability. For that reason President Cleveland was persuaded not to travel to Indiana for the Vice President's funeral.

From the time of Hendricks' death on November 25, 1885, until December 7, 1885, there was no man in line to succeed Cleveland. Then John Sherman was elected Senate President Pro Tem—thus becoming the first in line.

In 1888 Cleveland sought reelection, but was defeated by Senator Benjamin Harrison of Indiana. Elected Vice President was Levi P. Morton of New York, a long-time crony of Roscoe Conkling and a man who had been considered for the national ticket for many years.

Born at Shoreham, Vermont, Morton later moved to New York and organized a Wall Street banking company. He served one term in Congress, then was appointed U. S. Minister to France. As Vice President, Morton was noted as one of the fairest presiding officers in the Senate's history. He refused to join forces with his fellow Republicans in ruling on procedural questions—insisting on protecting the rights of the

Democratic minority. During one controversial debate some Republicans suggested to Morton—in an attempt to get him out of their way—that he looked ill and should take a vacation trip to Florida. Morton replied that he felt fine and would stay in Washington, whether the Republican senators liked it or not. Later in the debate Morton stopped going out to lunch so that the Republicans could not take advantage of his absence to force their will on the minority.

The results of Morton's insistence on scrupulous fairness were mixed. On the one hand the senators of both parties thought so much of him that they gave him a farewell banquet when he left the vice presidency. On the other hand, although President Harrison was renominated, Morton was dropped from the ticket for the 1892 election. His spot on the ticket was taken by Whitelaw Reid, editor of the *New York Tribune* and one-time Minister to France. Morton went on to become Governor of New York.

In the 1892 election Grover Cleveland turned the tables on Harrison and became the only President ever to serve two terms that were not consecutive. Cleveland won renomination on the first ballot at the Democratic convention, and had little trouble defeating the incumbent President in the November election. He drew 277 electoral votes to Harrison's 145.

Elected Vice President was Adlai E. Stevenson of Illinois, whose grandson and namesake was to be a two-time Democratic candidate for the Presidency more than a half century later. The elder Stevenson, like his grandson, was a man of intellect and wit. He had shown great popularity with the electorate in Illinois by winning two congressional races against heavy odds in a strongly Republican district. He had later served as the first Assistant Postmaster General.

Stevenson was fond of poking fun at his own role as Vice President. In later years he would advise his young grandson never to seek or take the office (the advice was followed). Nonetheless, the elder Stevenson ran for Vice President twice. As we shall see, he was successful only once.

CHAPTER EIGHT

The End of the Century

THE presidential elections of 1896 and 1900 pitted the nation's greatest orator of the time against one of its most skilled political professionals.

The orator was silver-tongued William Jennings Bryan. Bryan, the Democratic candidate, won the nomination in 1896 on the fifth ballot. President Cleveland, after serving his second term, went into retirement. Bryan was a Bible-quoting, phrase-turning speaker who seemingly could charm the apples from the trees. A religious fundamentalist, he later would be the prosecutor in the Scopes "monkey trial" in Tennessee. For all his fine attributes, Bryan was far from an expert at winning elections. His running mate in 1896 was Arthur Sewall of Maine.

The Republican standard-bearer in both races was William McKinley—a man who looked like a President, commanded personal affection and *was* an expert at winning elections. McKinley had served in Congress for more than a decade, then become Governor of Ohio. In the House he had served as chairman of the powerful Ways and Means Committee and been a leading advocate of the high protective tariff.

McKinley's running mate in 1896 was Garret A. Hobart of New Jersey. An attorney, Hobart served in the legislature from 1873 to 1885—part of the time as president of the state senate. He was defeated in a race for United States senator in 1884, but remained prominent in national Republican activities.

McKinley conducted what came to be known as "the front porch campaign." He stayed at his home in Canton, Ohio, receiving visiting delegations from all parts of the country on his front porch. Bryan, meanwhile, traveled the country— making 600 speeches in four tours that carried him 13,000 miles through twenty-nine states.

The business community rallied behind McKinley and Hobart with a zeal that sometimes overstepped the bounds of propriety. Some manufacturers warned their workers that their plants would close if the Democrats won the election. Others placed supply orders containing clauses that permitted cancellation in case of a Democratic victory.

Helped by these acts of intimidation, the McKinley-Hobart ticket swept to victory by a popular-vote margin of 7,111,607 to 6,509,052. The electoral vote went to the Republicans by 271 to 176.

Vice President Hobart left little mark on the nation's second highest office. Perhaps his most important niche in history was carved by his death during the third year of his term. This made it possible for one of the most dynamic figures in American political annals to serve as his successor.

The successor was the bombastic, vigorous Governor of New York, Theodore Roosevelt. He became Vice President not because of his many sterling qualities but because his enemies wanted to "bury" him politically in a job they considered relatively unimportant.

Teddy Roosevelt had served as a member of the New York state legislature and the federal Civil Service Commission before being appointed Assistant Secretary of the Navy under McKinley. During McKinley's first term Roosevelt was one of the chief agitators for war with Spain over Cuba. When the Spanish-American War finally erupted, he left Washington to become a lieutenant colonel in charge of a disorganized band of volunteers known as the "Rough Riders."

Roosevelt won international fame as a swashbuckler by

leading the "Rough Riders" in the celebrated charge up San Juan Hill. He returned to the United States from Cuba as a hero and set his sights on higher political office.

In 1898 he was elected Governor of New York. But the term lasted only two years. Thus, in 1900, he would have to stand for election again if he wanted to remain governor.

Some New York Republicans, however, were determined to go to any lengths to get Roosevelt out of the Governor's Mansion. They were led by that crusty, formerly discredited Conkling man, Thomas C. Platt. After taking a back seat for several years, Platt had fought his way back into the Senate and had become the Republican state chairman.

It was a foregone conclusion that President McKinley would be renominated in 1900. The major focus at the Republican convention thus would be on the nomination for a successor to the late Vice President Hobart.

Platt decided to try to persuade Roosevelt to abandon the governorship and run for Vice President. Roosevelt, after being flattered at first by the proposal, later saw through Platt's scheme and wrote to him: "The more I have thought over it, the more I have felt that I would a great deal rather be anything, say professor of history, than Vice President."

Nonetheless, there was considerable sentiment among delegates to the Republican convention—some inspired by Platt and some resulting from genuine admiration of Roosevelt—in favor of making him McKinley's running mate. Republican National Chairman Mark Hanna was aghast at the thought of Roosevelt, whom he called a "madman," standing one heartbeat away from the Presidency.

Hanna appealed to McKinley to head off the boom for Roosevelt. But the President sent word to the convention that he had no favorite candidate for the vice presidency and would accept anyone chosen by the delegates.

When Roosevelt entered the convention hall in Philadelphia—wearing a broad-brimmed hat of the type made famous by the "Rough Riders"—he was greeted by tumultuous applause. Still, he insisted that he would not take the vice-presidential nomination.

Delegates from Western states—where Roosevelt was extremely popular because he had been a North Dakota rancher for a time and had been a champion of Western conservation measures—rallied behind the former "Rough Rider." It became clear that Roosevelt was the heavy favorite of the convention. And Roosevelt, his past reluctance cast aside, announced: "I cannot disappoint my Western friends. . . . I cannot seem to be bigger than my party."

McKinley and Roosevelt were nominated unanimously.

The Democrats again nominated Bryan, this time with former Vice President Adlai Stevenson as his running mate. During his previous vice-presidential term Stevenson had differed with President Cleveland on economic policy and, as a result, had been allowed to enter only the fringes of the administration's inner circle. He had surrounded himself with advisers, also opposed to the Cleveland policy, who were sneeringly called by their enemies "the Stevenson Cabinet." Nonetheless, Stevenson made many friends while serving as Vice President. He was considered an excellent presiding officer of the Senate. Thus his nomination as Bryan's running mate was generally popular among party members.

This campaign was more vigorous than the one in 1896, largely because of Roosevelt's arrival on the scene. He was a crowd-pleasing speaker—no match for Bryan at oratorical elegance, but an arm-swinging, flamboyant platform performer who captured every bit as much attention as the Democratic standard-bearer.

The Democrats accused the Republicans of imperialistic foreign policy, demanded independence for the Philippines and denounced the McKinley program for Puerto Rico. The Republicans hammered at the theme that theirs was the party of prosperity and that economic disaster lay with the election of the Democrats.

McKinley and Roosevelt were elected by an even larger

margin than the one given McKinley and Hobart in 1896.

Roosevelt settled somewhat uncomfortably into the Vice President's office. At the age of forty-two he felt confined by the relatively inactive position. His immediate plans called for completing his law-school education (he had attended for only one year) while he was Vice President. After that, who knew what would happen? Roosevelt harbored hopes of becoming President someday. But he was preparing for any eventuality. With a law degree he might enter some prestigious law firm after leaving the vice presidency.

However, a seemingly inconsequential little man named Leon F. Czolgosz—previously unknown to Roosevelt—was to play a surprise role in his career.

Czolgosz, a former factory and farm worker who had turned into an aimless drifter and a political anarchist, hated government and rulers—whether kings, presidents or prime ministers.

In early September of 1901 Czolgosz found himself in West Seneca, New York, a suburb of Buffalo. By coincidence, President McKinley had scheduled a visit to Buffalo for September 5 and 6, at which he would participate in ceremonies at a Pan-American Exposition.

Czolgosz, who felt McKinley represented the business interests that oppressed poor working people, decided to try to assassinate the President.

McKinley, who took a light view of his own safety, was under scant guard at the exposition. The Secret Service, in those days, provided only casual, informal protection to the President. It was not even empowered to do so by law. Thus only three Secret Service agents were assigned to accompany McKinley.

On the afternoon of September 6, the President was the guest of honor at a public reception in the ornate Temple of Music at the exposition. Hundreds of citizens lined up to shake his hand. Among them was Leon Czolgosz.

It was a hot, humid day, so many of the persons inside the

Temple of Music were using handkerchiefs to mop their brows. And several places ahead of Czolgosz in the line waiting to meet the President was a man with a bandaged right hand. When it became this man's turn to shake the President's hand he pointed to the bandage and said: "Excuse my left hand, Mr. President."

Seizing on the idea—and the abundance of handkerchiefs in use—Czolgosz stealthily removed a revolver from his pocket and wrapped a handkerchief around it to simulate a bandaged hand. When it became his turn to meet McKinley, Czolgosz extended his left hand. The President reached to shake it.

But Czolgosz suddenly slapped McKinley's hand aside, leaped forward and fired two shots in quick succession through the handkerchief. The President quivered, then sank into the arms of the men near him. Secret Service agents and other officers seized Czolgosz and hustled him off to jail to protect him from an angry mob.

The President clung to life for eight days after the shooting. One of the bullets had hit his breastbone but failed to penetrate his body. The other had torn into his abdomen, ripped through his stomach walls and lodged in his back muscles. Shortly after the shooting he had been rushed to an emergency hospital on the exposition grounds, where surgeons had tried in vain to find and remove the second bullet. Later, the President was taken to the home of a Buffalo attorney in the hope that he might recover.

Vice President Roosevelt was attending a meeting of Vermont conservationists on an island in Lake Champlain at the time of the shooting. He rushed to Buffalo on a special train shortly after learning of the assassination attempt. When he arrived, McKinley seemed to be progressing satisfactorily, and the doctors told the Vice President that they were sure the President would recover.

The diagnosis was sufficiently optimistic that Roosevelt soon left on a mountain-climbing expedition in the Adirondacks. However, on September 12, McKinley's pulse abruptly weakened. He rallied briefly, but on September 13 realized that the end was near. He said goodbye to his wife, whispered a passage from a favorite hymn—"Nearer My God to Thee"—and then spoke his last words: "Goodbye, all. Goodbye. It is God's way. His will be done."

McKinley sank into a coma from which he never emerged. He died at 2:15 A.M. September 14.

Leon Czolgosz was tried for the President's murder, convicted and sentenced to death. As he was strapped into the electric chair, he showed no trace of remorse. "I killed the President because he was the enemy of the good people—the good working people. I am not sorry for my crime."

Roosevelt had been eating lunch beside a mountain brook on the afternoon of September 13 when a courier brought word that McKinley was dying. The Vice President descended from the mountain, then began a race by buckboard and special train to the President's side. But he did not arrive in Buffalo until more than eleven hours after McKinley's death.

Two hours after his arrival, in an attorney's office eight blocks from the site where McKinley's body lay in state, Theodore Roosevelt took the oath of office as President.

Mark Hanna was inconsolable. "I told William McKinley it was a mistake to nominate that wild man at Philadelphia," Hanna said. "Now look. That damned cowboy is President of the United States."

"That damned cowboy" turned out, however, to be a much more vigorous President than McKinley. While pledging to carry on McKinley's policies, Roosevelt made it clear that he was his own man.

The new President told newsmen shortly after taking the oath:

> I was voted for as Vice President, it is true, but the Constitution provides that in the case of the death or inability of the President the Vice President shall serve as President and, therefore, due to the act of a madman, I am President and shall act in every word and deed precisely as if I and not Mc-

Kinley had been the candidate for whom the electors cast the vote for President.

He grasped control of the government firmly—in a way that none of his predecessors had managed to accomplish. The nation had entered the twentieth century, and it had at its helm a man who represented the modern era in politics and government. Neither the Presidency nor the vice presidency would be quite the same again.

Roosevelt was already a popular figure among the electorate at the time he became President. He became even more popular in the White House. The citizenry loved the picture of this young, vigorous man who enjoyed hunting, exercising, romping with his children and traveling around the country to meet the public.

Unlike his predecessors as "accidental" President, Roosevelt soon seemed destined for election to a full presidential term of his own.

Roosevelt was nominated in 1904 with Charles W. Fairbanks of Indiana as his running mate. The Democrats convened to choose their candidates in an atmosphere of defeatism. Roosevelt and Fairbanks seemed unbeatable. Nominated for President was Alton B. Parker, chief judge of the New York State Court of Appeals. Parker had little taste for the political life. A measure of his anonymity is provided by the fact that, of all the major party candidates for the Presidency, he is the only one who has never been the subject of a biography.

His vice-presidential candidate was eighty-one-year-old Henry G. Davis of West Virginia. The convention had chosen Davis in the hope that he could put West Virginia in the Democratic column and, as a millionaire banker and railroad executive, would be a heavy contributor to the campaign coffers. (He failed on both counts.) The recent assassination of McKinley only served to remind voters that this aged man stood one life from the Presidency. In addition, Parker was being assailed at the time as a friend of big business—and the choice of a millionaire as his running mate heightened the criticism.

The campaign was dull. And the election was both a disaster for the Democrats and a personal triumph for Roosevelt.

The President was returned to office with a popular vote of 7,628,785—400,000 more than McKinley's total in 1900 and 2,500,000 more than Parker's total. Parker carried only the South, plus Kentucky and Maryland.

After the election neither Roosevelt nor his Vice President made any secret of the fact that they were not getting along. Although he had previously advocated giving the vice president a seat in the Cabinet and a permanent vote in the Senate, Roosevelt did not pursue the matter on behalf of Fairbanks.

The Vice President, for his part, joined forces with Roosevelt's enemies in Congress in an attempt to defeat the President's programs. The bitterness between the two men became so notorious that, upon hearing that Roosevelt was considering taking a submarine trip, humorist Finley Peter Dunne advised the President not to do so "unless you take Fairbanks with you."

Roosevelt became the first modern President to carve out a role as a legislative leader. He was not always successful in this regard, but his assumption of the role was highly significant. In addition, he was notable as a great publicizer of change— change in both the public image of a president and change in government policies.

He inaugurated numerous government reforms, launched the construction of the Panama Canal (though his political methods in bringing this project about were severely criticized), sent the United States fleet around the world and staved off a threatened war.

In 1908 Roosevelt prepared to bow out as President—but pushed through the Republican convention the presidential nomination of William Howard Taft. A huge man with a walrus mustache, Taft had been Roosevelt's Secretary of War and had been sent by the President on a number of special missions to such places as Panama, Cuba and the Philippines. He previously had served as a judge in his native Ohio, as a federal appeals judge and as U. S. Solicitor General.

The convention delegates, who were not pleased about having Taft forced upon them by Roosevelt, decided to retaliate by choosing a conservative as vice-presidential nominee. The candidate was Congressman James Schoolcraft Sherman, an upstate New York lawyer, businessman and banker. Sherman had served as Mayor of Utica before being elected to Congress. He was known as an expert parliamentarian, but otherwise had not distinguished himself in Congress. The voters were again faced with a Republican ticket composed of men with differing views.

The Democrats turned once more to William Jennings Bryan as presidential nominee. His running mate was John Kern of Indiana, an unknown who added virtually nothing to the ticket.

Predictably, Roosevelt's continuing popularity carried his candidate, Taft, to victory. Taft's popular vote of 7,677,000 was slightly higher than the total given Roosevelt four years earlier. But Bryan got 6,407,000 and the Democrats made gains in gubernatorial elections and other races.

Taft and Sherman, like Roosevelt and Fairbanks, did not get along well. Shortly after their election Taft asked Sherman to serve as the administration's liaison man with the House of Representatives. The President did so because he intensely disliked the House Speaker, Joe Cannon, and wanted nothing to do with him. But Sherman was a friend of Cannon's and refused to take the liaison assignment. "I am Vice President," he told Taft. "And acting as a messenger boy is not part of the duties of a Vice President." The President and Vice President later had an even more serious disagreement over control of the Republican organization in Sherman's home state of New York. Sherman, became increasingly hostile toward Taft.

Roosevelt himself eventually had a falling out with Taft.

The former President became convinced—somewhat unfairly —that Taft had betrayed previous Roosevelt programs. Taft had pushed through the Congress a number of progressive antitrust, health and conservation measures whose passage Roosevelt had been unable to achieve.

At any rate, in 1912, Roosevelt attempted a political come-back in an effort to unseat Taft. The two men battled for the presidential nomination at the Republican convention, with Taft winning. Roosevelt then led his backers out of the convention to form a party of their own—the Bull Moose Party. (Roosevelt was fond of boasting: "I'm as strong as a bull moose.")

By the time the Taft-Roosevelt fight at the Republican convention was over, the delegates were drained of energy and seemingly convinced that the intraparty battle would cost them the election. Therefore, little attention was paid to the nomination of a vice-presidential candidate. Sherman was re-nominated. He became the first Vice President since John Calhoun to win renomination.

Sherman, however, was not destined to serve a second term. He died several days before the election, but 3,500,000 persons, not knowing he was dead, voted for him and Taft on the Republican ticket. Even if he had lived, he would not have served again. For Taft was not to be reelected. Neither was Roosevelt.

The new President was to be Woodrow Wilson, Governor of New Jersey and former president of Princeton University. He was to defeat Roosevelt by more than 2,000,000 votes and Taft by almost 3,000,000.

But despite Wilson's obvious qualifications—among them great intellect, compassion and vision—it had taken the delegates to the Democratic convention in Baltimore 46 ballots to agree upon him as the nominee. It seemed imperative to the delegates that they balance the selection of the progressive Easterner with a more conservative candidate from another section.

They chose Thomas Riley Marshall of Indiana, himself something of an intellectual. Marshall, an attorney and philosopher, had been governor of his state. Indiana had swung its 29 delegate votes to Wilson at a critical point in the convention. Thus his choice seemed both wise and practical.

Marshall, as Vice President, would be confronted with a challenge that had previously faced only one of his predecessors. How he met that challenge would play a major role both in American history and in shaping the future concept of the vice president's place in government.

❧❧❧

CHAPTER NINE

Politics and the Great War

I T IS one of the ironies of history that Thomas Riley Marshall is best remembered for a lighthearted remark he once made rather than for his struggles to cope with one of the most difficult dilemmas ever to face an American Vice President.

The remark that made Marshall famous was uttered one day while he was presiding over the Senate. The debate on the floor featured a long, dull speech by Senator Joe Bristow of Kansas on the subject of "What This Country Needs." Vice President Marshall leaned toward a Senate aide and commented in a stage whisper that could be heard across the chamber: "What this country needs is a really good five-cent cigar!"

The comment was typical of Marshall. He had a dry sense of humor that made him extremely popular as a public speaker. In fact, to make ends meet on the relatively low salary he made as Vice President, he earned extra money as a touring lecturer. He said he clung stubbornly to the rule advocated by the silver-tongued orator William Jennings Bryan: "Always get your money before you step onto the platform."

As Indiana's governor, Marshall had put together an impressive record that earned him the approval of political leaders in several other midwestern states. He pushed through progressive legislation on such subjects as labor, conservation and social welfare. Nonetheless, he was considered more conservative than Woodrow Wilson.

After his easy victory in the presidential race, Wilson

launched a program of national reform called the New Freedom. He made little effort to draw upon his Vice President's talents by assigning him special duties commensurate with his abilities.

But Marshall proved valuable to the Wilson administration in his position as presiding officer of the Senate. He gave the Democrats every possible break in Senate debates. In addition, he was active behind the scenes in helping devise the strategy for pushing Wilson's program through the Senate.

Yet Marshall was well aware of the limited scope of his duties. He viewed philosophically his place in the government—saying he had decided "to acknowledge the insignificant influence of the office; to take it in a good-natured way; to be . . . loyal to my chief and at the same time not to be offensive to my associates."

Marshall's humble view of his own importance, and his quiet way of getting things done for the Wilson administration, won him many admirers. Still, he had some detractors. As the Democratic National Convention of 1916 approached, some Democrats initially opposed renominating Marshall.

Wilson, however, put an end to the talk of dumping Marshall from the ticket. Wilson had come to appreciate Marshall's ability and good humor. Defending Marshall against those who wanted him replaced on the ticket, the President said: "He has given me every reason to admire and trust him." The dump-Marshall movement quickly evaporated.

Ahead lay a presidential contest that was to pit in political battle two of the most able candidates ever offered the American electorate. Wilson's Republican opponent was Charles Evans Hughes—Associate Justice of the Supreme Court, former Governor of New York and a man who possessed as much integrity as any presidential candidate in history. Hughes' running mate was Charles W. Fairbanks, who had served as Vice President under Teddy Roosevelt. Marshall and Fairbanks were the first opponents for the vice presidency ever to come from the same state.

Charles Evan Hughes was perhaps the most reluctant presidential candidate in history. He was the only one on record to threaten that he would file suit to prevent his name from being placed in nomination.

Nonetheless, the Hughes-for-President boom persisted. It was not generated by the professional politicians, who felt the upright Hughes would be hard to handle in matters of patronage and policy. It was a genuine grass-roots drive. And it succeeded. At the Republican National Convention Hughes received one-fourth of all the votes on the first ballot. By the third ballot the nomination was his—with all the votes except 18 from dyed-in-the-wool Teddy Roosevelt supporters.

There was great doubt at the time that Hughes would accept the nomination. But, in the end, he accepted, saying he felt the two-party system must be preserved and that his campaign would foster that objective.

The campaign was hard-fought. There was a multitude of weighty issues involved. World War I was in progress, although the United States had not yet entered the conflict. German submarines were menacing American ships. Mexican raids on border areas had brought about skirmishes with American troops and destruction of U. S. property.

Throughout the campaign Vice President Marshall was a tower of strength. His past speaking tours had made him a favorite with the public, and he cashed in on his reputation to bring voters into line behind the Wilson administration.

The election was one of the closest in American history. Wilson and Marshall drew 9,129,606 popular votes to 8,538,-221 for Hughes and Fairbanks. The electoral vote was even closer, 277 to 254. In fact, it was not until two days after the election that California's electoral votes went to the Democrats and assured them of victory. Commenting on the narrow margin, Marshall said: " 'Tis not so deep as a well nor so wide as a church door, but 'tis enough. 'Twill serve."

During the second term of Wilson and Marshall the United States entered the war and pressed on to victory. Marshall's stature continued to rise. He made frequent speeches spelling out Wilson administration programs and rallying support for the war effort. Former critics began to speak in glowing terms of the Vice President. The New York *Times*, which previously had intimated that Marshall did not have "the mental equipment . . . for an understanding of what is required," now called him "an American patriot . . . whose words have a sense and sanity that are urgently needed."

After the war Wilson went to France to help negotiate a peace treaty and to bring into being the League of Nations. At Wilson's request, while the President was away, Marshall became the first Vice President to preside over Cabinet meetings.

The Vice President did so only reluctantly, for he feared it might be unconstitutional. He governed with wisdom and dignity over the Cabinet during the President's absence. And when Wilson returned from Europe the Vice President smoothly slipped back into his old routine—presiding over the Senate and helping plan legislative strategy.

Wilson was confronted by serious opposition in the Senate to some of the terms of the League of Nations covenant. Since Senate ratification was necessary in order for the United States to join the League, the President decided to try to mobilize public opinion behind the covenant in an attempt to force Senate approval. In the fall of 1919 Wilson embarked on a speaking tour of the West aimed at drumming up support for the League.

Already exhausted from the strain of the European negotiations, the President was in no physical condition for such an arduous tour. His physician, Admiral Cary Grayson, later described the tour as a "prolonged agony of physical pain" for Wilson. "The terrific strain which he had been under for more than a year was telling, and his exertions on the Western trip were sapping his vitality very fast," Grayson said. "From the time we reached Montana the President suffered from asthmatic attacks and severe headaches, which seriously interfered with his rest. Frequently I was summoned during the night to give him necessary aid and to assist him in breathing. It was necessary for him to sleep a good part of the time sitting up, propped up with pillows in a chair."

On September 26 Wilson broke completely under the strain. He had been suffering since the previous day with a headache that was so severe he could hardly see. Admiral Grayson was awakened early in the morning to treat the President. "He was suffering very much," Grayson recalled.

> I found that he was on the verge of a complete breakdown. . . . It was with great difficulty that I could persuade him to turn back to Washington and omit the remainder of the itinerary. He insisted that he must go on, saying: "I should feel like a deserter. My opponents will accuse me of having cold feet should I stop now." Mrs. Wilson added her pleas to my urgent medical advice, and at last he turned to me and said sadly: "I guess you are right." And tears ran down his cheek as he added: "This is the greatest disappointment of my life."

Grayson announced that the President had suffered a "complete nervous breakdown," but released no details on Wilson's ailments. On September 28, when the presidential train returned to Washington, Wilson was hustled behind the closed doors of the White House. Grayson later issued a series of optimistic medical bulletins, which obscured the seriousness of Wilson's condition.

As Grayson was to report much later: "On the evening of October first he seemed quite bright and cheerful. . . . But early the next morning the crash came. He fell stricken with a thrombosis."

The cerebral thrombosis left Wilson near death. The left side of his body was paralyzed. Not only the public, but also Vice President Marshall, lacked information on the true nature of the President's condition. Marshall was told nothing. All he could do was read the daily press reports and wait.

Wilson's collapse could not have come at a worse time. The capital, and indeed the nation, stood divided on the issue of U.S. entry into the League. Wilson had submitted the League covenant to the Senate for ratification in July, but Republican Majority Leader Henry Cabot Lodge, Sr., and Senator Hiram Johnson of California had led a group of "irreconcilables" in a series of interminable delaying tactics.

Now, with the President gravely ill, no one could predict what action the Senate would take. Navy Secretary Josephus Daniels, a Wilson intimate, advised Admiral Grayson to issue a complete, candid report to the public. Daniels anticipated that such a report would bring a tide of sympathy for Wilson. However, the President's family—feeling that Wilson did not want pity—chose to keep the public in the dark.

Meanwhile, the legal question of presidential disability hung over the White House. Today there is little question among scholars that Wilson—for at least a month—was disabled under the terms of the Constitution. He took no official action, considered no legislative matters, made no appointments to office and issued no state papers. Even after he passed the initial crisis he was unable to assume the full responsibilities of the Presidency for months.

Members of Wilson's inner circle contemplated the possibility of having the President resign and/or having Vice President Marshall assume the powers of the Presidency. Wilson's wife, who was to play a major role during the period of crisis, discussed her husband's possible resignation with one of his physicians, Francis Dercum.

"For Mr. Wilson to resign would have a bad effect on the country and a serious effect on our patient," Dr. Dercum said. "He has staked his life and made his promise to the world to do all in his power to get the treaty ratified and make the League of Nations complete. If he resigns, the greatest incentive to recovery is gone."

Mrs. Wilson decided against permitting her husband to resign. Instead, without the benefit of constitutional authority, she assumed the power to serve as a buffer between the President and the machinery of government. Mrs. Wilson called this her period of "stewardship." But critics described it in far less complimentary terms. Some claimed Mrs. Wilson actually was serving as President.

Mrs. Wilson denied that she was playing a substantive role in government. Her power, she said, was merely in deciding what was brought to her husband's attention. "I studied every paper sent from the different secretaries and senators," she later recalled. "I tried to digest . . . the things that had to go to the President. I, myself, never made a single decision regarding the disposition of public affairs. The only decision that was mine was what was important and what was not."

Of course, she was making important decisions in just sifting what she considered important and unimportant. For, without her say-so, her husband did not even learn of the existence of essential information. And what he did upon receiving such information became a major mystery. For weeks important messages sent to the President were not even acknowledged—much less answered. Bills passed by Congress took effect without his signature and without any indication that he had even considered whether to approve or veto them. Wilson's advisers, after making urgent requests to see him on matters of national consequence, were sent away.

"I am not interested in the President of the United States," Mrs. Wilson insisted. "I am interested in my husband and his health."

A week after Wilson was stricken in Colorado, Secretary of State Robert Lansing suggested that Vice President Marshall take over the duties of the President. He cited to Joseph Tumulty, the President's secretary, the disability section of the Constitution.

Tumulty was livid at the suggestion. However, the Secretary of State was not easily dissuaded. He proposed that either Tumulty or Admiral Grayson issue a public statement that the President was disabled under the terms of the Constitution. Tumulty's rage rose to fever intensity.

"You may rest assured that, while Woodrow Wilson is lying in the White House on the broad of his back, I will not be a party to ousting him," Tumulty stormed. "He has been too kind, too loyal and too wonderful to me to receive such treatmet at my hands."

Historians might well ponder whether Wilson's kindness and loyalty were the issue, as opposed to the national interest. But, at that moment, the national interest seemed secondary to those holding the nation's fate in their hands.

While Tumulty and Lansing sat glaring at each other, Admiral Grayson entered the room.

"I am sure that Dr. Grayson will never certify to the President's disability—will you, Grayson?" Tumulty asked. Both the physician and the President's secretary vowed to stand together to oppose any future efforts by Lansing or anyone else to hand the reins of government over to Vice President Marshall.

Failing to bring about Wilson's resignation, Lansing nonetheless took steps to assure some continuity of government action. As the top-ranking member of the Cabinet—and its most formidable figure—he began calling Cabinet meetings to deal with whatever business was possible in the President's absence.

Wilson later would contend that the calling of the Cabinet meetings by Lansing was indicative of a lack of loyalty. Eventually, he would force Lansing to resign.

Vice President Marshall was told nothing at first about the true nature of Wilson's condition. Although he shuddered at the thought of assuming Wilson's duties, he felt that, as Vice President, it was incumbent on him to know the facts so that he could prepare himself for what lay ahead.

Ultimately, Wilson's closest advisers decided that Marshall should be told the truth. They feared, however, that if the information were provided formally Marshall might initiate a movement to oust the President. They arranged for the Vice President to be briefed unofficially by an intermediary from outside the government.

A newspaperman, J. Fred Essary of the Baltimore *Sun*, was chosen as the intermediary. Essary made a discreet visit to the Vice President's office and told him that the President was near death and that Marshall might become chief executive at any moment.

Despite the unofficial nature of Essary's visit, Marshall never doubted that the newspaperman was telling the truth. The Vice President was so shaken by the dire report that he sat motionless and silent as the embarrassed reporter—not knowing what else to do—rose and left the office. Marshall could not even tell Essary good-by. The prospect of assuming the Presidency had virtually struck him dumb.

Marshall soon confided to a few close friends the substance of the report given him by Essary. Leaks developed from other sources. Shortly the seriousness of Wilson's condition—if not all the medical details—became common knowledge in government circles.

And, with these developments, Thomas Riley Marshall was confronted by a haunting dilemma. Should he make a bold try for the Presidency, in spite of his fear that he was inadequate for the job? Should he feign indifference to the office while permitting others to nudge him toward it? Or should he simply do nothing and let nature take its course?

Friends of the Vice President deluged him with advice.

Both Democrats and Republicans insisted that he should proclaim himself President by virtue of Wilson's disability. Influential congressmen told him that the legislative branch would stand behind him.

There were those who already considered Marshall Acting President. Some foreign governments sent official messages to him rather than to Wilson. So did some U. S. officials. Democratic Party functionaries consulted him about patronage appointments.

As he wrestled with his conscience Marshall concluded that he must try to work out a reasonable solution by talking directly with Wilson. But Mrs. Wilson, still conducting her "stewardship" program, refused to permit Marshall to see her husband.

He decided that he would assume the Presidency only if a number of circumstances prevailed: Congress must pass a resolution declaring that Wilson was disabled and that Marshall had a legitimate right and duty to become President. Moreover, both Mrs. Wilson and Admiral Grayson must approve in writing of the takeover.

The gravity of the situation was not lost on Marshall. He once told his wife: "I could throw this country into civil war— but I won't."

Marshall's personal secretary, Mark Thistlethwaite, insisted that the Vice President's conditions could never be satisfied. He wanted Marshall to set some alternative terms under which he would take over from Wilson. But the Vice President told Thistlethwaite: "I am not going to seize the place and then have Wilson, recovered, come around and say, 'Get off, you usurper!' "

Nonetheless, Thistlethwaite pressed Marshall to make some preparations for the possibility of assuming the Presidency, if not by virtue of Wilson's disability, then because of Wilson's death. At the very least, Marshall should carry with him constantly a prepared statement that could be released if the President died. The statement would pledge Marshall to carry out Wilson's policies. But Marshall rebelled at this idea. If he did become President, he said, he would have his own programs.

"All right," Thistlethwaite said. "Change later, but first announce a continuation of the previous policies."

Marshall refused. And that ended that.

Still, the pressure to make Marshall President persisted. One senator proposed a bill that would oust Wilson "whenever for any reason whatsoever" he became "unable for a pe-

riod of six weeks to perform the duties devolved upon him."
Senator Albert Fall of New Mexico told the Foreign Relations
Committee that the elected President was not in office. He
declared: "We have petticoat government! Mrs. Wilson is
President!"

Cries arose for Congress to adjourn until a "legitimate"
President was in office. Some said Mrs. Wilson had become
the nation's first "Presidentess." Others said she had changed
her title from First Lady to "Acting First Man."

Wilson's advisers decided something must be done to assure the country that the President's condition was not so dire
as rumored. An opportune occasion presented itself during a
visit to the United States by the King and Queen of the Bel-
gians.

Vice President Marshall served as official host—as he was to
do for several other members of European royalty who visited
Washington during the period Wilson was incapacitated.
Marshall resented having this duty thrust upon him for several
reasons. For one, it imposed a presidential responsibility upon
him without the presidential office. For another, it was expen-
sive—and he was compelled to pay the expenses out of his
$12,000-a-year salary. During the periods when he was serving
as official host, Marshall refused to preside over the Senate.
He complained that he could not do justice to the President's
role as entertainer of royalty one minute and as presiding officer of the Senate the next.

As evidence that Wilson was able to continue serving as
President his advisers arranged for him to receive the Belgian
King and Queen at the White House on October 30, 1919.
This was little more than a month after he had been stricken
in Colorado. A great clamor attended the visit, for the Bel-
gians were the first persons other than White House insiders
and medical personnel to see the President since he had fallen
ill.

Mrs. Wilson greeted the King and Queen, served them tea,
then took them upstairs to see her husband. The President,

wearing a dressing gown, received them in bed. The King and Queen were pleased to note that he seemed to be in possession of his faculties and was able to carry on a conversation, although his speech was somewhat halting and indistinct.

As the Belgian royalty left the White House a swarm of reporters waited to fire questions about the President's condition. The King and Queen assured the newsmen, although using vague terms, that Wilson was doing quite well.

Vice President Marshall embarked on another lecture tour to raise some money. On November 23 he spoke at the civic auditorium in Atlanta, Georgia. Marshall was praising the accomplishments of Washington and Lincoln when he noticed a policeman rushing up an aisle to the platform. The officer approached a prominent Atlanta citizen and told him word had just been received by telephone that President Wilson had died. The citizen stepped up to the Vice President, asked him to stop his speech and whispered that Wilson was dead. Marshall's knees sagged, and it appeared that he might fall. But, in a few seconds, he regained some of his composure. He raised his hands to get the attention of the audience.

"I cannot continue my speech," he said. "I must leave at once to take up my duties as Chief Executive of this great nation."

Marshall asked the audience to pray for him. At his request, the organist struck up "Nearer My God to Thee." Police surrounded Marshall and rushed him away to his hotel.

It was not until he reached the hotel—and phone calls were placed to news services and the White House—that Marshall discovered the telephone report of Wilson's death was a practical joke.

"A most cruel hoax," Marshall said. He later told friends this was the worst hour of his life. A $100 reward was posted by the state of Georgia for the arrest of the person who had perpetrated the haox, but he was never found.

Marshall never got any closer to the Presidency. Wilson ultimately weathered the crisis and served out his term as President. Marshall was left to preside over the historic Senate debate on the United States' entry into the League of Nations. It was here that Wilson perhaps suffered the most from his illness. Unable to take an aggressive role and shielded from knowing all the facts during his period of ill health, Wilson made a series of miscalculations.

The most serious of these was a basic misinterpretation of the will of the Senate. Although a majority of the senators favored the idea of the League of Nations—and the public was clearly behind creation of the international organization—a number of senators felt some compromise was necessary to assure that the United States would not surrender any significant measure of sovereignty. Senators Lodge and Johnson were in the forefront of those demanding changes in the League covenant. Wilson felt that one of the proposed changes would nullify a key section of the covenant pledging each League member to help defend every other member's territorial integrity and independence against outside aggression.

The Senate debate developed into a test of strength. The odds were stacked against the President. For one thing, Lodge and Johnson held the spotlight on the floor of the Senate while Wilson lay flat on his back at the White House. For another, Wilson received his news of the debate second-hand from his wife and his secretary, Joseph Tumulty. And this news was colored to make it appear as optimistic as possible, for Mrs. Wilson and Tumulty feared that the truth might kill the President. Thus, Wilson was confident that he was winning the struggle when actually he was losing.

Senator Gilbert Hitchcock of Nebraska, the Democratic minority leader, called at the White House to plead with the President. Hitchcock said it would be impossible to bring about U. S. entry into the League without resorting to compromise with Lodge.

"It *is* possible! It *is* possible!" Wilson insisted. "Let Lodge compromise!"

"Well, of course, he must compromise also," Hitchcock said. "But we might well hold out the olive branch."

"Let Lodge hold out the olive branch!" Wilson replied.

With that, Hitchcock was ushered out of the White House. As he left, the chances of bringing about ratification of the League convenant left with him.

After months of debate, the Senate finally voted. The Democrats were under orders from Wilson to vote against the first measure presented to them—one which would approve U. S. entry into the League with the reservations proposed by Lodge and Johnson. The measure was defeated, 55 to 39. Next, the senators voted on a measure that omitted the reservations— thus providing for ratification of the convenant in the form favored by Wilson. This, too, was defeated. The vote was 53 to 38.

Wilson's dream was dead. Despite future efforts to revive the issue and reverse the vote in the Senate, the United States would never enter the League of Nations. And, without U. S. participation, the League would fade into oblivion.

Woodrow Wilson continued to live in a virtual dream world for the remainder of his term. He actually believed—in spite of his health problems and his political defeats—that the Democrats might nominate him for a third term as President. He was supported in this belief by his new Secretary of State, Bainbridge Colby, who had replaced Robert Lansing. Colby went to the Democratic National Convention in San Francisco in 1920 prepared to engineer Wilson's renomination. But Dr. Grayson was convinced that another political campaign would kill Wilson. He prevailed upon other members of the Cabinet to persuade Colby to drop the renomination plan, and the renomination campaign was over before it had begun. Both Wilson and Vice President Marshall faded from the political scene. From the time he fell ill in Colorado until he left office, Wilson saw his Vice President only once—a brief encounter just before the inauguration of his presidential successor.

In the aftermath of the Wilson incapacitation, four bills seeking to improve the method of declaring a president disabled were introduced in Congress. But, once the crisis was passed, the issue was all but forgotten. All four bills died in committee.

In retrospect it seems clear that the nation's interests would have been better served if Marshall had assumed the Presidency. The Vice President had grown in experience, popularity and political skill during his two terms in Washington. As an emergency replacement for Wilson, Marshall logically could have expected to win the sympathy of the citizenry. As a man in good health, he would have been better able than the stricken Wilson to cope with the debate over the League. And, having won many friends in the Senate during his service as presiding officer, he might have been able to bring about an acceptable compromise.

Of course, no one can say with certainty if the course of history might have been changed. But it does seem justifiable to speculate that Marshall might have been able to bring the United States into the League. There are those who go so far as to maintain that U. S. membership would have saved the League and, consequently, might have prevented World War II.

In any event, the crisis precipitated by Wilson's illness once again focused attention on the importance of electing capable men to the vice presidency. It represented an important milestone in the evolution of the vice president's office. Ahead lay further challenges and further milestones in that evolution.

CHAPTER TEN

Scandal and the Roaring Twenties

THE Republican National Convention of 1920 put the term "smoke-filled room" into the American political vocabulary. It has remained there, as a cliché, ever since.

It was in the celebrated "smoke-filled room" of Chicago's Blackstone Hotel that a group of Republican bosses chose Warren Gamaliel Harding as their party's presidential candidate. Harding, a Senator from Ohio, had been given little attention at the start of the convention. Such distinguished men as General Leonard Wood, who had been responsible for the program that eradicated yellow fever in Cuba, and Frank O. Lowden, a former Governor of Illinois, were considered far more promising candidates than the Ohio senator.

For nine ballots the convention was deadlocked. The party bosses then went looking for a dark-horse compromise candidate. At a 2:00 A.M. meeting in the "smoke-filled room," they chose Harding. He won the nomination officially on the convention floor later in the day—but actually it had been signed, sealed and delivered at the early-morning meeting.

Most observers assumed that the nomination of the vice-presidential candidate would be a mere formality. The bosses who had chosen Harding had picked Senator Irvine H. Lenroot of Wisconsin to be his running mate. Now it was just a matter of having the delegates go through the motions of nominating Lenroot. Or so it seemed.

But there was an undercurrent of dissatisfaction among some delegates. They resented the fact that the nomination of Harding had been shoved down their throats. And they were determined to assert some measure of independence from the bosses.

When Senator Medill McCormick of Illinois began his speech placing Lenroot's name in nomination, he was interrupted by a cry of "Coolidge!" McCormick plunged ahead with his speech but was interrupted again. "Coolidge," another voice called. Then came a chorus of shouts: "Coolidge! Coolidge! Coolidge! Coolidge!"

McCormick hastily concluded his nominating speech. Perfunctory seconding speeches were delivered on behalf of Lenroot—to the accompaniment of continuing cries of "Coolidge." Under the bosses' plan it was now time to close the nominations and hand the second spot on the ticket to Lenroot without a contest. Some of the delegates were already leaving the convention hall.

However, a virtually unknown Oregon delegate named Wallace McClamant stood atop a chair on the convention floor and waved insistently at the platform—demanding to be recognized. The chairman gave him the floor.

McClamant's speech was short and punchy. He placed in nomination for Vice President the name of Governor Calvin Coolidge of Massachusetts. The speech was greeted by tumultuous cheers from rebellious delegates. In short order these delegates pushed through the nomination of Coolidge by a vote of 674½ to 146 over Lenroot.

Coolidge seemed the prototype of the laconic, conservative New Englander. Born in Plymouth, Vermont, the son of a storekeeper who enjoyed moderate success in state politics, Coolidge cherished the simple virtues. He was economical, temperate and cautious.

After his graduation from Amherst College, Coolidge entered the practice of law in Northampton, Massachusetts. He soon began a political career that was to see him hold a great variety of public offices—city councilman, city solicitor, county court clerk, mayor, state legislator, president of the state senate, lieutenant governor and governor.

One of his proudest accomplishments as governor was enactment of the eight-hour day for Massachusetts workers. Coolidge was highly popular with the state's voters, a fact that puzzled some of his friends. As one of them put it: "In appearance he was splendidly null, apparently deficient in red corpuscles, with a peaked, wire-drawn expression. You felt that he was always about to turn up his coat collar against a chilling east wind." It was certainly not an outgoing personality that led to his popularity. Coolidge was known as a man of few, well-chosen words.

Once three prominent citizens tried to persuade him to increase a state appropriation. One member of the trio gave Coolidge a lengthy sales talk on the subject. "Anybody else got anything to say?" Coolidge asked. A second man echoed the sentiments of the first. "I understand you all agree on what you want," Coolidge said. "Yes," the three men chorused. "Can't be done," Coolidge snapped. "Good-bye."

Several years later a woman approached Coolidge at a dinner party and told him she had bet someone that she could make him say more than two words. "You lose," Coolidge replied.

Coolidge was a popular figure when the Republicans convened in Chicago in 1920 to choose their national ticket. When the spirit of rebellion swept over the convention, enough interest in Coolidge had been generated to make him a logical alternative to the vice-presidential candidate chosen by the bosses.

In Boston he received word of his nomination by telephone. A wave of congratulatory messages arrived at the Massachusetts State House. Among the messages was a telegram from Vice President Marshall. "Please accept my sincere sympathy," wired the disillusioned Vice President.

Two weeks after the Republican convention the Democrats convened in San Francisco. With President Wilson reluctantly retiring from office, there were no fewer than seventeen potential candidates for the presidential nomination.

Among the leading contenders were Treasury Secretary

William G. McAdoo, Wilson's son-in-law; Attorney General A. Mitchell Palmer; Ohio Governor James M. Cox; John W. Davis, Ambassador to the Court of St. James's, and New York Governor Alfred E. Smith. But, through 43 ballots, no candidate was able to secure the nomination. From the tenth ballot on it was a two-man contest between McAdoo and Cox.

With each succeeding ballot Cox gained strength. He had much to recommend him. He had risen from a $35-a-week janitor to a $200,000-a-year newspaper publisher. He had served in Congress and put together an excellent record as a progressive governor.

On the 44th ballot Cox finally won the nomination. Chosen by acclamation as his vice-presidential candidate was Assistant Secretary of the Navy Franklin D. Roosevelt.

During the campaign Harding stayed at his home in Marion, Ohio, greeting visiting delegations on his front porch. Coolidge hit the campaign trail, urging the citizenry to fight against government interference in business. Cox and Roosevelt toured the country. At the insistence of Wilson they made American participation in the League of Nations a key campaign plank. The Republicans, while opposing the League covenant, did not repudiate the idea of international cooperation. They favored an "Association of Nations."

While there was no great enthusiasm for the Harding-Coolidge ticket, the public was in the mood for a change from Democratic to Republican administration. Harding seemed to appeal to a tired-of-idealism public that yearned for a "return to normalcy." Harding and Coolidge received 16,152,200 popular votes to 9,147,353 for Cox and Roosevelt. The Republican ticket captured 404 electoral votes to 127 for the Democrats.

As President, Harding used Coolidge to some extent as a liaison man between the legislative and executive branches of government. He also invited his Vice President to attend Cabinet meetings regularly. This was considered a major advance in broadening the scope of the Vice President's activities.

Coolidge usually remained silent at the Cabinet meetings, speaking up only when specifically asked for his views. But his attendance at the meetings gave him a familiarity with the workings and problems of the executive branch that was to serve him in good stead later.

By background and temperament, Coolidge was ideal for his role as presiding officer of the Senate. He had become an expert on parliamentary procedure during his service as a Massachusetts legislator. And, unlike some Vice Presidents who found the presiding officers's chores monotonous and dissatisfying, Coolidge genuinely enjoyed these duties. "I was entertained and instructed by the debates," he said.

President Harding appointed to office a number of his political cronies who were to bring disgrace to the administration. Interior Secretary Albert B. Fall was implicated in the Teapot Dome scandal, involving the leasing of government oil reserves to private oil interests. He was eventually convicted of accepting a bribe and given a one-year sentence, thus becoming the first Cabinet member ever sent to prison. Charles R. Forbes, appointed by Harding to head the Veterans Bureau, also was imprisoned on corruption charges. A congressional investigation established that half of the bureau's annual budget was devoted to sheer graft. The bureau's legal counsel shot himself in a home he had bought from Harding. Another crony of the President committed suicide in the apartment of Attorney General Harry M. Daugherty. The Attorney General, who had been Harding's campaign manager, later was discredited by other scandals.

Disillusioned and worried over the scandals, Harding sought a respite from the pressures of life in Washington by making a transcontinental tour during the summer of 1923. The President and his wife, accompanied by a large party of friends, set out by train from the capital on June 20. But Harding got little rest, for he was called upon to make numerous speeches during the trip. His betrayal by long-time friends preyed constantly on his mind.

The presidential party went to Alaska, then returned to Seattle on July 27. There the President became ill. When he reached San Francisco two days later, he was in serious condition. He spent several days in bed and seemed to rally. But then, on the afternoon of August 2, he died. His death was variously attributed to food poisoning, bronchopneumonia and a heart ailment.

At the time of Harding's death Vice President Coolidge and his wife were in summer residence at his father's farm home in Plymouth, Vermont. The family went to sleep at 9 P.M. The Vice President's father, John Coolidge, did not have a telephone. The only phone in the village was at a general store operated by Miss Florence Cilley.

At 10:30 P.M. ten miles away in Bridgewater, the operator of a private telephone exchange, W. A. Perkins, received a call from the Western Union office in White River Junction, asking Perkins to inform Vice President Coolidge that a telegram had arrived from President Harding's secretary, George Christian. The telegram said simply that the President was dead. It gave no details.

Perkins wrote down the message, cranked up his Model-T Ford and set out over a bumpy road for the neighboring village. At Plymouth he woke Miss Cilley, who advised rousing the Vice President and took him to the Coolidge home. Their knocking brought John Coolidge to the door in his nightshirt, carrying an oil lamp. Perkins and Miss Cilley spilled out the news and Perkins handed the written message to the Vice President's father.

John Coolidge thanked his visitors, then headed upstairs to the guest bedroom. He woke his son, who read the message by lamplight and, without a word, began to dress. (Asked years later to describe his initial reaction upon learning he had inherited the Presidency, he answered: "I thought I could swing it.")

Calvin Coolidge shaved unhurriedly, then finished dressing. After waking his wife and telling her the news, he went downstairs to the parlor. Within a short time newsmen began arriving outside the house. Coolidge sent word out to them that he would soon issue a statement. He immediately began dictating the statement to his assistant secretary, E. C. Geiser, who took it down directly on a typewriter.

The statement read:

> Reports have reached me, which I fear are correct, that President Harding is gone. The world has lost a great and good man. I mourn his loss. He was my chief and friend. It will be my purpose to carry out the policies which he has begun for the service of the American people and for meeting their responsibilities wherever they may arise. For this purpose I shall seek the cooperation of all those who have been associated with the President during his term of office. Those who have given their efforts to assist him, I wish to remain in office that they may assist me. I have faith that God will direct the destinies of our nation. . . .

Coolidge was in no particular hurry to take the presidential oath of office. He planned to have his father, who was a notary public, administer the oath later in the day. But one of the men who hurried to his side during the night, Congressman Porter Dale of Vermont, urged him to take the oath immediately. "The country is without a President, Mr. Coolidge," Dale said. "The United States has no President. . . . No President. . . . The country should never be without a President."

Dale's plea persuaded Coolidge. But, before being sworn in by his father, he wanted to be sure that it was legal for the oath to be administered by a notary public. He sent a message to William Howard Taft, who had become Chief Justice of the United States after leaving the Presidency, and asked for advice on the question. It was 2:35 A.M. before Coolidge was handed Taft's reply: "Procedure legal. Best wishes. Taft."

At 2:47 A.M., by the light of an oil lamp, Coolidge placed his left hand on a Bible once owned by his mother, raised his right hand and was sworn in by his father as thirtieth President of the United States.

As President, Coolidge's first major problem was how to deal with the scandals that had blossomed during the Harding administration. Some of those tainted by the scandals had left the government, but others remained.

Coolidge appointed a pair of special prosecutors to investigate the corruption and seek criminal convictions against the guilty parties. It was as a result of these prosecutors' work that former Interior Secretary Fall and several other persons were eventually sent to prison. Coolidge's personal integrity was so highly regarded that, despite his role in the Harding administration, there was never any serious attempt to hold him even partly responsible for permitting the corruption to exist.

Coolidge had assumed the Presidency just ten months before the Republican National Convention of 1924. Not surprisingly, he wanted the nomination for a full four-year presidential term. His short tenure in the White House had given him little opportunity to establish a record of his own, but he captured the nomination with ease.

The delegates' choice for the vice presidency was former Governor Frank O. Lowden of Illinois. Lowden, who disapproved of Coolidge's agricultural policy, served notice that he would not accept the nomination. The convention nominated him just the same. True to his word, Lowden refused to run. He thus became the second vice-presidential nominee in American history to reject the nomination. (The first, it will be recalled, was Senator Silas Wright, who refused to run with James K. Polk in 1844.)

The delegates now nominated Charles G. Dawes of Illinois. He was the architect of the Dawes Plan for handling German reparations payments following the war—a service for which he was awarded the Nobel Peace Prize.

The Democrats were hampered in 1924 by deep factional splits. Their national convention at New York's Madison Square Garden lasted from June 23 to July 10—the longest political convention in the nation's history. Northern Democrats supported New York Governor Alfred E. Smith for the presidential nomination. Those from the South and West backed William G. McAdoo. On the 103rd ballot, the nomination went to a compromise candidate, John W. Davis, of West Virginia.

Davis had served in Congress and had been U. S. Solicitor General and Ambassador to the Court of St. James's. At the time of his nomination Davis was a prominent Wall Street lawyer. Nominated as Davis' running mate was Governor Charles Bryan of Nebraska, the brother of William Jennings Bryan.

The nation's economy was thought to be healthy, and Coolidge campaigned on the theme that he would keep it that way. He pledged to hold down government spending. "I am for economy," he said. "After that, I am for more economy." In actuality, however, only some sectors of the economy were healthy—e.g. automobile manufacturing, electrical equipment production, road and housing construction. Harold Faulkner pointed out in *American Economic History* that coal mining, cotton manufacturing, shipbuilding and, most especially, agriculture were "stagnant or declining." The Democrats made Republican corruption a major campaign issue. But their inability to link Coolidge with any of the wrongdoing weakened their case.

Coolidge and Dawes rolled to an easy victory. They captured 15,725,000 popular votes and 382 electoral votes. Davis and Bryan received 8,386,000 popular votes and 136 electoral votes. A third-party ticket, the Progressive slate of Wisconsin Senator Robert M. La Follette for President and Montana Senator Burton K. Wheeler for Vice President, polled 4,822,-000 popular votes and 13 electoral votes.

The new Vice President posed an interesting contrast to his President. Dawes was as colorful as Coolidge was colorless. He believed in positive action; Coolidge believed in what newspaper columnist Walter Lippmann called "alert inactivity." Dawes favored stirring things up; Coolidge preferred smoothing them over. While Coolidge was a man of few words, Dawes was a man of many. And his language was both blunt and imaginative.

This language had tagged Dawes with a colorful nickname. During his World War I service he had been in charge of procuring supplies for the Army. After the armistice a congressional committee launched an investigation in search of waste and corruption in the wartime purchasing system. Dawes appeared before the committee to defend the system. He told the congressmen: "Hell and Maria, we weren't trying to keep a set of books; we were trying to win the war." He thus became known as "Hell and Maria" Dawes.

A man of genuine ability, Dawes could have been a great asset to the Coolidge administration. But his value was seriously undermined by a number of blunders he committed.

The first of these came even before he had taken office as Vice President. Shortly before Inauguration Day Dawes wrote a letter to Coolidge saying that he would decline any invitation from the President to attend Cabinet meetings. He said he was afraid his attendance at Cabinet meetings would set a precedent obligating some future President to invite to Cabinet meetings a Vice President he considered "unsuitable."

Dawes' letter was presumptuous in the extreme. Coolidge had not even invited him to attend Cabinet meetings. Moreover, Dawes publicly embarrassed the President by notifying the press that he had written the letter.

The consternation caused by the letter had not yet died when Dawes created an even greater furor. This one resulted from his Inauguration-Day speech. Immediately after taking the oath of office as Vice President, Dawes launched a bitter assault on the Senate's filibuster rule. The rule, permitting unlimited debate, enables a minority of senators to block passage of legislation by discussing it at such length that the measure never comes to a vote.

Dawes told the inaugural gathering that the filibuster rule handed "a minority of even one senator, at times, power to defeat the measure" being discussed. He demanded a change in the rule. He asked "who would dare oppose" such a change. And he cautioned that failure to alter the rule would "lessen the effectiveness, prestige and dignity of the United States Senate."

The speech stirred up a tempest among members of the Senate. They felt they had been lectured like schoolboys and that it had not been the Vice President's place to deliver such a lecture. Many complained that Dawes had shown poor judgment and even poorer taste. One commented that the Vice President's performance had been "brutal and clownish."

Aside from other considerations, Dawes's speech had done a disservice to Coolidge. Coolidge had considered the day of his inauguration to a complete four-year presidential term as the most important day of his life. He had written a major speech on government economy for the occasion. But, to his dismay, the press and the public paid far more attention to the Vice President's remarks than to the President's.

Dawes urged the public to support his demand for a change in the filibuster rule. His call was greeted with apathy by the citizenry. The issue eventually did come to a vote in the Senate, but the proposed rule change was defeated.

Only five days after his inaugural speech Dawes was involved in another unfortunate episode. Coolidge had appointed Attorney General Harlan F. Stone to the Supreme Court and had designated Charles Warren to replace Stone in the Cabinet. Warren's nomination was sent to the Senate for confirmation. There was strong opposition to the nomination because Warren had been closely connected with monopolistic sugar interests. Dawes knew that the balloting on Warren's confirmation would be so close that he might be called upon to cast a tie-breaking vote.

On the afternoon of March 9, 1925, Dawes asked the Senate majority and minority leaders whether a vote would be taken that day on the nomination. He was told there would be no vote during the afternoon, since a number of senators still wanted to speak on the question. Thus assured, the Vice President assigned a senator to take over the presiding officer's chair and retired to his hotel room for a nap.

But, as Dawes slept, some of the senators scheduled to speak on the Warren nomination decided to pass up the opportunity. The debate ended earlier than expected and the voting began. One of the Vice President's aides frantically phoned the hotel and woke Dawes. The Vice President rushed out of the hotel, hopped into a taxi and headed toward Capitol Hill.

Meanwhile, Republican senators did everything they could to make the roll-call vote proceed as slowly as possible. But the roll was completed before Dawes could return. The vote, as anticipated, resulted in a tie. Once again the Republicans resorted to delaying tactics in the hope that Dawes would arrive in time.

When the Vice President's taxi finally arrived outside the Capitol, he ran full speed up the steps and through the corridors to the Senate chamber. He was gasping for breath as he entered the hall. But his race had been in vain. During the delay a Democratic senator who had initially voted to confirm Warren's nomination had been persuaded to change his mind. The tie vote was a tie no longer. It was now 41-39 against confirmation. Dawes' absence had cost Warren the Attorney General's post.

The Vice President was subjected to merciless ridicule. It was pointed out that he was the great-great-grandson of William Dawes, the revolutionary patriot who accompanied Paul Revere on his celebrated ride. Sarcastic comparisons were made between the taxi ride of the Vice President and the ride of his great-great-grandfather. Other famous rides were recalled. Senator George Norris of Nebraska went so far as to take the floor of the Senate and recite a parody on the poem "Sheridan's Ride." Part of the parody read:

> And when his statue is placed on high,
> Under the dome of the Capitol sky,

> Be it said, in letters both bold and bright:
> O, Hell and Maria, he has lost us the fight!

The series of blunders committed by Dawes seriously impaired his future effectiveness. Although Dawes later was accorded considerable respect for his skill in presiding over the Senate, President Coolidge made no effort to bring him into the inner councils of the administration.

By 1927 there was widespread speculation among political observers about whether Coolidge would seek reelection. While vacationing in South Dakota on August 2, 1927, he distributed to the press slips of paper bearing the message: "I do not choose to run for President in 1928."

However, speculation about Coolidge's plans continued. In an attempt to halt the discussion, Coolidge issued another message: "My statement stands. No one should be led to suppose that I have modified it."

Coolidge was in a position that had faced no previous "accidental" President. His succession to the Presidency had come just nineteen months before the end of Harding's four-year term. Thus he had become the first "accidental" President to serve less than half of his predecessor's term. The question was whether another four-year term—added to the full term Coolidge was then serving and the nineteen months of Harding's unexpired term—would violate the two-term tradition. Coolidge did not think that the nineteen months should count as a presidential term. His decision against seeking reelection was determined by other considerations.

A number of senators contended that a Coolidge candidacy in 1928 would set a dangerous precedent. On January 31, 1928, Senator Robert M. La Follette, Jr., of Wisconsin, who had replaced his late father in the Senate in 1925, introduced a resolution declaring that it was

> . . . the sense of the Senate that the precedent established by
> Washington and other Presidents of the United States in re-
> tiring from the presidential office after their second term has

become, by universal concurrence, a part of our republican system of government, and that any departure from this time-honored custom would be unwise, unpatriotic and fraught with peril to our free institutions.

La Follette introduced a second resolution advising Coolidge to take due notice of the warning and to govern himself accordingly. The Senate debated the La Follette resolutions on February 7. Three days later a majority of senators voted for the first resolution. The specific warning to Coolidge was defeated.

There is strong evidence that Coolidge was sincere all along and had no intention of seeking another term. However, some of his close associates felt he wanted to be drafted for renomination. The passage of the La Follette resolution put an end to any draft-Coolidge movement.

When the Republicans gathered for their national convention they turned to Secretary of Commerce Herbert Hoover as their presidential nominee. Hoover, originally named to the Cabinet by President Harding, was not one of Coolidge's favorite subordinates. Coolidge had once said of him in jest: "That man has offered me unsolicited advice for six years—all of it bad." But Hoover had little trouble capturing the nomination on the first ballot, collecting 837 of the 1,084 delegate votes.

Hoover had several important assets in his quest for the Presidency. He had become one of the best-known men in the world through his humanitarian work as administrator of refugee and relief programs in Europe during and after World War I. He had served effectively as Secretary of Commerce. And he had put together the nucleus of an efficient political organization during the preconvention maneuvering.

A native of West Branch, Iowa, Hoover moved to Oregon as a boy, following the death of his parents, and was reared by relatives. He was graduated from Stanford University, then worked for a time as a mining engineer. He later went to

China, where he became a business manager, promoter and consultant.

By the time World War I began, he was a successful financier in London. The war confronted millions of Europeans with possible starvation. Many of them were homeless. Hoover plunged into a series of relief programs to aid these war victims. His skill as an administrator and his spirit of selfless service won him worldwide acclaim.

Warren Harding insisted that a Cabinet position be reserved for Hoover and offered to appoint Hoover either Secretary of Commerce or Secretary of the Interior. Hoover chose the Department of Commerce. As Commerce Secretary under both Harding and Coolidge, he enlarged facilities for domestic commerce and helped reduce waste and duplication in American industry. In addition, the department, through the use of commercial attachés in embassies and consulates throughout the world, became more aware of the economics of other nations. The ease with which he gained the presidential nomination—although he was not a Republican Party "regular"—attested to his national popularity.

As the vice-presidential candidate, the Republicans nominated a man who was the epitome of a party "regular." The nominee was Senate Majority Leader Charles Curtis of Kansas, a veteran member of the Senate "club." Curtis, nicknamed "Indian" because his mother was a member of the Kaw tribe, was many things to many people. To the influential Senator William Borah of Idaho, Curtis was "a great reconciler, a walking political encyclopedia." But to Oswald Garrison Villard, a noted writer of the period, he was a "mediocrity who is as faithful and devoted to his party as he is dull and dumb."

Some ticket-balancing considerations entered into the selection of Curtis as Hoover's running mate. Since some Republicans considered Hoover too liberal, the nomination of a reactionary vice-presidential candidate would help balance the ticket. Curtis seemed to be a thoroughly committed reactionary. Moreover, it was regarded as essential to the Republican ticket that the vice-presidential nominee be acceptable to the farm states. Farmers generally were unhappy with Coolidge's agriculture policy, and Hoover was closely identified with that policy.

The Democrats convened in Houston, Texas, and nominated New York Governor Alfred E. Smith for President on the first ballot. Smith's nomination had been virtually assured when he had made a splendid showing in a series of presidential primaries. Chosen as his running mate was Senator Joseph T. Robinson of Arkansas.

Al Smith had been the first man in nearly a century elected to more than two terms as New York's chief executive. Born into a poor family in a tenement on New York City's lower East Side, Smith had never finished grammar school. He had grown interested in politics as a boy and had risen through the Democratic Party ranks to become an influential state legislator before his four-term election to the governorship.

As governor, he had instituted numerous reform programs —including compulsory education for children, adult education, alleviation of slum conditions and rebuilding of dilapidated state hospitals and prisons. He had a relaxed air and a keen sense of humor. When a campaign manager in one of his gubernatorial races urged him to stop cocking his hat on the back of his head, saying it did not appear dignified, Smith replied: "The people of this state don't care how the outside of my skull looks. They want to know what's inside of it." Smith's attitude won for him the nickname "the Happy Warrior."

Smith had one decided liability in his race for the Presidency—his religion. He was the first Catholic nominated for the Presidency. And many Protestants vowed to keep Smith from reaching the White House.

Some ministers and officials of Protestant churches openly urged their people to vote against Smith. Influential publications carried articles suggesting that Smith might be unduly influenced by the Catholic Church if elected President. A tide of pamphlets, letters and anonymous newspapers revived some of the most vicious libels ever published about the Catholic religion. If Smith were elected, it was said, the Catholics would rule the country and only Catholics would be allowed to hold public office. A tunnel would be built to connect the White House with the Vatican. Protestant children would be forced to attend Catholic schools. A Catholic political party, with Smith as its head, would take the place of the Democratic Party.

Smith countered by pointing out that his New York State Cabinet consisted of two Catholics, thirteen Protestants and one Jew. He said:

> I recognize no power in the institution of my church to interfere with the operations of the Constitution of the United States or the enforcement of the law of the land. I believe in absolute freedom of conscience for all men and in equality of all churches, all sects before the law as a matter of right.

Smith attacked what he called the big-business monopoly of government in the Coolidge administration, the corruption of the Harding regime and the Republican farm policies. He lashed out at the Ku Klux Klan and other hate groups.

Hoover and his running mate, Senator Curtis, campaigned chiefly on the prosperity issue. Times were good, they said, and would continue to be good if the Republicans remained in power. Hoover said:

> We in America today are nearer to the final triumph over poverty than ever before in the history of any land. The poorhouse is vanishing from among us. We have not reached the goal, but, given a chance to go forward with the policies of the last eight years, we shall soon with the help of God be in sight of the day when poverty will be banished from this nation.

These words would later return to haunt Hoover.

Nearly 75 per cent of the nation's eligible voters went to the polls on Election Day. The result was a decisive victory for Hoover and Curtis. They carried forty states, received 21,429,-109 popular votes to 15,005,497 for Smith and Robinson and captured 444 electoral votes to the Democratic ticket's 87.

When Charles Curtis became Vice President he was almost seventy years of age. He was not destined by either age or temperament to bring any bold innovations to the office. And, since he and Hoover were not particularly congenial, the President made no move to broaden the scope of the Vice President's duties. He did, however, invite Curtis to attend Cabinet meetings—thus reestablishing the custom that had been broken during the Coolidge-Dawes administration.

Curtis, although he committed no major blunders, sometimes displayed an insensitivity that caused the Republican administration embarrassment. On one occasion, when a group of Negroes and whites called at his office, Curtis pointedly refused to shake hands with the Negroes. Another time he remarked that the average voter was "too damn dumb to understand" Republican policies.

He subjected himself to ridicule by abandoning his former "regular-fellow" attitude and adopting a pompous air. This apparently was an honest attempt by Curtis to live up to the dignity he felt the vice president deserved. But his former colleagues laughed at the fact that Curtis threw away his old sombrero and replaced it with a top hat. They were even more amused by Curtis' refusal to have them call him "Charley" any longer. "Where do you get that 'Charley' stuff?" Curtis once asked. "Don't you know I am Vice President now?"

It was during Curtis' term that the musical play *Of Thee I Sing*—with the laughable Vice President named Alexander Throttlebottom—appeared on Broadway. Curtis' detractors considered it no coincidence that a play poking fun at the vice presidency should make its bow while he was serving in the nation's second highest office.

In 1929 the nation's prosperity bubble burst. The stock market crashed on October 23 and the country subsequently

sank into the Depression. Unemployment mounted to 7,000,-
000 within a year, ultimately reaching 15,000,000. Those lucky
enough to find work received greatly reduced wages. Bread-
lines became familiar sights. Despair became the prevailing
mood.

As the Republican National Convention of 1932 approached, it seemed extremely doubtful that the GOP could
win the fall election. Backers of both Hoover and Curtis argued that Republican chances would be enhanced if the other
man were left off the ticket. But in the end, at a convention in
which delegates made no secret of their discouragement, both
the President and the Vice President were renominated.

The presidential election of 1932 ushered in a dramatic new
era in American political life. This era brought with it new
importance for the vice presidency and men of stature to fill
the office.

❦

CHAPTER ELEVEN

The Depression and World War II

IF EVER a man set his sights early in life on becoming President of the United States and then worked relentlessly to reach the White House, that man was Franklin Delano Roosevelt.

As a young lawyer Roosevelt confided that he did not intend to practice law for the rest of his life. He planned to seize the first opportunity that arose to run for public office. For he wanted to be President someday, he said, and he felt that he had a genuine chance to reach his goal. Roosevelt's colleagues did not take his statements seriously. But he himself was in dead earnest.

For a man whose political career was to be identified closely with his appeal to the "common people," Roosevelt hardly came from humble beginnings. A cousin of Theodore Roosevelt, he was born in 1882 to wealthy, socially prominent parents. He was reared with the help of governesses and tutors on the family's estate at Hyde Park, New York. He went to the "best" schools—Groton, Harvard, Columbia Law School. After his admission to the bar in 1907, he joined a prestigious New York City law firm.

His political career was launched in 1910 when, at the age of twenty-eight, he was offered the Democratic nomination for state senator from Dutchess County. The heavily Republican county had never elected a Democrat. He not only won a surprise victory in the election but was reelected two years later.

Roosevelt assumed a progressive political image early in his career and maintained it throughout his life. In 1912 he led an enthusiastic group of upstate New Yorkers in a series of demonstrations on behalf of the presidential candidacy of Woodrow Wilson at the Democratic National Convention. His support brought him to the attention of the candidate's aide Josephus Daniels. When Wilson was elected and named Daniels Secretary of the Navy, Daniels brought Roosevelt into the Federal Government as his Assistant Secretary.

A year after entering the Navy Department, Roosevelt sought the nomination for a United States Senate seat from New York without getting the cooperation of the leaders of Tammany Hall. He was beaten decisively in a primary fight for the nomination. Roosevelt continued in the Navy Department post, serving a total of seven years in Washington and picking up valuable governmental experience. In the meantime he patched up his differences with the Tammany leaders.

In 1920, when the Democrats nominated James Cox for the presidency, it was Tammany boss Charles F. Murphy who suggested Roosevelt for the vice-presidential nomination. Chosen by acclamation for the second spot on the ticket, Roosevelt threw himself enthusiastically into the campaign—although he knew the Democrats had little chance of winning the election. He barnstormed throughout the country, using the opportunity to acquaint himself with local party leaders and with the problems confronting various sections of the nation. All of this was to prove invaluable later. Roosevelt's campaign tours attracted attention that rivaled, and sometimes overshadowed, those of Cox. And when the campaign ended in defeat for the Democrats, it was Roosevelt who emerged as the recognized leader of the national party.

But in 1921 an event occurred that threatened to put a premature end to Roosevelt's political career. He contracted polio. His legs were paralyzed, and some members of his family became convinced that he would spend the remainder of his life as a helpless cripple. His mother had never thought well of his political activities and now urged that he resign himself to the life of an invalid country squire. However, Roosevelt's wife, Eleanor, and his long-time aide, a former newspaperman named Louis M. Howe, persuaded him to retain a close interest in politics while undergoing rehabilitation efforts. Roosevelt spent much of his time in hydrotherapy in the warm mineralized water at Warm Springs, Georgia. Meanwhile, Howe kept him in the public eye by carrying on a steady political correspondence in Roosevelt's name.

The rehabilitation efforts, while they did not restore normal use of Roosevelt's legs, strengthened other parts of his body and helped keep him in good health. He remained an active, vigorous man. His example, which received wide publicity, provided incentive to many other handicapped persons.

In 1924, when Al Smith unsuccessfully sought the presidential nomination at the Democratic National Convention, it was Roosevelt who placed his name in nomination. He hobbled to the rostrum of New York's Madison Square Garden on crutches and delivered a highly acclaimed speech that lambasted Republican policies, praised Smith's record and castigated anti-Catholic bigots. The address later came to be known as the "Happy Warrior" speech, for that phrase was used for the first time to describe Smith.

Four years later, when Smith succeeded in becoming the presidential candidate, it was again Roosevelt who placed his name in nomination. After the campaign had begun, Smith realized that his chances of election were slim—that he might, in fact, fail to carry his home state. He felt that Roosevelt could strengthen the Democratic ticket in New York by running for governor. Roosevelt was reluctant to make the race because he sensed that this would be a Republican year. But Smith and other state party leaders persuaded the state convention to nominate Roosevelt and talked him into accepting.

Roosevelt waged an energetic campaign, making it clear that his handicap would not prevent him from becoming a dynamic, full-time governor. When the election returns were counted, Al Smith had been defeated for President and had failed to carry his native state. Roosevelt had been elected governor by a small majority.

Roosevelt served effectively in Albany. He organized an unemployment relief system, expanded welfare programs begun by Smith and pushed through legislation beneficial to the state's farmers. Meanwhile, he narrowed his sights on the Presidency. His initial plan was to make the presidential election of 1936 his target year. He originally felt the Republicans would be virtually unbeatable in 1932. But, with the onset of the Depression, he moved up his timetable. His confidence in his vote-getting ability was bolstered in 1930 when he was elected governor by the largest margin ever given any candidate in the state's history.

Because of the probability of a Democratic victory in the 1932 election, the presidential nomination was a prize sought by numerous contenders. Roosevelt was foremost among them. The others included Al Smith, who felt he deserved another chance; House Speaker John Nance Garner of Texas; Maryland Governor Albert C. Ritchie; and Newton D. Baker, who had been Woodrow Wilson's Secretary of War.

Roosevelt held a majority of delegate votes on the first three ballots at the Democratic National Convention, but he was about 100 votes short of the two-thirds margin necessary for nomination. There were indications that some of Roosevelt's delegates would defect to other candidates on later ballots. But Speaker Garner, with strong backing from publisher William Randolph Hearst and William G. McAdoo, controlled enough votes from Texas and California to swing the nomination to Roosevelt if he turned his delegates over to the New York governor.

Garner feared another prolonged deadlock such as the 103-ballot shambles at the 1924 convention. He decided that Roosevelt should be nominated and instructed his floor manager, Congressman Sam Rayburn of Texas, to switch his delegates to Roosevelt on the next ballot. However, many of Garner's backers refused to budge unless he were given the vice-presidential nomination. Garner did not want to be Vice President. He felt that his position as House Speaker was the second most powerful in the government. But he agreed, out of party loyalty, to become Roosevelt's running mate. A deal was quickly worked out, and the Roosevelt-Garner ticket was nominated.

Roosevelt conducted a typically vigorous campaign. He charged that the Depression had resulted from blunders by the Hoover administration. He described the administration's record as "the most reckless and extravagant of any peacetime government anywhere at any time." He pledged his own administration to economy, financial reform and a balanced budget.

In the election, Roosevelt and Garner swept to a stunning victory. They polled 22,809,000 popular votes to 15,758,000 for Hoover and Curtis. Hoover and Curtis carried only six states.

The new Vice President could hardly have possessed a background more different from the President's. John Nance Garner was born in a log cabin in northeast Texas on November 22, 1868. His family faced a harsh frontier existence. The last of the Indian struggles were still being fought in Texas.

Although a sickly boy, he was fired by a fierce determination to accomplish anything on which he set his mind. At the age of ten he was told that he was not strong enough to pick 100 pounds of cotton in one day. He thereupon picked the cotton, sold it, bought a mule, then sold the mule at a handsome profit. When he was twenty he was told at Vanderbilt University in Tennessee that his previous education was inadequate and that he would have to leave. (Years later, when he was a national figure, Vanderbilt offered him an honorary degree. He refused to accept it.) Young Garner studied enough law privately to be admitted to the Texas bar at the age of twenty-one.

Meanwhile, a physician advised him that he had tuberculosis and that he would die unless he moved to a drier climate.

Garner moved across the state to Uvalde in southwest Texas —an area so dry it was dotted with cactus. Garner later became known as "Cactus Jack." He looked very much like a typical desert inhabitant. A stubby man with leathery red skin, he had bushy eyebrows and piercing blue eyes. (Garner's move to Uvalde apparently agreed with his health. Contrary to his doctor's warning of an early death, he lived longer than any other vice president or president in the nation's history. He was ninety-eight when he died in Uvalde on November 7, 1967.)

In 1898 Garner won a seat in the Texas legislature. He made his first race for Congress in 1902. Garner campaigned on foot, on horseback, in a horse and buggy and by stagecoach. He shook hand after hand and delivered speech after speech at outdoor rallies, church revival sessions and ranch barbecues. He built up such overwhelming support that his opponent withdrew from the race. This support never wavered during the next three decades as he was reelected to his House seat fifteen times.

When he first arrived in Washington other congressmen tended to laugh him off as a cowboy with an inflated idea of his own importance. But within a matter of weeks he made friends with many of his colleagues and was on a first-name basis with scores of them. He was always brutally frank. He once told Republican President Theodore Roosevelt: "Come to Texas, Mr. President. The people of Texas love you. They'll do anything in the world for you but vote for you."

Garner set his sights early in his congressional career on the influential post of House Speaker. He cultivated a friendship with Speaker Champ Clark, learned how to obtain and use power in Washington and became an expert in parliamentary procedure.

Garner was a firm believer in the art of compromise. "The most constructive laws on our statute books have been put there by intelligent compromise," he said. Garner was greatly admired by his congressional colleagues, and he did most of his effective work behind the scenes in the committee rooms.

He was chiefly credited, for example, with bringing about the graduated income-tax system that taxes citizens according to what they earn.

When the nation was plunged into the Depression, Garner refused to be drawn into rigid opposition to all of President Hoover's proposals for easing the economic distress. He supported those Hoover policies that he considered practical. "I astonished people here in Washington once by saying I was for the welfare of the country first and that of the Democratic Party second," Garner explained.

It was one of the ironies of Garner's career that, after longing to be House Speaker for three decades, he got to serve in the office for only a bit longer than one year. He became Speaker in 1931 and was elected Vice President the following year. As Speaker he initiated what he called his "board of education" meetings. Groups of congressmen were invited to his office to "sit a spell" and "strike a blow for liberty" (have a drink) before talking out their differences. Later, as Vice President, he played host at similar sessions for members of the Senate.

Once, as Speaker, he became impatient with several balky congressmen during a budget debate. "All those who wish to balance the budget please rise," Garner shouted. He gave all members present time to get to their feet. "Let the record so note," Garner said. "Let all those who do not wish to balance the budget stand." Not one member rose for the second call. While presiding over the Senate as Vice President, Garner was asked by the rambunctious Senator Huey Long of Louisiana: "How should a senator, who is half in favor of this bill and half against it, cast his vote?" Garner shot an icy glance at Long. "Get a saw and saw yourself in half," he replied. "That's what you ought to do anyhow."

President Roosevelt made extensive use of Vice President Garner as a liaison man between the executive and legislative branches. Garner's knowledge of the intricacies of the government, and the esteem in which he was held by members of Congress, proved invaluable.

Roosevelt called his program the New Deal. It was more than new; it was revolutionary. Its overriding purpose was to promote the American people's economic well-being through the Federal Government. After one brief effort to keep his campaign pledge to reduce federal expenditures, Roosevelt made it clear that the government would use borrowed money, if necessary, to put his program into effect.

New government agencies were brought into being in such numbers that the public could scarcely keep track of all of them. The National Recovery Administration (later ruled unconstitutional by the Supreme Court) set up programs aimed at bringing about increased employment, reducing the length of the work week, providing higher wages, preventing unfair business competition and eliminating overproduction. Agencies such as the Public Works Administration, the Civilian Conservation Corps and the Work Projects Administration put the unemployed to work on government projects. The Social Security Board was created to administer a series of programs designed to provide citizens with insurance against the hazards of illness, unemployment and old age. The Tennessee Valley Authority provided inexpensive electrical power, flood control and other services to parts of eight states lying between Virginia and the Mississsippi River. The Agricultural Adjustment Administration (later declared unconstitutional) sought to increase agricultural prices by subsidizing farmers who refrained from raising surplus crops.

Vice President Garner, more conservative than Roosevelt, might have been expected to resist some of the liberal New Deal legislation. But, at least at first, he gave the President unstinting support. He did so out of a sense of loyalty to Roosevelt and out of conviction that strong medicine was needed to cure the nation's desperate economic illness.

He not only attended Cabinet meetings but was an active

participant. He provided expert analyses of the inner workings of Congress to some of Roosevelt's political neophytes. In addition, Garner convinced Roosevelt of the wisdom of initiating weekly meetings with the Senate and House leaders and was an active participant in these meetings.

Garner was the first Vice President to visit a foreign country on official business. He achieved this distinction in 1935 when he represented the United States at the inauguration of Manuel Quezon as President of the Philippines.

In 1936 both Roosevelt and Garner were renominated at the Democratic National Convention in Philadelphia. The Roosevelt administration was riding the crest of a wave of national popularity.

Former President Herbert Hoover denounced the Roosevelt program as "a cold-blooded attempt by starry-eyed boys to infect the American people by a mixture of European ideas, flavored with our native predilection to get something for nothing." But Republican campaign strategists decided that the party's chief hope lay in promising the public even more benefits than those offered by the New Deal.

The Republicans chose as their presidential candidate Kansas Governor Alfred M. Landon, who had been the only Republican governor in the nation reelected in 1934. Picked as his running mate was Colonel Frank Knox, owner of the Chicago *Daily News*.

Roosevelt and Garner were given one of the most sweeping political endorsements ever accorded a national ticket. They captured every state except two, Maine and Vermont. They drew 26,484,000 popular votes to 17,469,000 for Landon and Knox. And they won the electoral vote by the count of 523 to 8.

During their second term Garner did his best to exert a restraining influence on the President. He periodically advised Roosevelt at Cabinet meetings: "Mr. President, you know you've got to let the cattle graze." But Roosevelt disagreed.

Buoyed by the proportions of his 1936 election victory, he was determined to keep pressing for additional New Deal legislation. Gradually, relations between Garner and Roosevelt became strained.

These relations sank to a new low when Roosevelt proposed his so-called "court-packing" bill. The President had been frustrated and angered by a series of Supreme Court decisions which had ruled unconstitutional seven major pieces of New Deal legislation. By Roosevelt's second term six of the nine Supreme Court justices were past seventy years of age—but none showed any inclination to retire.

To cope with the situation Roosevelt hit upon the idea of "packing" the court with liberal justices who would be inclined to favor his programs. He proposed giving the president power to add one member to the court—up to a maximum of six—for each justice who had reached the age of seventy, had served for at least ten years and had failed to retire.

In February of 1937, he called in the Vice President and congressional leaders and presented them with a word-for-word copy of the bill he wanted pushed through the Congress. Garner was taken aback both by Roosevelt's handling of the matter and by the proposed legislation itself. He later publicly showed his disdain for the proposal by holding his nose and giving a thumbs-down signal in a lobby outside the Senate chamber.

The Vice President was far from alone in his distaste for the bill. Many members of both parties in Congress argued that Roosevelt's proposal threatened the constitutionally guaranteed independence of the judiciary and that it would be dangerous to appoint to the court justices whose chief qualifications would be harmony with the political philosophy of the party in power.

Roosevelt declared: "A constant and systematic addition of younger blood will vitalize the courts and better equip them to recognize and apply the essential concepts of justice in the light of the needs and facts of an ever-changing world." But the Senate Judiciary Committee, reporting adversely on the bill, said: "Let us of the 75th Congress declare that we would rather have an independent court, a fearless court, a court that will dare to announce its honest opinion in what it believes to be the defense of the liberties of the people, than a court that, out of fear, or sense of obligation to the appointing power, or factional passion, approves any measure we may enact."

As the full Senate debated the measure and the time for its crucial vote approached, Garner left Washington for a vacation in Texas. The Vice President and his wife had been planning the vacation for half a year. But Roosevelt felt that Garner had deserted his post at a critical time. He urged him to come back to the capital. Garner refused.

The major burden of pressing for passage of Roosevelt's bill fell to Senate Majority Leader Joseph T. Robinson of Arkansas. Robinson drove himself relentlessly during this period, working long hours at a frenzied pace. On July 14, 1937, he suffered a heart attack and died. Following his death, the ranks of those supporting the "court-packing" bill dwindled.

Garner returned from Texas and reported to Roosevelt that the measure was doomed to defeat. The President asked him to try to work out some kind of compromise. Garner tried without success. On July 24 the Senate killed the bill by sending it back to committee.

After Senator Robinson's death, Democratic Senators had to elect a new majority leader. A contest developed between Senators Alben Barkley of Kentucky and Pat Harrison of Mississippi. Both Roosevelt and Garner promised not to intervene in the contest, but Roosevelt exerted strong pressure on certain senators to vote for Barkley. Garner disapproved of the President's action, feeling it represented improper meddling in the conduct of Senate business.

A year later Garner became even more upset when Roosevelt opposed in primaries throughout the nation those senators who had voted against his court-packing bill. Garner complained that Roosevelt was endangering the future of the

Democratic Party by trying to convert it into a personal party shaped in his own image.

The electorate delivered a stinging setback to Roosevelt by voting to renominate most of the senators he opposed in the primaries. The general elections of 1938 saw the Republicans make their first national gains at the polls in ten years. They boosted their membership in the Senate from fifteen to twenty-three and in the House from eighty-eight to 170. The number of Republican governors was increased from five to eighteen. Garner blamed Roosevelt for bringing about the Republican gains. With increasing frequency the President and Vice President quarreled at Cabinet meetings. A further worsening of relations between the two men developed when Roosevelt came to suspect Garner of revealing to outsiders what had taken place behind the closed doors of the Cabinet Room. The President and members of his Cabinet became reluctant to speak with complete frankness at the meetings. Individual members took to staying after the meetings to discuss confidential matters with Roosevelt in private. Garner, who resented these private sessions, derided them as "prayer meetings."

The final break between the President and Vice President came in 1940 when Roosevelt decided to ignore the two-term tradition and run for a third presidential term. World War II had broken out in Europe. And, while the United States had not yet joined the conflict, it was clear that perilous times lay ahead. Roosevelt and his supporters felt that these times called for an experienced man to lead the nation. Although he did not at first announce his intention to seek a third term, Roosevelt encouraged his backers to arrange for the Democratic National Convention to "draft" him for renomination.

Garner was dead set against Roosevelt's reelection. "I would be against a third term on principle even if I approved every act of Roosevelt's two terms," he said. "I would oppose my own brother for a third term . . . No man should exercise the great powers of the Presidency too long."

At age seventy-one Garner was so opposed to Roosevelt's candidacy that he announced he would seek the presidential nomination himself. His name was put before the convention. But the convention delegates voted overwhelmingly to "draft" Roosevelt for a third term.

Even before Garner had opposed Roosevelt's third-term candidacy at the convention, the President had decided to seek another running mate. He had sounded out Secretary of State Cordell Hull on the possibility of running for Vice President, but Hull had declined. Roosevelt then decided he wanted Secretary of Agriculture Henry A. Wallace to occupy the second spot on the ticket.

The choice of Wallace was destined to set off a furor among professional politicians. Wallace was one of the most controversial figures in Washington. A man of ability and courage, he was also an unabashed idealist. Even some of those Democrats who supported the most liberal New Deal programs considered Wallace too ultraliberal for their taste. But Roosevelt had the utmost confidence in him.

Shortly before the Democratic convention the President asked Democratic National Chairman James A. Farleys' advice on a possible Wallace candidacy for Vice President. Farley raised the question of Wallace's potential succession to the Presidency if Roosevelt should die. "I would not like to see him Vice President, though I like him personally, because I think it would be a terrible thing to have him President," Farley said. "The people look on him as a wild-eyed fellow."

But Roosevelt viewed the question differently from Farley. "A man with paralysis can have a breakup any time," he told the party chairman. "While my heart and lungs are good and the other organs functioning along okay, nothing in this life is certain. It's essential that the man who runs with me should be able to carry on." He said he considered Wallace such a man.

Roosevelt was in Washington when the Democratic convention in Chicago nominated him for a third term. He instructed his representative at the convention, Harry Hopkins, to advise party leaders that Wallace was his choice for Vice President.

When word of Roosevelt's decision reached the convention delegates, a budding revolt developed. Hopkins phoned the President to give him the news. Roosevelt was livid. "They will go for Wallace or I won't run," he roared. "And you can jolly well tell them so."

The President listened to the convention on the radio. Each time Wallace's name was mentioned, Roosevelt could hear boos resounding through the convention hall. He took up a pen and angrily started scribbling a letter. He gave the letter to an aide, Samuel Rosenman, and told him to get it ready for possible release to the press. It was to be released if the convention refused to nominate Wallace. It announced Roosevelt's rejection of the presidential nomination.

Rosenman took the letter outside the President's office and showed it to General Edwin M. (Pa) Watson, Roosevelt's appointment secretary. Watson suggested destroying the letter. Rosenman rejected Watson's suggestion, followed Roosevelt's instructions and got the letter ready for release in the event that the convention refused to nominate Wallace.

Meanwhile, at the convention, Roosevelt's preference for Wallace was being accepted reluctantly by many of the participants. A number of other contestants for the vice-presidential nomination withdrew their names from consideration. House Speaker William B. Bankhead remained the lone formal candidate in the running against Wallace. Confidants of Roosevelt scurried from one delegation to another, appealing for Wallace's nomination. When the balloting ended, Wallace had been nominated by a narrow majority. Except for the fact that the Democrats had abandoned the traditional two-thirds rule four years earlier, his margin would have been too small for nomination.

The Republicans convened in Philadelphia and, on the sixth ballot, gave their presidential nomination to Wendell Willkie, an Indiana-born lawyer who had never before run for public office. Willkie, president of the Commonwealth and Southern Corporation, had led the fight against establishment of the Tennessee Valley Authority. On many other issues of domestic and foreign policy, however, he took positions that did not seem to differ markedly from Roosevelt's. Nominated as Willkie's running mate was Senator Charles McNary of Oregon.

The third-term issued played a major part in the campaign. Willkie's supporters pasted stickers on their cars reading: "NO THIRD TERM." Roosevelt's backers responded with stickers of their own: "BETTER A THIRD-TERMER THAN A THIRD-RATER."

During the campaign Wallace's past connections with members of a small, offbeat religious group threatened to cause the Democratic ticket serious embarrassment—if not worse. Some years earlier Wallace had become acquainted with a mystical, bearded man named Nicholas Konstantino-vich Roerich. Roerich had studied art, law and archeology, had traveled widely and had painted thousands of pictures. He had made archeological expeditions to such colorful places as Tibet, Sikkim and Kashmir. During one of these expeditions he claimed to have found some aged Buddhist writings pur-portedly disclosing that Jesus Christ had journeyed to India in his youth.

Wallace became persuaded that indications of the Second Coming of Christ might be discovered somewhere in central Asia. While serving as Secretary of Agriculture in Roosevelt's first term, Wallace appointed Roerich to head a government expedition to Mongolia. The stated purpose of the expedition was to hunt for grasses capable of withstanding periods of drought. Actually, Roerich hoped to uncover evidence of the Second Coming.

Finally Wallace soured on him and ousted him from his gov-ernment job. Roerich did not come back to the United States. But some of his followers, feeling Wallace had been disloyal to him, vowed to get even. One of them threatened to make public several embarrassing letters Wallace was said to have written to Roerich and his backers.

Some of these letters fell into the hands of anti-Wallace newspapers during the 1940 election campaign. The papers' editors made painstaking attempts to establish their authenticity. Some of the letters were signed with Wallace's name, some with his initials. Some were typed, some in longhand.

One letter contained the following mysterious passage: "I have thought of the new country going forth, to meet the seven stars under the sign of the three stars. And I have thought of the admonition, 'Await the stones.'" In another letter the writer told of spending a wearisome day and then finding that his eyes would not focus properly. "I remembered the lovely gift of musk and rose, and a pinch of it cleared up my vision like magic," the letter said.

Handwriting specialists were called in to try to determine if the letters actually had been written by Wallace. They reported that some of the letters were in his handwriting. But those that were potentially most embarrassing had been typewritten and the specialists differed over whether Wallace had signed them.

The matter caused great consternation among top Democratic leaders. They were prepared to mount a massive public-relations campaign to offset the effects of the letters in the event that the letters were published.

One determined newsman, who hounded Wallace for information about the letters, finally prompted a response. Wallace gave him a written statement that said in part: "Your publisher must know that the material in question is composed of malicious, spurious, fraudulent and forged matter."

In the end, the newspapers did not publish them. The storm blew over. Roosevelt made light of the affair. But some political observers have speculated that, if the newspapers had published the letters during the campaign, the outcome of the election might have been changed.

As it turned out, Roosevelt and Wallace won the election by a plurality of 4,900,000 votes, with 27,200,000 to 22,300,-000 for Willkie and McNary. The voter turnout was the largest in the nation's history. The Democrats carried thirty-eight states with 449 electoral votes, the Republicans ten states with 82 electoral votes.

The election brought to the vice presidency one of the most unusual men ever to hold the office. Born in 1888, Wallace was a member of an Iowa family renowned in the field of agriculture. His grandfather had founded the nation's leading farm journal, *Wallace's Farmer*. His father had served as Secretary of Agriculture from 1921 to 1924. And he himself was regarded as an expert in both the scientific and economic aspects of farming.

Possessed of a restless, inquiring mind, Wallace refused to accept many of the agricultural clichés that had satisfied generations of farmers. Even as a boy he had conducted tests proving to his satisfaction that corn long thought to be the most nutritious—because it looked most attractive—was actually inferior to some "ugly" corn. After studying agricultural science at Iowa State University, he pioneered in developing a new strain of hybrid corn—which he marketed through his Hi-Bred Corn Company.

When his father was appointed Secretary of Agriculture Wallace took over from him the editorship of *Wallace's Farmer*. He proceeded to shake up many of the publication's readers with some of his seemingly revolutionary ideas. His references to such subjects as comparative religion, in relation to agricultural problems, befuddled some subscribers.

But if Wallace's unorthodox ideas were disturbing to conservative readers, they were nonetheless interesting to other influential persons. One of Franklin D. Roosevelt's confidants became acquainted with Wallace just before Roosevelt made his initial race for the Presidency. When the time came for Roosevelt to formulate an agricultural policy during the 1932 campaign, Wallace was invited to discuss his ideas with the candidate. Roosevelt was taken with Wallace's intelligence, energy and inquisitive nature. When he was elected to the Presidency, he appointed Wallace his Secretary of Agriculture.

Wallace joined the Cabinet at a time when the nation's farmers—as well as members of other segments of the economy—were in deep trouble. Agricultural prices were disastrously low. Wallace decided that the best way to provide relief to the farmers was by reducing the oversupply of agricultural products. At his insistence farmers slaughtered 6,000,000 pigs and plowed under 10,000,000 acres of cotton land. These policies brought down the wrath of political conservatives on Wallace. The slaughter of the pigs prompted one newspaper to brand him as "the greatest butcher in Christendom."

Wallace retorted that it was a tribute "to the humanitarian instincts of the American people that they sympathize more with little pigs which are killed than with full-grown hogs." He suggested that some people might oppose killing pigs at any age. "Perhaps they think that farmers should run a sort of old-folks home for hogs," he said. "But we have to think about farmers as well as hogs. And we must think about consumers and try to get a uniform supply of pork from year to year at a price which is fair to farmer and consumer alike." Within a year, hog prices had risen by more than 50 per cent.

Wallace did not restrict his interests or activities to the field of agriculture. He ranged over the whole spectrum of American life. He became one of the leading spokesmen for the New Deal—a tireless speechmaker and writer. A veritable torrent of words rushed from his lips and his pen. In just one year he wrote three books, twenty articles and delivered eighty-eight speeches. Again and again he spoke on behalf of the "common man" in his fight against the vested interests.

His curiosity seemed limitless. One day he would be investigating the mysteries of the boomerang. The next day he would be studying one of the world's great religions. The day after that he would be looking into the relationship between technological advancements and the eradication of poverty.

Wallace grasped before many other Americans the danger of Adolf Hitler's Nazi government in Germany. He attempted to mobilize American opinion against Hitler's racist theories even before the outbreak of World War II. Ridiculing Hitler's claims that Aryans made up a "master race," Wallace commented: "The color of a cow's hair has nothing to do with her ability to produce milk. And there is no reason to think that the color of a man's hair has anything to do with his ability to produce ideas."

Nor was Wallace satisfied to lash out only at bigotry on the far side of the Atlantic. He was equally outspoken in criticizing racial and religious discrimination in the United States.

Wallace's vitality, curiosity and liberalism were among the qualities that influenced Roosevelt to choose him as Vice President. They were also some of the very qualities that prevented him from being welcomed into the inner circle of congressional leaders. These men, by and large, considered the Vice President an outsider—and a rather odd one at that. His ability to serve as a legislative liaison man for Roosevelt was limited.

But Roosevelt had other duties in mind for Wallace that would significantly broaden the scope of the vice presidency and prepare the way for even greater expansion of the vice president's functions under future presidents. Roosevelt decided in mid-1941 to assign the Vice President some executive responsibilities.

Four months before the United States entered World War II, the President created a new government agency called the Economic Defense Board (renamed the Board of Economic Warfare after the declaration of war). Wallace was appointed to head the board, which included seven members of the Cabinet. The board had vast powers concerning accumulation of strategic materials, import-export policy, American investments abroad, the communications industry, shipping and patents. Wallace was given final authority to make crucial decisions on matters under the board's jurisdiction. Roosevelt also appointed him chairman of the Supply Priorities and Allocations Board and a member of a five-man advisory committee on atomic energy, which ultimately recommended that the United States try to build an atomic bomb.

Wallace became one of the President's most influential advisers on other issues. He emerged as a major architect of government policy. No previous vice president had exerted such a powerful influence on the executive branch.

It soon became apparent that there was an overlapping of interests between Wallace's Board of Economic Warfare (BEW) and the Reconstruction Finance Corporation (RFC). The RFC was under the jurisdiction of Secretary of Commerce Jesse H. Jones. Like the BEW, the RFC was engaged in acquiring strategic goods from foreign sources. Jones was a conservative buyer—shopping around painstakingly until he found the lowest price. But Wallace felt that the demands of the war effort made it necessary to buy up huge quantities of materials with the greatest possible speed, sacrificing economy in the name of expediency. His agency sent representatives throughout the globe on massive purchasing expeditions.

Wallace was impatient with what he regarded as the slow pace of Jones's agency. Within four months of the United States' entry into the war, he publicly denounced the RFC program.

A month later, at Wallace's urging, Roosevelt signed an executive order giving the BEW authority to direct the RFC to buy any materials wanted by the BEW at any price determined by the BEW. The executive order also gave Wallace the power to serve as an adviser to the Secretary of State on administration of the Lend-Lease Act—under which the United States provided material aid to its allies.

Both Jones and Secretary of State Cordell Hull were disturbed by the order and told Roosevelt so. The President informed Wallace he never would have issued the order if he had known Jones and Hull would object. Wallace said he had not asked for the opinions of the two Cabinet members because he knew, without asking, that they would oppose the order. Roosevelt moved to resolve the differences between the Vice President and the State Department by signing a new executive order making clear Hull's authority over the conduct of foreign affairs while reaffirming Wallace's role in economic programs. The difficulties between Wallace and Jones remained unresolved.

Early in 1943 the Vice President—on his own authority—issued an order granting BEW sole right to stockpile, purchase and sell foreign strategic goods. Jones, aghast at the order, refused to obey it. He argued that Congress had given the RFC power to engage in such activities and that the Vice President had no authority to take away what Congress had granted.

A vitriolic struggle ensued, with liberal Democratic members of Congress generally lining up behind Wallace and conservatives behind Jones. Stung by congressional attacks, Wallace and one of his key aides, Milo Perkins, prepared a lengthy written report that castigated Jones as an obstructionist who had hampered the war effort through "hamstring bureaucracy." Jones retaliated by branding the charges "dastardly" and "maliciously false."

Efforts were made by intimates of the President to bring about a truce between Wallace and Jones. But the feud had become much too serious for that. Bitter words continued to fly.

Roosevelt was forced to act. He said the necessities of the war effort did not permit "sufficient time to investigate and determine where the truth lies." So he removed both Wallace and Jones from responsibility for the programs that had created the dissension. The President disbanded the BEW and stripped Wallace of all his executive duties. Simultaneously, he took away Jones's authority over international economic programs of the RFC and created a new Office of Economic Warfare. A close friend of Jones, Leo Crowley, was named to head the new agency. Because of their friendship, some observers interpreted the appointment as a victory for Jones. The Secretary of Commerce supported this interpretation. Wallace merely said that he would not question Roosevelt's judgment.

Despite the sour taste it left, the experiment in assigning executive duties to the Vice President established an important precedent. Future presidents would not hesitate to call upon their vice presidents to carry out important executive responsibilities.

Wallace plunged into a new series of activities with the same zeal he had given his BEW work. He made a highly successful good-will tour of Latin America in 1943. He began the strenuous tour by playing two sets of tennis in Bolivia, while his Latin hosts marveled at his stamina. Wallace was extremely popular in South America and drew large, enthusiastic turnouts at virtually every stop on the tour.

The Vice President continued to build his reputation as a prolific speechmaker. Hardly a week seemed to pass without a major Wallace speech on one subject or another. The most celebrated of all his speeches was delivered in 1942 to the Free World Association in New York. It came to be known as his "Common Man Speech." Wallace said:

> Some have spoken of the "American Century." I say that the century on which we are entering, the century which will come out of this war, can be and must be the century of the common man. We shall not rest until all the victims under the Nazi yoke are freed. We shall fight for a complete peace as well as a complete victory. The people's revolution is on the march, and the devil and all his angels cannot prevail against it. They cannot prevail, for on the side of the people is the Lord.

During the war one of Wallace's political liabilities became increasingly apparent—his blind spot to the menace of communism. Though not a Communist himself, he allowed himself to be used by the Communists on a number of occasions. During the early 1930s Wallace had spoken out against the "violence and brutality" of the Communist government in Russia. But a decade later he was describing the Soviet regime in glowing terms. (Russia at this time was an ally of the United States against Hitler.) In a New York speech before the Congress of American-Soviet Friendship—a forum which his critics said he should not have addressed in the first place —the Vice President declared in 1942 that the Soviet Union and the U.S. were trying to reach the same goals. In other addresses he spoke out against what he called an "anti-Russian bias" in this country.

As the presidential election of 1944 approached it was a foregone conclusion that President Roosevelt would run for a fourth term. He would not voluntarily retire with the war still in progress. But would Wallace again be his running mate? The Vice President had influential supporters, chiefly union officials and liberal leaders, who wanted him kept on the ticket. However, he also had numerous political enemies, who insisted that he be dumped in favor of some other vice-presidential candidate.

What would follow would be one of the most curious—yet significant—battles ever waged over a vice-presidential nomination.

❦❧❦

CHAPTER TWELVE

The End of the War

THE circumstances surrounding the selection of the 1944 Democratic vice-presidential candidate were among the most fascinating in the annals of American politics. And the outcome of the contest for the nomination was destined to have a profound impact on world history. Much of the fascination generated by the selection process stemmed from a bitter struggle for power, an involved series of behind-the-scenes machinations and the strange reluctance of a usually decisive President to make clear his choice of a running mate.

Any study of the Democrats' choice of a vice-presidential candidate in 1944 must take into account the poor state of President Roosevelt's health at the time. A series of illnesses had sapped the President's strength. He looked thin, drawn and tired. He had trouble sleeping. His physicians instructed him to work only four hours a day. Many political insiders doubted that he would live to serve out another full four-year term. For that reason the choice of a vice-presidential candidate assumed additional significance.

Against this background a movement developed to dump Henry Wallace and find another vice-presidential candidate. But if Wallace were to be dumped, the obvious question became who would replace him on the Democratic ticket. Numerous names were considered in the preconvention maneuvering.

An early favorite for the nomination was James F. Byrnes. A respected former Senator and Governor from South Carolina, Byrnes had long been a member of Roosevelt's inner circle.

The President had appointed him to the Supreme Court in 1941. Byrnes had resigned from the bench a year later to take on the burdensome responsibilities of serving as the nation's director of war mobilization. Byrnes's long record of effective service gave him some strong selling points for the vice-presidential nomination. But because he came from a segregationist Southern state, it was feared that he would drive Negro and liberal votes away from the Democratic ticket. It was also feared that he would cost the ticket votes among union members, since he had differed sharply with labor leaders during his service as mobilization director. Lastly, there was speculation that Catholic voters would oppose him. Although born a Catholic, Byrnes had left the religion after marrying a Protestant.

Other leading contenders for the nomination were the Democratic leaders of both houses of Congress—House Speaker Sam Rayburn of Texas and Senate Majority Leader Alben W. Barkley of Kentucky. Both had lengthy records of loyal service to their party and their country. They had been instrumental in pushing much of Roosevelt's New Deal legislation through Congress.

Among liberals there was strong support for Supreme Court Justice William O. Douglas. Many who favored the renomination of Wallace saw Douglas as an attractive second choice.

Last, but far from least, in the list of chief contenders was Senator Harry S Truman of Missouri. A few years earlier Truman would have been given scant attention for a place on the national ticket. But during the war he had moved into a position of national prominence. He had traveled a long, difficult road to reach this position.

Truman was born into a farm family of modest means at Lamar, Missouri, in 1884. The family moved to Independence when he has six, and he went through school there while his father worked at a succession of jobs as a laborer. Truman sought appointments to West Point and Annapolis—but was rejected because of poor eyesight. He then went to work, first for a contractor and then for a bank. Later, he joined his father and brother in running a 600-acre farm. No matter how the family tried, it was seldom able to get out of debt.

Truman joined the National Guard, went on active duty when the United States entered World War I and was sent to France as commander of a field-artillery battery. He rose to the rank of captain before his discharge in 1919.

He then went into the haberdashery business in Kansas City with an army friend. The business venture was a terrible failure—leaving Truman $20,000 in debt.

It was after the collapse of the business that Truman first entered politics. He was recommended to the Pendergast brothers, Tom and Jim, who ran the Democratic political machine in Kansas City. With their support he was elected in 1922 as county court judge for Eastern Jackson County. In 1924 Truman was defeated in a bid for reelection but two years later he was elected, again with Pendergast support, as presiding judge of the county court.

Truman did an outstanding job as presiding judge, bringing a higher degree of efficiency and honesty to the county government than had ever prevailed in the past. Although the Pendergast machine had been notorious for its corruption, not a breath of scandal tainted Truman's record as he presided over the expenditure of more than $60,000,000 on public-works projects.

In 1934 Truman intended to seek a seat in the House of Representatives. However, Pendergast persuaded him to run instead for the Senate. He swept to victory by a margin of 250,000 votes.

Truman became a member of the Senate's inner circle through steady attendance at Vice President Garner's "board of education" meetings and cultivation of friendships with influential members.

In 1941 Truman's stature as a public figure began to rise sharply. The United States, although not yet a combatant in World War II, was engaged in a vast defense mobilization program. In anticipation of the country's possible entry into the war, millions of dollars worth of government contracts were hurriedly being awarded to defense plants, companies involved in building military bases and others.

Truman introduced a Senate resolution calling for creation of a Special Committee to Investigate the National Defense Program. The resolution was passed, and Truman was appointed chairman of the committee. Under his direction the committee did an outstanding job in a watchdog role both before and after the United States' entry into the war. It delved deeply into every phase of the defense program and was credited with saving the taxpayers at least $15,000,000.

Truman became a national figure. In 1944, when Washington newspapermen compiled a list of the "ten most valuable men in Washington in the war," he was the only member of the Congress included. He found himself possessed of new power and prestige. When the time came for consideration of a 1944 vice-presidential nominee, it seemed natural that Truman should be among those in contention.

Henry Wallace made it plain that he was determined to fight for renomination. Among his most influential backers was Sidney Hillman, president of the Amalgamated Clothing Workers of America. A confidant of Roosevelt, Hillman headed the powerful Political Action Committee (PAC) of the Congress of Industrial Organizations—the chief political voice of the labor movement. Hillman was destined to play an important, controversial role in the selection of the vice-presidential nominee.

By the beginning of 1944 the anti-Wallace Democratic leaders were making headway in their campaign to get Wallace dumped from the ticket. The President conferred with Democratic leaders about the vice-presidential nomination in January. Among those sitting in on the meeting were Democratic National Chairman Robert E. Hannegan; his predecessor in that job, Postmaster General Frank Walker; National Committee Treasurer Edwin W. Pauley; and New York boss

Edward J. Flynn. The conferees considered the qualifications and vote-pulling appeal of the chief prospects for the nomination—Wallace, Truman, Byrnes, Barkley, Rayburn and Douglas. Of the six contenders, Truman received the strongest support at the meeting. Roosevelt spoke affirmatively about the Missouri senator's assets as a potential running mate. But the talk was merely exploratory. All the original contenders were still considered in the running when the meeting ended.

The first to fall out of the running was Senator Barkley. He and Roosevelt got embroiled in a dispute over a tax measure that grew so bitter as to preclude the possibility of their becoming running mates.

Next, Speaker Rayburn dropped out of contention. Voters in his home state of Texas had been growing increasingly disillusioned over what they considered an erosion of states' rights. In early 1944 the Supreme Court handed down a decision holding that it was illegal for Texas' Democratic Party to bar Negroes from voting in primaries. This ruling created additional resentment among Texas Democrats.

At the Texas Democratic state convention a revolt developed against the Roosevelt administration. The state party split with only half the delegates remaining loyal to Roosevelt. These loyalists bolted the state convention and elected their own slate of delegates to the national convention. A dispute ensued over which delegation the national convention should seat. Ultimately, both delegations were seated—with the state's votes split between the two groups. Rayburn realized that it was politically impractical for him to become Roosevelt's running mate. He urged his supporters to back some other vice-presidential hopeful.

In mid-May, Roosevelt set off waves of new speculation by sending Henry Wallace on a mission to China. Since the Democratic National Convention would begin July 19, Wallace would be out of the country until a few days before it opened. Did Roosevelt want Wallace out of the way during the critical preconvention maneuvering? Was he planning to dump the Vice President? Or did he hope that the mission abroad would demonstrate his trust in the Vice President's ability, thus enhancing Wallace's prestige? Nobody, except Roosevelt, was certain what the President had in mind.

Roosevelt was behaving with uncharacteristic indecisiveness. He made numerous contradictory statements—leading several of the candidates to believe they had his support for the nomination.

During the early summer Roosevelt seemed to favor Jimmy Byrnes as his running mate. On June 14, the President urged Byrnes to seek the permanent chairmanship of the Democratic National Convention as a possible stepping stone to the vice-presidential nomination.

Roosevelt soon had second thoughts about Byrnes. Union leader Sidney Hillman warned him that Byrnes's candidacy would not sit well with the labor movement or Negro voters. Hillman wanted Wallace renominated. Only two weeks after urging Byrnes to seek the convention chairmanship, the President advised confidants that he would like to have Wallace as his running mate once again. But he quickly launched into a discussion of the merits of other possible candidates—further confusing an already confused situation.

Ed Flynn reported to Roosevelt in early July that Wallace's name on the ticket would swing several key states to the Republicans. Flynn doubted that any of the vice-presidential hopefuls would substantially strengthen the ticket. He thought the question, instead, was which one would least hurt Roosevelt's chances. He and Roosevelt concluded that Senator Truman was the least likely to lose votes for the ticket. Truman had a responsible Senate record and a tide of favorable publicity. He had alienated none of the nation's traditional voting blocs. Roosevelt told Flynn he planned to invite a group of Democratic leaders to dinner at the White House on the evening of July 11, at which time the vice-presidential nomination would be discussed. He asked Flynn to speak on behalf of Truman's candidacy at the dinner.

On the morning of July 11, Roosevelt formally announced that he would be a candidate for a fourth term. He indicated that the Democratic convention would be left free to make its own choice of a vice-presidential candidate, but most knowledgeable observers agreed that the President would have the final say on a running mate.

At midday Vice President Wallace—just back from his Asian trip—was Roosevelt's guest for lunch. The President had asked a White House aide to break the news gently to Wallace in advance that he would not be renominated. But the Vice President arrived at the White House with an advance copy of the results of a Gallup poll showing that 65 per cent of Democratic voters favored his renomination. He also claimed that his supporters had already lined up almost 300 of the 589 convention votes needed for nomination.

Roosevelt was taken aback. Wallace seemed to have more support than the President had suspected. Roosevelt had dreaded having to tell Wallace that he would not be on the ticket. Now he could not bring himself to do it. Instead, he promised to write a letter endorsing Wallace's renomination.

This did not stop the President from having a full discussion about all the potential candidates that same evening at his dinner with party leaders. Roosevelt's guests were Bob Hannegan, Ed Flynn, George Allen, Ed Pauley, Frank Walker and Ed Kelly. The President's son-in-law, John Boettiger, joined the group after the meal had ended.

Over coffee and after-dinner drinks, the talk turned to the vice-presidential nomination. Each of the prospects' assets and liabilities were assessed.

Wallace was given short shrift in the discussion. Roosevelt did not mention that he had promised earlier in the day to write the letter endorsing Wallace's candidacy. Byrnes was ruled out. Roosevelt initiated a discussion of Justice Douglas —saying he had a sort of Boy Scout quality about him that might be appealing to voters and, besides, played a good game of poker. But the party leaders were not enthusiastic about

Douglas. Moreover, Douglas did not want to run and had asked friends to keep his name from being placed in nomination.

Flynn brought Truman's name into the discussion. The President said he considered Truman capable, loyal to the administration and politically astute. Several of the party leaders also spoke up on Truman's behalf.

Roosevelt said one thing troubled him about Truman—the senator's age. The President was under the impression that Truman was sixty. Roosevelt himself was sixty-two. And neither major political party had ever fielded a ticket composed of two men past sixty. Hannegan and Pauley—knowing that the President's estimate of Truman's age was accurate—tried to change the subject. But Roosevelt sent his son-in-law to get a copy of the *Congressional Directory* and look up Truman's exact age.

When Boettiger returned with the directory, Pauley grabbed the book from him and held it unobtrusively on his lap. Roosevelt smiled at Hannegan and said: "Bob, I think you and everyone else here want Truman."

Although he did not put it into a flat statement, the President seemed to his guests to be in agreement with this decision. Postmaster General Walker suggested to Hannegan before they left the White House that an attempt be made immediately to get Roosevelt to put his approval of Truman's candidacy in writing.

Hannegan returned to the President's study after the others had left and told Roosevelt that it would be helpful to have a written expression of support for Truman. The President picked up an envelope and scrawled on the back: "Bob, I think Truman is the right man. FDR." He said he would write a more formal endorsement in the next few days.

By this time Roosevelt had pledged support to three men— Truman, Wallace and Byrnes. He felt he could not go back on his promise to write a letter endorsing Wallace, but hoped to

get Byrnes to pull out of the race. Shying away from the un-
pleasant task of confronting Byrnes, he asked Walker to tell
him that Truman would be the candidate. When Brynes
heard the news he phoned Roosevelt and said bluntly: "I
would like to know if you have changed your opinion about
my being a candidate."

Roosevelt simply could not bear to slam the door in the face
of his loyal aide. "You are the best qualified man in the whole
outfit and you must not get out of the race," he told Byrnes.
"If you stay in, you are sure to win." Later, in a face-to-face
conversation, Roosevelt and Byrnes agreed that Wallace could
not win the nomination. Byrnes, therefore, did not object
when the President told him he had promised to write a letter
endorsing Wallace. But he did extract a pledge that, aside from
this letter, Roosevelt "would not express a preference for anyone."

The letter Roosevelt had promised Hannegan he would
write on Truman's behalf was hardly the clear-cut endorsement
Hannegan desired. It said:

> DEAR BOB,
> You have written me about Harry Truman and Bill Doug-
> las. I should, of course, be very glad to run with either of them
> and believe that either one of them would bring real strength
> to the ticket.

The President had thus kept his promise to Byrnes. By
mentioning both Truman and Douglas, he had managed to
avoid expressing a preference for any single candidate. But
why he chose Douglas' name to include in the letter remains a
mystery. Hannegan had done nothing to advance a Douglas
candidacy.

The letter Roosevelt had promised to write for Wallace also
turned out to be less than the decisive endorsement Wallace
had hoped to receive. The letter was addressed to Senator
Samuel D. Jackson of Indiana, who was to be permanent

chairman of the Democratic convention. Roosevelt asked that
the letter be read by Jackson to the convention. The letter
said:

> MY DEAR SENATOR JACKSON:
>
> In the light of the probability that you will be chosen as
> permanent chairman of the convention, and because I know
> that many rumors accompany all conventions, I am wholly
> willing to give you my personal thought in regard to the selec-
> tion of a candidate for Vice President. I do this at this time
> because I expect to be away from Washington for the next
> few days.
>
> The easiest way of putting it is this: I have been asso-
> ciated with Henry Wallace during his past four years as Vice
> President, for eight years earlier while he was Secretary of
> Agriculture, and well before that. I like him and I respect him
> and he is my personal friend. For these reasons I personally
> would vote for his renomination if I were a delegate to the
> convention.
>
> At the same time I do not wish to appear in any way as dic-
> tating to the convention. Obviously the convention must do
> the deciding. And it should—and I am sure it will—give great
> consideration to the pros and cons of its choice.

The last paragraph of the letter substantially weakened the
endorsement. In addition, the President seemed to be putting
his support of Wallace on a personal rather than a professional
basis. Moreover, while he had said in his letter to Hannegan
that Truman or Douglas "would bring real strength to the
ticket," he had made no such claim for Wallace. In a convention bent on finding the running mate who would least hurt
Roosevelt's chances, this point would work to Truman's advantage.

Roosevelt departed from Washington July 13, six days before the opening of the convention, for a visit to his Hyde Park
home en route to a secret strategy meeting with military officials in California. The next day Jimmy Byrnes discussed the

nomination with Hannegan and Walker. To his surprise and dismay they told him their current understanding was that Roosevelt favored Truman or Douglas as the candidate. Byrnes told them that, only a day earlier, the President had urged him to stay in the race and called him "the best qualified" of the hopefuls. Hannegan and Walker confessed they were bewildered by this turn of events.

Byrnes phoned Roosevelt at Hyde Park. The conversation really settled nothing, for Roosevelt did some more equivocating. "I am not favoring anybody," he said at the outset. When Byrnes said Hannegan and Walker had concluded that he preferred Truman first and Douglas second, Roosevelt replied: "That is all wrong. That is not what I told them. It is what they told me. . . . They asked if I would object to Truman and Douglas and I said no. That is different from using the word 'prefer.' That is not expressing a preference because you know I told you I would have no preference."

Byrnes relayed the substance of the conversation to Hannegan. "I don't understand it," the Democratic national chairman muttered.

Curiously enough, during all the maneuvering on his behalf, Harry Truman had done nothing to advance his own vice-presidential candidacy. Now, from his home in Independence, Missouri, he announced that he would not be a candidate. Byrnes was elated to hear the news. He immediately phoned Truman, who was preparing to leave for the Chicago convention. As Truman later recalled the conversation: "He told me that President Roosevelt had decided on him as the new nominee for Vice President, and he asked me if I would nominate him at the convention. I told him that I would be glad to do it if the President wanted him for a running mate."

Truman did not know at the time that Roosevelt had expressed support for his own vice-presidential candidacy and had written the longhand note to Hannegan. He later concluded that Byrnes had deceived him in the phone conversation. However, at the time, Truman took Byrnes at his word and worked diligently for Byrnes's nomination in the early stages at Chicago.

On July 15, Roosevelt's train stopped in Chicago on its way to the West Coast. Hannegan, who was in the city making advance arrangements for the convention, boarded the train. Determined to prevent Wallace from being renominated, he still hoped to persuade Truman to run, but he needed an alternate candidate.

Roosevelt saw Byrnes as the logical man. "Jimmy has been my choice from the very first," he told Hannegan. "Go ahead and name him." He made it clear, however, that Truman was acceptable if he chose to run.

Before the meeting ended, Roosevelt gave Hannegan a brief but fateful order: "Clear it with Sidney." The "Sidney" mentioned by the President was the controversial labor leader, Sidney Hillman.

The next morning, before Hannegan had attempted to "clear" anything with him, Hillman had breakfast with Harry Truman in Chicago. Truman asked him if he would support Byrnes. Hillman shook his head. "Labor's first choice is Wallace," he said. "If it can't be Wallace, we have a second choice —but it isn't Byrnes."

"Who then?" Truman asked.

"I'm looking at him," Hillman replied.

Truman told him that he was not a candidate and that he intended to nominate Byrnes. Later the senator met with Philip Murray, president of the CIO, and A. F. Whitney, president of the Brotherhood of Railroad Trainmen. Both took positions identical to Hillman. William Green, president of the American Federation of Labor, was even more pro-Truman than the other labor leaders. He told the senator that the AF of L, unlike the CIO, was opposed to Wallace. Green said Truman was his organization's first choice for the nomination.

That evening a group of party leaders met with Byrnes and told him they were now willing to support his candidacy.

Then Hannegan—who was one of the group—remembered his most recent discussion with Roosevelt—the instruction to "Clear it with Sidney." Hannegan said he would talk to Hillman the following day.

The next day, July 17, Ed Flynn was told by Hannegan that the nomination was in the bag for Byrnes. Flynn was incredulous. He was certain that Roosevelt wanted Truman nominated. At Flynn's insistence a meeting of the leaders was convened.

Attending the meeting were Kelly, Walker and Hillman, in addition to Hannegan and Flynn. It quickly became clear that Byrnes's nomination could not be "cleared with Sidney." Hillman found Byrnes totally unacceptable to the labor movement. Hillman repeated to the President by telephone his objections to Byrnes. And Byrnes's candidacy promptly evaporated.

Flynn took over the phone and urged Roosevelt to tell the other party leaders flatly that he preferred Truman as his running mate. The President agreed, and the phone was passed from man to man so that each could hear the message.

The next day Byrnes formally withdrew from the race. Truman was now free to fend for himself. But he had still not decided to become a candidate.

Increasing pressures, however, were nudging him toward entry into the race. Byrnes's withdrawal caused numerous delegates to shift allegiance to Truman. Bob Hannegan showed Truman the note Roosevelt had scribbled on the envelope: "Bob, I think Truman is the right man. FDR." Still, the Missouri senator told Hannegan he did not want to be Vice President. "I bet I can go down on the street and stop the first ten men I see and that they can't tell me the names of two of the last ten Vice Presidents," he said.

When the Missouri delegation conducted its first caucus in advance of the convention's formal opening, Truman was swiftly chosen as delegation chairman. The next item of business was a resolution endorsing Truman for the vice-presidential nomination. Truman ruled the resolution out of order on the ground that he was not a candidate. But, at that point, someone called him to the door of the meeting room. The delegation's vice chairman, Sam Wear, quickly called for a vote on the resolution that Truman had just ruled out of order. The vote was unanimously in favor of endorsing Truman for the vice presidency.

Even so, Truman refused to announce his candidacy. But Hannegan and other party leaders informed key delegates that Roosevelt wanted Truman nominated and that the senator eventually would be persuaded to accept.

Henry Wallace remained as zealous as ever. He arrived in Chicago on the morning of July 19, only hours before the opening of the convention, with a vow to "fight to the finish" for the nomination.

Hannegan called the convention to order at noon. During the evening session Wallace walked onto the convention floor and took his place as a delegate in the Iowa contingent. A mixture of cheers and boos from the galleries greeted his appearance.

The following day Senator Jackson, permanent chairman of the convention, read to the delegates the letter he had received from Roosevelt regarding Wallace's candidacy. The letter came as no surprise. Its contents had been disclosed by Jackson three days earlier and had been interpreted in various ways.

Now Senator Barkley placed Roosevelt's name in nomination for a fourth term as President. One speaker after another took the rostrum to second the nomination. Then came word from the Iowa delegation that one of its members wanted to deliver a seconding speech. And who should come walking forward—to tumultuous applause from supporters in the galleries—but Henry A. Wallace. His appearance on the platform shocked many of the delegates, for tradition barred such speeches by anyone considered a candidate for nomination at a convention. But Wallace was never one to let tradition stand in his way.

He delivered a rousing speech, emphasizing the policies he felt the Democratic Party must follow. It was a seconding speech in name only. In reality, it was a speech advancing Wallace's own candidacy.

The speech ended with a new roar of approval from Wallace's backers. In short order the formality of handing the nomination to Roosevelt was accomplished.

Full attention now centered on the vice-presidential contest. Wallace's supporters were making extravagant claims of delegate strength. And the opposition forces had still not been able to coax Truman into the race.

On the afternoon of Roosevelt's renomination Hannegan phoned Truman and asked him to come to a meeting of party leaders. As Truman later recalled: "They all began to put pressure on me to allow my name to be presented to the convention, but I continued to resist."

Hannegan once again produced for Truman the longhand note from Roosevelt. In addition, he showed the Missouri senator for the first time the typed letter in which the President had said he would be "very glad" to run with either Truman or Justice Douglas.

Meanwhile, Ed Flynn put in a telephone call to the President, who was in San Diego, California. When Roosevelt came on the line, Flynn handed the phone to Hannegan. Since Roosevelt normally used such a loud voice on the telephone that it could hurt his listener's ear, Hannegan held the receiver well away from his head. It was thus possible for Truman and everyone else in the room to hear both ends of the conversation.

"Bob," the President asked, "have you got that fellow lined up yet?"

Hannegan answered: "No. He is the contrariest Missouri mule I've ever dealt with."

Roosevelt's voice then roared through the phone: "Well, you tell him if he wants to break up the Democratic Party in the middle of a war, that's his responsibility!"

The sound of Roosevelt banging down the phone was all that followed. "I was completely stunned," Truman later recalled. At last Truman told the party leaders: "Well, if that is the situation, I'll have to say yes, but why the hell didn't he tell me in the first place?"

A short time later Truman made public his decision to enter the race for the nomination. "I am a candidate and I will win," he said.

On the night of July 20, only hours after Roosevelt had been renominated, he was scheduled to deliver his acceptance speech to the convention by radio from California.

The Democratic leaders' initial plan called for trying to get the convention to name Truman as the vice-presidential candidate that same night. However, events at the convention arena forced a change in the plan.

The leaders learned that the Wallace forces had counterfeited convention tickets (a common practice at political conventions) and packed the galleries with whooping, chanting, sign-waving Wallace enthusiasts. The pro-Wallace flavor was heightened by the convention organist, who played again and again the Vice President's theme song, "Iowa—That's Where the Tall Corn Grows." An uproar swept across the convention hall. Entrances and aisles were jammed. Delegates were forced to fight their way through swarms of spectators to reach their seats.

Some measure of order was restored during the period when Roosevelt's radio speech was being piped through the convention public-address system. Once the speech had ended, however, the uproar began anew. First came a cry from one of the galleries: "We want Wallace." It was picked up by others. Soon the arena was filled with thunderous chants: "We want Wallace . . . We want Wallace . . . We want Wallace."

Once again the organist struck up "Iowa—That's Where the

Tall Corn Grows." Wallace backers began marching around the convention floor. A Wallace fever seemed to have invaded the convention. True, it was hardly spontaneous, for it had been carefully contrived by Sidney Hillman and other Wallace supporters. But, even so, the pro-Truman party leaders recognized that the atmosphere was far from conducive to the nomination of their candidate that night. As George Allen described the situation: "It could have been Wallace if the vote had been taken. It almost was a stampede."

The full house gave the party leaders an excuse to stall for time. Ed Kelly, in his capacity as Chicago mayor, declared that a fire hazard existed. He ordered the hall cleared. Convention Chairman Jackson entertained a motion to recess until the next day. A voice vote was taken. Although the no votes clearly seemed to outweigh the ayes, Jackson ruled that the motion had carried. The convention stood in recess.

During the recess, frantic maneuvering for delegate votes ensued. A number of favorite-son candidates entered the contest. By the time the nominating speeches were concluded the next day, sixteen candidates were in the race.

Shortly before 5 P.M. on July 21 the vice-presidential balloting finally began. Truman took an early lead, but a surge of Wallace votes soon put the Vice President in front. Wallace maintained his lead throughout the remainder of the first ballot. However, he was unable to capture the necessary 589 votes. A second ballot would be necessary.

During the lull between the ballots Truman's managers appealed to the favorite-son candidates to pull out of the race and throw their support to the Missouri senator. When the second ballot began, the lead seesawed back and forth between Wallace and Truman. Gradually, some of the favorite sons withdrew and gave their support to one man or the other —with Truman picking up more of these votes than Wallace. But, by the time the entire roll of states had been called, both men were again short of the crucial 589-vote mark.

However, convention rules permitted delegates to change

their votes before the results became final. Now, Alabama's favorite son, Senator John Bankhead, withdrew and handed his state's 22 votes to Truman. The Indiana delegation switched another 33 from its favorite son, War Manpower Chief Paul V. McNutt, to Truman.

These changes opened the gates for a tidal wave of shifts to Truman. Bandwagon psychology took over. Nearly everyone now wanted to be recorded on Truman's side. Delegation chairmen shouted frantically to be recognized. The final tally gave Truman an overwhelming 1,031 votes to Wallace's 105. Thus did Harry Truman become the Democrats' vice-presidential candidate.

Roosevelt immediately wired him a message of welcome to the ticket. Shortly after the convention Roosevelt and Truman met in Washington to discuss campaign plans. Roosevelt said he would be so busy directing the war effort that Truman would have to do much of the campaigning for both of them.

To oppose Roosevelt the Republicans nominated for President the Governor of New York, Thomas E. Dewey. Before being elected Governor Dewey had achieved national renown as a racket-busting district attorney in New York City. His prosecution of top gangland figures had promoted him to hero status. Novels, motion pictures and plays had been based upon his exploits. Dewey was still riding the crest of this popularity when nominated for the Presidency. Chosen as his running mate was Ohio Governor John W. Bricker.

Dewey and Bricker waged a fighting campaign. The Republicans made a major campaign issue of Sidney Hillman's influence within Democratic ranks. They latched onto the phrase "Clear it with Sidney," which was being widely misquoted at the time as "Clear everything with Sidney," and used the latter version in countless radio broadcasts. Governor Bricker lashed out at what he described as the Democrats' "vicious alliance with Sidney Hillman and the Political Action Committee." Both Bricker and other Republicans accused the

Roosevelt administration of turning control of the government over to Communists.

The Democrats concentrated their strategy on persuading the voters that, since the nation was involved in a war, it was no time to "change horses in midstream." Senator Truman hammered at this theme repeatedly in a rigorous whistle-stop tour of the country.

In a characteristic speech in his birthplace, Lamar, Missouri, Truman said:

> We cannot expect any man wholly inexperienced in national and international affairs to readily learn the views, the objectives and the inner thoughts of such divergent personalities as those dominant leaders who have guided the destinies of our courageous allies. There will be no time to learn, and mistakes once made cannot be unmade.
>
> Our President has worked with these men during these trying years. He talks their language—the language of nations. He knows the reasons which govern their decisions. Just as he respects them and their opinions, so do they respect him. At no time in our history has the President possessed such knowledge of foreign leaders and their problems. None has ever so completely won their confidence and admiration.

When Truman's campaign tour reached Peoria, Illinois, a crisis developed. Word was telephoned to the campaign train that the Hearst newspapers were publishing a copyrighted article charging Truman had once belonged to the Ku Klux Klan. The charge, unless adequately rebutted, could have dealt a serious blow to the Democratic campaign—particularly among Negro and liberal voters. George Allen, assigned to represent the Democratic National Committee on Truman's tour, hurried to the candidate's private railroad car to discuss the crisis with him. The car was filled with politicians, so Allen led Truman into "the only place available for a private conference"—the men's room.

If the charge of Klan membership were true, Allen said,

Truman would have to remain silent and hope the affair would soon blow over. But, if it were false, Allen advised him to file a libel suit immediately against the Hearst papers.

"We sue," Truman snapped.

A New York libel lawyer quickly filed suit on Truman's behalf against the Hearst organization. The suit was dropped after the election, but served during the campaign as an effective rebuttal to the charge. It was later revealed that Truman had rejected many years earlier an invitation to join the Klan. Moreover, he had led a movement to bar Klansmen from his local Masonic lodge.

Truman's whistle-stop tour was highly successful—giving him campaign experience that later would prove invaluable. For much of the race, Roosevelt stuck to his strategy of remaining off the campaign trail, preferring to rely on his image as Commander in Chief. But late in the race, stung by Republican attacks and by hints that he was so ill that he could not campaign, the President returned to the hustings. In one notable episode designed to counter rumors that he was actually on his deathbed, he sat through a driving rainstorm in New York City with water rushing down his cheeks—waving gaily to spectators under umbrellas—and emerged without so much as a sniffle.

The high point of Roosevelt's campaign came in a speech before a Teamsters Union dinner in Washington, one of the most frequently quoted of all his speeches. He accused the Republicans of loving labor unions only at election time. He scoffed at Dewey's criticism of his economic policies, pointing to the bread lines of the Hoover era. He denounced Dewey as an isolationist. And, in the most memorable portion of his speech, he ridiculed Republican charges that he had once sent a Navy vessel on a mission to retrieve his forgotten pet Scotch terrier, Fala.

"These Republican leaders have not been content with attacks upon me, or on my wife, or on my sons—no, not content with that, they now include my little dog, Fala," Roosevelt scoffed. "Unlike the members of my family, he resents this. Being a Scottie, as soon as he learned that the Republican fiction writers had concocted a story that I had left him behind on an Aleutian island and had sent a destroyer back to find him—at a cost to the taxpayers of two, or three, or eight, or twenty million dollars—his Scotch soul was furious. He has not been the same dog since."

On Election Day Roosevelt and Truman received 25,602,504 popular votes to 22,006,285 for Dewey and Bricker. The Democratic ticket drew 432 electoral votes to the Republicans' 99 votes. The victory margin was the smallest of Roosevelt's four presidential campaigns, but he had nonetheless carried thirty-eight of the forty-eight states. Shortly after being sworn in as Vice President, Truman told newsmen: "I want to bring the administration and Congress closer together on the methods of attaining the goal all of us have in common and, if I can create a better understanding, I feel that I can render an important public service." But Truman was to get precious little opportunity to achieve this ambition during his vice presidency.

One of the few noteworthy tasks given the new Vice President by Roosevelt concerned winning Senate approval for the appointment of Henry Wallace to a Cabinet post. Wallace had campaigned tirelessly for the Democratic ticket. Roosevelt, grateful for this support, offered to name Wallace to any Cabinet position he wanted with the exception of Secretary of State. Wallace chose the job of Secretary of Commerce. This forced the President to oust from the Commerce post Wallace's long-time enemy, Jesse Jones. The ouster touched off a storm of protest in the Senate, posing a serious threat to Wallace's confirmation. Truman performed important behind-the-scenes duty in persuading a number of recalcitrant senators to approve the Wallace nomination.

Truman was called upon to cast only one tie-breaking vote as Vice President. The vote was on an amendment to restrict provisions of the Lend-Lease extension bill. The amendment was designed to eliminate presidential power to carry out post-war Lend-Lease deliveries under contracts drawn up during the war. Truman broke the tie by voting to defeat the amendment.

Truman served only eighty-two days as Vice President before being elevated to the Presidency by Roosevelt's death. During those eighty-two days Roosevelt was in Washington less than a month. The President and Vice President conferred only twice in that period. Truman would later comment that he was the most poorly prepared man for the Presidency since Andrew Johnson had succeeded Abraham Lincoln.

"But now the lightning had struck, and events beyond anyone's control had taken command," Truman would recall. "America had lost a great leader, and I was faced with a terrible responsibility."

How he met that responsibility would play an important role in the development of both the Presidency and the vice presidency.

‑‑‑✥‑‑‑

CHAPTER THIRTEEN

The Postwar Years

Although Harry Truman left no doubt from the very first that he was in command of the Ship of State, he repeatedly lamented in the early days that he was inadequate for the responsibilities of the Presidency. This was perhaps natural. Truman had warned during the 1944 election campaign that it takes a new president at least a year to learn the fundamentals of his job. Now he had unexpectedly been catapulted into the Presidency as successor to the man who had occupied the White House far longer than any other—a man who had mastered to an exceptional degree the techniques of exercising presidential power. World War II was still raging. The United States and its allies looked to the American president for leadership. The monumental task of drawing plans for formation of the United Nations was already under way.

Truman's expressions of inadequacy proved unnerving to government officials, newsmen and the public. Only a day after taking the presidential oath, he told reporters: "Boys, if you ever pray, pray for me now. I don't know whether you've ever had a load of hay fall on you. But when they told me yesterday what had happened, I felt like the moon, the stars and all the planets had fallen on me."

Truman's close friends were concerned that his repeated assertions of unfitness for the Presidency would result in a lack of public confidence in him. They warned him of the danger inherent in continuing to make such statements. Senate Majority Leader Alben Barkley was perhaps the most eloquent in delivering such advice. Barkley said:

Mr. President, I respect you for your humility. But you are President of the United States, and I hope you will no longer minimize your ability to carry on the task to which you have been called. God raises up leaders. We do not know the process. But, in the wisdom of Almighty God, you have been made President. . . . Have confidence in yourself. If you do not, the people will lose confidence in you. However humble and contrite you feel, you have got to go forward and lead this nation out of war. Have faith in the God who brought this about and He will enable you to do what you have to do.

Truman followed the advice, and he began to speak and act with more self-assurance. He decided to address a joint session of Congress at the earliest appropriate time following Roosevelt's funeral in order to outline the general policies his administration would follow and to seek bipartisan support. On April 16, four days after Roosevelt's death and one day after his funeral, a visibly moved President Harry S Truman stood before the members of the House and Senate. He was so stirred that he forgot to follow the established procedure he had witnessed many times before as a member of the Senate and as Vice President.

"Mr. Speaker," he said, intending to launch into his speech.

But House Speaker Sam Rayburn immediately interrupted him. "Just a minute, Harry," Rayburn murmured. "Let me introduce you." Although Rayburn had whispered, his remarks had been picked up by the microphones and relayed all over the country by the radio networks.

"The President of the United States," Rayburn announced. Truman began again. He pledged to follow Roosevelt's war and peace policies. He emphasized his determination to work for a system of permanent world peace and security. He appealed for public support of a strong United Nations organization that would succeed where the League of Nations had failed. He expressed confidence in the nation's military leaders and reaffirmed the nation's demand for unconditional surrender by its enemies. And he called upon all Americans to help

keep the nation united in defense of the ideals expressed by
Roosevelt.

"At this moment I have in my heart a prayer," Truman
said. "As I have assumed my heavy duties, I ask only to be a
good and faithful servant of my Lord and my people."

Truman's speech was extremely well received. He embarked
on the honeymoon period usually given new presidents—particularly "accidental" presidents.

Almost immediately after becoming President Truman
began considering a Cabinet shakeup. He felt it was essential
to keep members of Roosevelt's Cabinet in office for a reasonable period in order to assure continuity of government and
maintain public confidence. But he also felt every president
should "have a Cabinet of his own choosing." After a brief
transition period, six of the ten Roosevelt appointees would be
replaced. And other changes would follow.

In addition to wanting men of his own choosing in the Cabinet, Truman was also concerned about the question of succession to the Presidency. The law provided for the secretary
of state to stand next in line behind the vice president in the
order of succession. If both the president and vice president
should die or otherwise leave office, the secretary of state
would inherit the Presidency. Behind him stood the secretary
of the treasury, followed by other Cabinet members.

Truman felt that any man elevated to the Presidency by the
death of the president and vice president should have held at
least one previous position to which he had been elected by
popular vote. Many Cabinet members through history had not
held such office. Truman's proposal would have the speaker of
the House be next in line behind the vice president because
he was elected to the House originally by popular vote and
then chosen speaker by the members of the country's most
numerous legislative body. Behind the speaker, under Truman's plan, would be the president pro tem of the Senate.
The Cabinet members would then follow in the line of succession.

Pending change he felt duty-bound to place in the office of secretary of state the man he considered best qualified to become president in case of his own death. The Secretary of State Truman had inherited from Roosevelt was Edward R. Stettinius, Jr., forty-four, former president of the U. S. Steel Corporation. Stettinius had held a variety of appointive government positions but had never been a candidate for elective office. He did not measure up to Truman's yardstick as a possible successor.

The man chosen by Truman to replace Stettinius was Jimmy Byrnes. He considered Byrnes the best qualified man as a possible successor to the Presidency and felt that the former aide to Roosevelt could make a major contribution as Secretary of State. There was a personal consideration involved in the choice. Byrnes had been deeply hurt by the failure of the Democrats to nominate him for Vice President at the 1944 convention. In Truman's words, "I thought that my calling on him at this time might help balance things up."

Stettinius was scheduled to lead the United States delegation to the conference beginning April 25 in San Francisco to organize the United Nations. Truman did not want to replace him until the conference had ended. Immediately after the conference closed on June 27, Stettinius resigned and the President named Byrnes to succeed him. Truman persuaded Stettinius to remain in the government as the U. S. representative on the United Nations Security Council.

Meanwhile, other Cabinet changes were undertaken. Postmaster General Frank Walker was replaced by Bob Hannegan; Attorney General Francis Biddle by Tom C. Clark; Secretary of Labor Frances Perkins by Lewis B. Schwellenbach; Secretary of Agriculture Claude R. Wickard by Clinton P. Anderson; and Treasury Secretary Henry Morgenthau, Jr., by Fred M. Vinson.

Even before Byrnes had taken office as next in line for the Presidency, Truman had presented to Congress his proposal for changing the succession law. The proposal provided for placing the House speaker and Senate president pro tem, in that order, at the head of the succession list. In addition, it called for the voters to choose a new president and vice president at the time of the midterm congressional elections in case both offices became vacant before their elected occupants completed two years of their terms.

Truman's bill aroused considerable controversy. Its backers argued that it would place in line for the Presidency men of wide political experience who would be more representative of the people than would Cabinet members. Its opponents claimed, among other things, that the special-election provision was impractical. Moreover, some said the drafters of the Constitution had never meant for such special elections to be conducted.

The bill passed the House in only four days, but died in a Senate committee. Truman did not give up on the proposal. Two years later a similar bill—omitting the special-election provision—was pushed through the Congress.

Less than a month after Truman became President, the war in Europe ended with the surrender of Germany on May 8. Truman warned in announcing the German surrender that the United States was now in a position to turn the greatest war machine in the history of the world loose in the Pacific. He said:

> The Japanese people have felt the weight of our land, air and naval attacks. So long as their leaders and the armed forces continue the war, the striking power and intensity of our blows will steadily increase. The longer the war lasts, the greater will be the suffering and hardships which the people of Japan will undergo—all in vain. Our blows will not cease until the Japanese military and naval forces lay down their arms in unconditional surrender.

At the time he made that statement, Truman knew that American and British scientists—working jointly in the United States—were in the process of developing the atomic bomb. But the first bomb had not yet been tested. The President had little hope of an early surrender by the Japanese at this point. He and his military leaders estimated that it would take until late fall of 1946, using conventional military tactics and weapons, to defeat Japan.

However, all this was changed by the successful test explosion of the first A-bomb on July 16, 1945, near Alamogordo, New Mexico. Word of the test's success was flashed to the President at Potsdam, Germany, where he was engaged in an historic conference with British Prime Minister Winston Churchill and Soviet Premier Joseph Stalin. On July 26 the American, British and Chinese governments issued what came to be known as the Potsdam Declaration (the Soviet Union had not yet declared war on Japan). The Declaration was an ultimatum to Japan to surrender or face "the inevitable and complete destruction of the Japanese armed forces and . . . the utter devastation of the Japanese homeland." The ultimatum set out the terms under which Japan must surrender.

The Japanese, however, announced their determination to continue fighting. They assailed the Potsdam Declaration as "absurd . . . presumptuous . . . and unworthy of consideration."

Now Harry Truman faced one of the most momentous decisions ever to confront an American President. Should he order the use of the most devastating weapon in the history of mankind?

A special committee of advisers, created to counsel the President on the implications of the new weapon, recommended that the bomb be used against the enemy as soon as possible. The committee also recommended that the bomb be used without specific warning against a target that would clearly demonstrate capacity. Top-level scientists working with the committee reported: "We can propose no technical demonstration likely to bring an end to the war; we see no acceptable alternative to direct military use."

Although Truman recognized that use of the bomb against Japan "would inflict damage and casualties beyond imagination," he indicated in his memoirs that he felt his choice was clear. "Let there be no mistake about it," he wrote. "I regarded the bomb as a military weapon and never had any doubt that it should be used. The top military advisers to the President recommended its use, and when I talked to Churchill he unhesitatingly told me that he favored the use of the atomic bomb if it might aid to end the war."

Truman ordered the War Department to use the bomb, with the proviso that it "be dropped as nearly as possible upon a war production center of prime military importance." The first bomb was dropped on the Japanese industrial complex of Hiroshima on August 6, wiping out 60 per cent of the city. A three-day pause followed, during which Japan was given another chance to surrender. When she did not, a second atomic bomb was dropped on Nagasaki, destroying one third of the city. The following day Japan finally expressed its willingness to end the war, with the condition that Emperor Hirohito be allowed to retain his throne. This condition was accepted by the Allies. Formal surrender ceremonies were conducted in Tokyo Bay abroad the battleship *Missouri* on September 2— bringing to an end at last the most terrible war in history.

In the postwar years the United States faced difficult new obligations and challenges. Truman met those responsibilities with decisive action that, by and large, was destined to win the approval of historians. He made containment of Communist aggression an integral part of American foreign policy. He put the Marshall Plan into effect—providing a multi-billion-dollar program of economic assistance to the impoverished nations of Europe, thus saving western Europe from both famine and Communist-inspired revolution. When the Russians tried to drive the Americans, British and French out of the divided city of Berlin by instituting a blockade, Truman ordered an airlift of supplies which frustrated the Soviet plan. The United States entered into the historic pact creating the North Atlantic Treaty Organization as a bulwark against Communist aggression. And when Communist troops attacked South Korea, it was Truman who dispatched American soldiers to defend the small Asian country.

On the domestic front Truman got Congress to put the atomic-energy program under civilian control, to unify the armed forces, to liberalize the Social Security Act and to appropriate large sums for national defense. He ordered the racial desegregation of the armed forces, appointed a Committee on Civil Rights and pressed for a variety of other civil-rights programs. While his Fair Deal domestic measures did not seem so revolutionary as those of the New Deal, they supplemented and expanded the scope of Roosevelt's innovations.

Some of Truman's most nettlesome difficulties were provided by two of the men who had been contenders for the 1944 vice-presidential nomination, Jimmy Byrnes and Henry Wallace. Truman had appointed Byrnes as his Secretary of State. Wallace, who had been Secretary of Commerce at the time of Roosevelt's death, had been kept in office by Truman through the first round of Cabinet shifts.

At the outset of his administration Truman gave his Cabinet members considerable freedom of action. Byrnes became so independent that he sometimes neglected to discuss important policy questions with the President before taking action. In one case, without Truman's permission, Brynes concluded a series of negotiations with the Russians on a declaration concerning control of atomic energy. Truman felt the declaration gave the Soviet Union undue concessions, and took Byrnes to task. The President and his Secretary of State also differed on other matters related to American-Soviet affairs.

Truman began to feel that Byrnes considered himself "an assistant President in full charge of foreign policy." He called the Secretary of State to the White House and made clear that he had no intention of abdicating his presidential responsibility to preside over foreign policy. Byrnes accepted Truman's position. The President then assumed more control over foreign policy, and Byrnes adopted a tougher line toward the Soviet Union.

This line, however, prompted new difficulties for Truman with Henry Wallace. In the fall of 1946 Wallace delivered a speech at New York's Madison Square Garden in which he sharply denounced what he described as Byrnes's "Get Tough with Russia" policy. He urged a policy of compromise with the Soviet Union.

Byrnes, who was attending a meeting of the Council of Foreign Ministers in Paris, wired Truman that it was hard for him to maintain his position as the U. S. representative there while another Cabinet member was criticizing the nation's foreign policy. He offered to resign. Truman made it clear in a subsequent transatlantic phone call to Byrnes that he was standing behind him and did not want his resignation. By this time the affair had stirred up a tempest in the press and in foreign capitals.

Truman decided he had to act. He phoned Wallace at his office and told him: "Henry, I am sorry, but I have reached the conclusion that it will be best that I ask for your resignation."

Wallace took the decision calmly. "If that is the way you want it, Mr. President, I will be happy to comply," he replied.

Later in the day Truman wrote to his mother and sister, Mary:

> Well, I had to fire Henry today, and of course I hated to do it. Henry Wallace is the best Secretary of Agriculture this country ever had unless Clint Anderson turns out as I think he will. Well, now he's out, and the crackpots are having conniption fits. I'm glad they are. It convinces me I'm right. . . .

Not long after Wallace left the government, Jimmy Byrnes followed. From the time of his initial disagreement with Byrnes over Soviet-American relations, Truman intended to replace his Secretary of State as soon as it became practical. His choice for the post was General George C. Marshall, the former Army Chief of Staff. But Marshall was on a vital mission to China for Truman, and the President wanted this assignment completed before any change was made in the State Department leadership. Byrnes later told Truman that he wanted to be relieved because of ill health.

Then General Dwight D. Eisenhower, who had succeeded Marshall as Chief of Staff, left on an inspection trip of the Far East. Truman asked Eisenhower to tell Marshall when he saw him in China that Byrnes intended to retire and that the President wanted to know whether Marshall would take the State Department job. Eisenhower returned to report that Marshall had said "Yes." As soon as Marshall's mission was over, Truman appointed him Secretary of State.

Truman and Byrnes remained on relatively friendly terms for several years. But they later drifted apart over Truman's civil-rights policy—and exchanged harsh words in both speeches and letters. Byrnes later would support four consecutive Republican presidential candidates.

In the congressional election of 1946 the Republicans toppled the Democrats from control of both houses. This development helped convince many Democrats that Truman could not win his own elected term as President in 1948—and perhaps could not even be nominated. The Democratic Party was torn by factionalism. Henry Wallace was leading a third-party movement designed to draw support from dissident left-wingers. Some Southern Democrats were threatening to bolt the party in protest of Truman's civil-rights policies. And a group of liberals—including Roosevelt's sons, James and Elliott—was seeking to dump Truman in favor of some alternate candidate. This group tried to draft General Eisenhower for the presidential nomination, although his party affiliation was unknown and he had given no indication that he would enter politics. However, the draft-Eisenhower boom fizzled when the general refused to run. An attempt was made to persuade Supreme Court Justice William O. Douglas to enter the race, but he also declined.

The Democratic National Convention at Philadelphia thus had little choice but to nominate Truman. The delegates, many of whom glumly assumed they were nominating a sure loser, gave the President a first-ballot victory over Georgia Senator Richard Russell by a vote of 947½ to 263. While Russell and some of his fellow Southerners remained loyal to the Democrats, others walked off the convention floor to form their own party. This party, the States' Rights Democrats (popularly called Dixiecrats), nominated South Carolina Governor J. Strom Thurmond for President and Mississippi Governor Fielding L. Wright for Vice President.

In advance of the Democratic convention, Truman tried several times to persuade Justice Douglas to join the ticket as the vice-presidential candidate. Each time, although giving the matter serious consideration, Douglas refused.

If Douglas was not to be the vice-presidential candidate, then who was? Attention turned to the Senate Democratic leader, Alben Barkley. By 1948 Barkley had been involved in politics for almost forty-five years—thirty-one of them in Congress. He had been considered a potential vice-presidential nominee at every national convention since 1928. At the 1948 convention he served as both keynote speaker and temporary chairman.

Barkley was interested in the nomination, but told a friend: "I don't want any biscuit that's been passed around the convention so long it comes to me cold." He made a rousing keynote speech to the convention, touching off a thirty-minute demonstration by delegates.

Truman, who remained in Washington during the early stages of the convention, congratulated Barkley on the speech by telephone. Barkley said he was being urged to enter the vice-presidential race. He asked whether Truman would object.

"Why didn't you tell me you wanted to be Vice President?" Truman replied. "It's all right with me."

The convention nominated Barkley by acclamation. Although Truman's acceptance of his candidacy seemed almost offhanded, the President actually considered Barkley an ideal running mate. He had long respected the Kentucky senator as one of the most able, hard-working men in Washington. He knew that Barkley was among the most popular figures in the Democratic Party. And, from a purely political standpoint, Barkley's acceptability to Southern voters was likely to help Truman in an area where he faced serious problems.

Barkley was born in Graves County, Kentucky, on November 24, 1877. He was seventy when nominated for the vice presidency, and his age, added to Truman's sixty-four years, made theirs the oldest ticket ever fielded by a major political party. Barkley was graduated from Marvin College in Kentucky in 1897 and admitted to the bar four years later. He served as a county prosecutor and a judge before being elected to the House in 1913. After seven terms there he was elected to the Senate in 1927. He was chosen as majority leader in 1937 and retained that post until the Democrats lost control of the Congress in the 1946 election. He continued to direct his party's Senate forces as minority leader during the next two years.

Perhaps the most colorful description of Barkley's physical appearance was given by George Allen. "The way Barkley looks is the way a politician should look. He has been battered into the mellow but still tough state of graceful wisdom that becomes the career politico."

Barkley was noted in Washington, a city filled with raconteurs, as one of the most accomplished of all political storytellers.

A favorite Barkley story concerned a constituent who was laggard in providing expected campaign support. "I took this fellow to task," Barkley would say. " 'Didn't I appoint your son postmaster?' I asked him. He admitted that I had. 'Didn't I send your nephew to West Point?' Again he conceded that I had. 'Didn't I get your brother out of that tax trouble he was in?' He acknowledged that I did. 'Then why are you letting me down in this campaign?' I demanded. He answered: 'It is true that you did all these things for me, and I appreciated them. But what have you done for me lately?' "

Another Barkley story concerned a Negro who tried to join an all-white church. The congregation rejected his application. The Negro appealed to the church's pastor, who advised him to take his case directly to the Lord through prayer. A few days later the Negro and the minister met by chance. The minister asked how things had turned out. The Negro answered: "I told the Lord I was afraid I wasn't going to get to join this church. And He said to me, 'Don't worry. I've been trying for twenty years to get into that church and I haven't made it yet.'"

Barkley's speechmaking ability was put to its greatest test during the 1948 election campaign. As Truman stumped the country by train, the vice-presidential candidate made the first truly national campaign tour in American political history by airplane. Using a chartered plane, Barkley campaigned across thirty-six states and delivered about 260 speeches during a six-week period. His amiability, his general popularity and his long record of achievement brought him warm receptions at virtually all the stops.

The Republicans had again nominated New York Governor Thomas E. Dewey. His running mate this time was California Governor Earl Warren, later to become Chief Justice of the United States.

The campaign was complicated by the entry of two new party tickets. In addition to the Dixiecrat ticket of Thurmond and Wright, there was the Progressive Party ticket of Henry Wallace for President and Idaho Senator Glen H. Taylor for Vice President. The Progressives campaigned for a reconciliation between the United States and the Soviet Union. To reports that Communists were masterminding his campaign, Wallace replied blandly: "If they want to help us out in some of these problems, why, God bless them, let them come along."

At the outset of the campaign Truman told Barkley: "I'm going to fight hard. I'm going to give them hell." And that he did, becoming known in some quarters as "Give-'em-Hell Harry." He lambasted the Republican-controlled Congress as "that do-nothing Congress." And he referred to his opponents as men "with calculating machines where their hearts ought to be."

Despite the vigor of the Democratic campaign, the polls were virtually unanimous in predicting a Republican victory. Only one pollster of repute, Louis Bean, forecast a Truman-Barkley triumph—and few took his prediction seriously. On the eve of the election, *Life* magazine published a full-page picture of Dewey with the caption: "THE NEXT PRESIDENT TRAVELS BY FERRY BOAT ACROSS THE BROAD WATERS OF SAN FRANCISCO BAY." And, while the election returns were still being tabulated, the Chicago *Tribune* came out with a banner headline: "DEWEY DEFEATS TRUMAN."

But the American people had decided otherwise. In a stunning upset, Truman and Barkley had swept to victory with 24,105,695 popular votes—carrying twenty-eight states with 303 electoral votes. Dewey and Warren had polled 21,969,170 popular votes, carrying sixteen states with 189 electoral votes. The Dixiecrat ticket had finished third, carrying South Carolina, Mississippi, Alabama and Lousiana. Wallace and Taylor brought up the rear, without a single electoral vote.

When Truman and Barkley returned to Washington after voting in their home states, a huge crowd was waiting to celebrate their victory with them. The two men rode to the White House together through cheering throngs. Outside the office of the Washington *Post*—which, like most American newspapers, had forcast a Democratic defeat—they spied a large sign: "MR. PRESIDENT, WE ARE READY TO EAT CROW WHENEVER YOU ARE READY TO SERVE IT." Truman sent the *Post* a message saying he had no desire to see anyone eat crow. But that did not prevent him from publicly performing a hilarious imitation of radio news analyst H. V. Kaltenborn, who had insisted throughout election night that although Truman was leading Dewey he would undoubtedly fall behind in the final tabulation.

Alben Barkley was seventy-one when inaugurated as Vice President—the oldest man to hold the office. He and Truman had an ideal relationship. As early as their inaugural ball, Truman told the guests: "You can't give (Barkley) . . . too much honor in my book. I don't think this country ever had a President and Vice President who were more congenial." This congeniality lasted through the years.

Barkley brought a new nickname to the vice presidency— "Veep." The word was coined by his grandson, who considered the title "Mr. Vice President" too fancy. Barkley casually mentioned his grandson's brain child at a news conference, and the term caught the public fancy. From that time on he was the "Veep." Countless newspaper headlines and picture captions used the title. But the name was never adopted for later vice presidents. Barkley's successor chose not to use the title, saying it was an honorary tribute to the popular Kentuckian.

Truman kept his promise to enlarge the Vice President's responsibilities. At his urging Congress passed in 1949 a statute making the vice president a member of the National Security Council. The council, one of the most important agencies of the executive branch, is charged by law with "the integration of domestic, foreign and military policies relating to national security." The passage of the law making the vice president a member of this body was considered the most meaningful advance in the vice presidency until that time. For this was not a temporary job but one that was permanently established by statute.

Barkley regularly attended meetings of the Cabinet and National Security Council, in addition to Truman's discussions with congressional leaders. His long experience and popularity in Congress made him ideal to help push Truman's programs through legislative roadblocks. He participated in the decision-making process on some of the most momentous questions to face the administration—including the military intervention against Communist aggression in Korea and the controversial ouster of General Douglas MacArthur as Far East commander for what Truman considered "insubordination."

The Vice President also represented Truman at all sorts of political meetings, community events and other occasions throughout the United States and abroad. One year he flew to Korea and ate Thanksgiving dinner with the troops. He was in constant demand to crown various beauty queens and generally was called upon to plant a kiss on the cheek of the winner —a practice he described as "this osculatory business."

Despite being the nation's oldest Vice President, Barkley was the only one to marry while in office. After his first wife's death in 1947 gossip columnists constantly speculated on his prospects for remarriage. "They were marrying me off with monotonous regularity to almost every eligible widow in the country," he once complained.

In the summer of 1949, he met Mrs. Jane Rucker Hadley, a widow from St. Louis. At thirty-seven, Mrs. Hadley was thirty-four years younger than the Vice President. However, the age disparity did not prevent them from falling in love. Their romance attracted voluminous coverage from the press and avid interest from the public. Barkley set what was believed to be a vice-presidential precedent by writing love letters while presiding over sessions of the Senate. "I would have tolerated anything, even the most outrageous sort of filibuster, to keep the senators talking so I could get my love letters written," he said. In November, 1949, a crowd of 10,000 persons jammed streets outside a St. Louis church as the Vice President and Mrs. Hadley were married. Barkley later wrote that he had been doubly blessed, "having had the good fortune of being married to two lovely and wonderful women."

The romance and marriage did not distract him from the responsibilities of his office. Anyone tempted to assume, for example, that he was not paying attention to Senate debates was swiftly straightened out by Barkley's alert mind and ready wit. When a senator once protested that his delivery of a speech had been greeted by a yawn from one of his colleagues,

Barkley ruled with a straight face: "The yawn of the senator from Illinois will be stricken from the record."

In 1951 the required number of state legislatures ratified a constitutional amendment approved by Congress in 1947— the so-called "two-term" amendment. The key passage of the Twenty-second Amendment provides: "No person shall be elected to the office of the President more than twice, and no person who has held the office of President, or acted as President, for more than two years of a term to which some other person was elected President shall be elected to the office of the President more than once." (The amendment places no similar restriction on a Vice President, but nobody has sought to serve more than two vice-presidential terms since its passage.)

The amendment had been passed largely in reaction to Franklin D. Roosevelt's election to four terms as President. Its supporters had argued that the longer any one man occupied the presidency the closer the nation moved to "dictatorship" and to destruction of the people's freedom. Although President Truman had been specifically exempted from terms of the amendment, he had decided even before its ratification not to seek reelection. As early as the day of his inauguration to a full presidential term in 1949, he had made up his mind not to run again. The following year he wrote a private memorandum to himself on the subject and locked it in his safe. The memorandum said:

I am not a candidate for nomination by the (1952) Democratic convention. In my opinion eight years as President is enough and sometimes too much for any man to serve in that capacity. There is a lure in power. It can get into a man's blood just as gambling and lust for money have been known to do. . . . I could be elected again and continue to break the old precedent as it was broken by F.D.R. It should not be done. That precedent should continue not by a constitutional amendment, but by custom based on the honor of the man in the office. Therefore, to reestablish that custom, although by a quibble I could say I've only had one term, I am not a candidate and will not accept the nomination for another term.

Truman did not at first make his decision public. He felt that, by the nature of the presidential office, "this is one secret a President must keep to himself to the last possible moment." He did, however, discuss the decision with some of his intimates, who tried to persuade him to change his mind. Finally, in a speech to a Jefferson-Jackson Day Dinner in Washington on March 29 of the election year, he announced:

I shall not be a candidate for reelection. I have served my country long, and I think efficiently and honestly. I shall not accept a renomination. I do not feel that it is my duty to spend another four years in the White House.

Truman tried to persuade Supreme Court Chief Justice Fred M. Vinson and Illinois Governor Adlai E. Stevenson to seek the Democratic presidential nomination, but found them both reluctant. About two weeks before the convention Vice President Barkley let it be known that he was interested in the presidential nomination. Truman and party leaders had previously given Barkley scant attention for the nomination because of his age (seventy-four), although they agreed that he was, in other respects, admirably qualified. Now, with no other candidate at hand, the President took into account that Barkley's "vigor and stamina defied time." He invited the Vice President to a meeting at the White House, attended by Democratic National Chairman Frank McKinney and several presidential aides. Truman told Barkley that those present were ready to support him for the nomination if he seriously wanted to run. Barkley made it clear that he could not be more serious.

The Vice President thus entered the convention with the backing of both the President and the national chairman. But this was not enough. When Barkley arrived in Chicago for the convention he met over breakfast with sixteen of the nation's top labor leaders to enlist their support. They were unanimous in opposing his candidacy because of his age. Convinced that he could not win the nomination in the face of labor's solid opposition, Barkley withdrew from the race. Although he delivered a moving farewell address to the convention—provoking one of the warmest ovations in convention history—Barkley left Chicago as a sorely disappointed man.

He served out the remainder of his vice-presidential term and then went into ostensible retirement. But the retirement was short-lived. Feeling the old lure for the political arena, he ran again for the Senate in 1954—and was elected at the age of seventy-six.

On April 30, 1956, Barkley addressed a gathering of students at Washington and Lee University in Lexington, Virginia. "I would rather be a servant in the house of the Lord than to sit in the seats of the mighty," he said. Those words were his last. He suddenly collapsed on the platform and, within a few minutes, was dead.

The Truman-Barkley years added much to the status and importance of the vice presidency. Truman's record as one of the most successful "accidental" Presidents emphasized anew the necessity for electing qualified men to the nation's second highest office. The assignment of new duties to the vice president—including the first major legal expansion of his role since the writing of the Constitution—further enhanced the office. The way was opened to even greater future changes. And, poised on the horizon, there loomed a man who stood ready—even eager—to bring about such changes.

❦

CHAPTER FOURTEEN

Nixon and the Fifties

THE man who unquestionably made the most of his role as Vice President was Richard Milhous Nixon.

As Vice President, Nixon assumed an executive role superior to any of his predecessors. He helped guide the country through three crises brought on by his President's illnesses. He presided over numerous meetings of the Cabinet and the National Security Council in the President's absence. He headed important committees of the executive branch. He visited fifty-four foreign nations on special diplomatic missions. He served as liaison between the administration and the Congress. And he was his party's chief political campaigner.

Circumstances were partly responsible for the broad scope of Nixon's role—circumstances that included the President's illnesses, the nonpolitical background and the executive philosophy of the President, the prevailing political conditions at home and the nature of American relations with governments abroad. But the background, personality and philosophy of Richard M. Nixon were also of major importance.

Nixon was the first Vice President born in this century, January 9, 1913, in Yorba Linda, California. His Quaker family was of modest means. His father, Francis Anthony Nixon, had followed a variety of occupations—streetcar conductor, oil-field worker, carpenter, lemon grower and grocer. The father owned a lemon grove at Yorba Linda when Nixon was born. But this business failed when the lemon market collapsed, and the family moved to Whittier, California. There the elder

Nixon operated a filling station, later expanded to include a grocery.

Richard Nixon possessed a fierce competitive spirit. He enjoyed all sorts of contests, from debating events to football games to elections. Even more, he enjoyed winning. From the time he was a fifth-grader, he won prize after prize in public speaking and debating contests. He also was highly successful in school elections, winning numerous student-body posts throughout his educational career.

At the age of nine he read a newspaper article that was to have a profound impact upon his life. The article concerned the Teapot Dome scandal. Nixon was to say later that it influenced his choice of a profession. He told his mother after reading the article: "You know what I'm going to be when I grow up? I'm going to be a lawyer who can't be bribed."

After his graduation from Whittier College, a small Quaker institution in his home town, Nixon won a scholarship to the Duke University Law School in Durham, North Carolina. He was president of the student body at both Whittier and Duke and finished third or higher scholastically in each school.

After his graduation from law school in 1937 he returned to Whittier and joined a local law firm. He quickly developed into a capable trial lawyer. After establishing a branch office of the law firm in nearby La Habra, Nixon assumed his first governmental position—a part-time job as town attorney of La Habra.

In his spare time he became an amateur actor in Whittier's "little theater" group. At a rehearsal of this group he met the woman who was to become his wife, Thelma (Pat) Ryan, a slender schoolteacher.

After the United States entered World War II, Nixon worked briefly as a lawyer in the tire-rationing section of the Office of Price Administration. He then was commissioned a naval lieutenant, junior grade, and sent to the Pacific as an operations officer with the South Pacific Combat Air Transport Command. His outfit ferried men and supplies to American forces fighting the Japanese on South Pacific islands. After fourteen months overseas, Nixon was sent back to Washington for training in Navy legal work. He was later assigned to perform legal duties for the Navy in New York, Philadelphia and Baltimore.

He was working in Baltimore in September, 1945, awaiting his Navy discharge, when he received a telegram from a banker named Herman Perry in Whittier, California, asking Nixon to phone him immediately. When Nixon called, Perry explained that Republicans in the Twelfth Congressional District of California were desperately seeking a candidate to run against the incumbent Democratic congressman, Jerry Voorhis. Although the district was traditionally Republican, it had elected Democrat Voorhis to five consecutive terms.

Republicans in the district organized a Committee of One Hundred in mid-1945 to search for a suitable candidate for the 1946 election. The committee took the unusual step of advertising in newspapers for possible candidates. The "want ads" sought a "congressman candidate with no previous political experience." They said: "Any young man, resident of district, preferably a veteran, fair education, no political strings or obligations, and possessed of a few ideas for betterment of country at large, may apply."

Members of the Committee of One Hundred also sought out other prospects. One man they approached was Walter Dexter, president of Whittier College during Nixon's student days there. Dexter declined to run, but urged the committee members to see if Nixon was interested in becoming a candidate.

Banker Perry was designated by the committee to approach Nixon. "Are you a Republican and are you available?" Perry asked him.

"I guess I'm a Republican," Nixon answered. "I voted for Dewey in 1944." He also said he would be available as soon as he received his Navy discharge.

"Fly out here right away," Perry urged him.

Nixon flew to California and talked to the committee for the ten minutes allotted to each prospect. "I will wage a fighting, rocking, socking campaign," he pledged. The committee members gave Nixon their endorsement—thus launching him officially on his political career.

Nixon did, indeed, wage a "fighting, rocking, socking campaign." He and his supporters accused Voorhis of being a tool of Sidney Hillman's CIO Political Action Committee (PAC), an enemy of free enterprise and a man who intended to help socialize the United States. Voorhis insisted that he did not want and did not have the support of the California PAC organization. But Nixon produced a report in which one local PAC chapter had recommended that the national organization support Voorhis. He claimed this proved Voorhis had PAC backing. Nixon referred repeatedly to high officials who "front for un-American elements, wittingly or otherwise, by advocating increasing federal controls over the lives of the people."

Three days before the election the Republican campaign headquarters released a statement by a former lieutenant governor that charged Voorhis with "consistently voting the Moscow-PAC-Henry Wallace line in Congress." The statement went on to discuss "the insolence of Moscow in telling the American voter to elect PAC candidates, such as Mr. Voorhis." And it concluded by calling Nixon "a man who will talk American and at the same time vote American in Congress . . . and fight in and out of Congress to perpetuate American ideals and American freedom."

Such tactics brought complaints from Voorhis backers and some neutral observers that the Nixon camp was indulging in unfair campaign practices.

This would not be the last time Nixon would be accused of unfair tactics. But his fighting campaign against Voorhis had been highly successful. When the ballots were counted, Nixon had 65,586 votes to Voorhis' 49,994. And so, at the age of thirty-three, Dick Nixon was on his way to Congress.

He went to Washington as a freshman member of the Eightieth Congress—the one President Truman denounced as "that do-nothing Congress." At his own request Nixon was given a place on the House Education and Labor Committee. In this capacity he helped write the controversial Taft-Hartley labor law. Although he did not request it, he was also assigned to the House Un-American Activities Committee.

An investigation of alleged infiltration into government by Communists, conducted by the Un-American Activities Committee, placed Nixon in the national spotlight for the first time. It centered about two men—one a confessed former Communist and the other a former high official of the State Department.

The admitted ex-Communist was Whittaker Chambers, a senior editor of *Time* magazine. The former State Department official was Alger Hiss, who had become president of the Carnegie Foundation for International Peace after leaving the government.

In 1948 Chambers was called before the House Un-American Activities Committee to testify about his past membership in the Communist Party. Chambers testified that, before leaving the party in 1938, he had been a member of a secret Communist espionage apparatus. He identified Hiss as a fellow member of the apparatus, who had given him secret government documents to be microfilmed and turned over to Russian agents.

Chambers' charges caused a sensation. Hiss was highly respected in government circles. He had served as secretary general of the San Francisco conference that created the United Nations, chief adviser to the American delegation at the first session of the United Nations, and chief adviser to the American delegation at the first session of the United Nations General Assembly. He had accompanied President Roosevelt at important international conferences. It seemed inconceivable to many observers that a man with such a record could possibly have been a Communist spy.

Hiss immediately demanded an opportunity to appear before the committee and answer Chambers' charges. Two days after Chambers' initial appearance, Hiss went before the committee and said he had never known a man named Whittaker Chambers. "I am not and never have been a member of the Communist Party," Hiss testified. "I have never followed the Communist Party line, directly or indirectly. To the best of my knowledge, none of my friends is a Communist."

Hiss made an effective witness for himself in this appearance. When he left the witness chair the general feeling in Washington was that the Un-American Activities Committee had committed a grievous blunder.

The committee went into closed session to decide what to do next about the affair. Nixon would later recall that "virtual consternation reigned among the members" at this point. Except for him, all members of the committee felt Hiss was telling the truth.

But Nixon was opposed to dropping the investigation. He felt that "Hiss was much too smooth . . . much too careful a witness for one who purported to be telling the whole truth without qualifications." Nixon argued that Chambers' charges were extremely serious and that, even if the committee could not firmly establish whether Hiss had been a Communist, it should at least pursue the question of whether Hiss had lied in denying ever knowing Chambers. The committee agreed to follow this approach.

If Chambers really had been a close friend of Hiss, Nixon reasoned that he should be able to provide considerable personal information about Hiss. Arrangements were made for the committee to question Chambers again in a secret session. Nixon prepared a lengthy list of questions regarding matters that a person normally would know about a close friend. Chambers replied to these questions with a mass of details about Hiss, other members of the Hiss family, their habits and personal interests. The depth of his answers convinced Nixon and other committee members that Chambers must, indeed, have known Hiss very well.

Hiss was recalled by the committee and asked numerous personal questions based on the information provided by Chambers. Many of his answers seemed to dovetail with the Chambers information. For example, Chambers had told the committee that Hiss was an avid bird watcher and had once been elated to spot a rare bird known as a prothonotary warbler in a swampy section near the Potomac. Hiss told the committee about seeing such a bird. Hiss had been shown photographs of Chambers and had said he did not recognize the man. But in his second appearance he began to hedge on this question. Shown another picture of Chambers, Hiss said: "The face is definitely not an unfamiliar face. . . .This man may have known me."

The committee arranged a secret confrontation in a New York hotel room between Hiss and Chambers. After viewing Chambers and hearing him speak, Hiss said he thought he recognized him. He denied ever knowing Chambers by the name Whittaker Chambers or by the name Carl—which Chambers had said was his code name within the Communist Party. Instead, Hiss said, he thought Chambers was a man he had known by the name George Crosley, a free-lance writer he had met while he was serving in the government.

Later the committee arranged a dramatic public confrontation between the two men in a congressional hearing room. Hiss positively identified Chambers as the man he said he had known by the name George Crosley. But he adamantly denied that they had been fellow Communists or that he had even suspected Crosley of being a Communist. He insisted their relationship had been perfectly innocent—that of a government official and a man who wrote about government affairs. Chambers denied ever using the name Crosley and continued to assert that he and Hiss had been fellow Communists.

Since statements made before congressional committees

cannot be used as the basis for libel suits, Hiss challenged Chambers to repeat his accusations outside the hearing room. He made it clear that, if Chambers did so, he intended to file a libel suit. Chambers accepted the challenge and repeated his charges on a radio program. A month later, Hiss filed the threatened suit.

While Chambers was preparing his defense against the suit, Nixon received word that Chambers had documentary evidence to back up his accusations. He went to Chambers' Maryland farm and asked him about it. Chambers conceded he had such evidence but was reluctant to produce it. Nixon had two committee investigators go back to the farm with a subpoena directing Chambers to hand over "all papers, documents and other matters you may have" concerning Hiss.

Chambers took the investigators to a pumpkin patch on his farm, picked up a pumpkin, hollowed out and dried like a jack-o'-lantern, lifted the top off the pumpkin, reached inside and withdrew five aluminum cylinders. Inside were rolls of microfilm, copies of secret State Department documents. Chambers said Hiss had taken documents home from his State Department office, copied them on a typewriter, then returned the originals. The copies had been microfilmed for relay to Russian agents, Chambers said.

The "pumpkin papers," as they came to be called, created still another sensation. FBI document experts examined them microscopically and testified that they had been typed on a Woodstock typewriter owned by Hiss. A grand jury eventually indicted Hiss on perjury charges, accusing him of lying when he denied turning over any secret documents to Chambers. His first trial ended in a hung jury, but he was convicted at a second trial and sentenced to five years in prison. After losing various appeals, Hiss entered prison on March 22, 1951.

Nearly three years passed between the opening of the congressional investigation and the imprisonment of Hiss. During that time the case was on the front pages much of the time. And so was Dick Nixon. He received enormous amounts of favorable publicity. He won a national reputation as a thorough, hard-digging investigator. In contrast to other congressional Communist-hunters accused of violating witnesses' constitutional rights, Nixon was generally regarded as scrupulously fair.

Riding the crest of national publicity, Nixon was easily re-elected to his House seat in 1948. In late 1949 he announced that he would try the following year to move up to the Senate. In his announcement, he charged that the Democratic Party "has been captured and is completely controlled by a group of ruthless, cynical seekers after power—committed to policies and principles completely foreign to those of its founders. Call it planned economy, the Fair Deal or social welfare—but it is still the same old socialist baloney, any way you slice it."

The California Senate campaign of 1950 was destined to be one of the most bitter in the state's history. Nixon's Democratic opponent in the race was Mrs. Helen Gahagan Douglas, a congresswoman and actress. She had won the Senate nomination only after a hard-fought primary campaign in which her rival accused her of being "soft on communism." Nixon made communism the central issue of his campaign against Mrs. Douglas.

At the outset of the race Nixon's campaign chairman charged that Mrs. Douglas' record in Congress "discloses the truth about her soft attitude toward communism." Nixon followed this up with a speech in which he said he was willing to run the political risk of criticizing a woman because "it just so happens that my opponent is a member of a small clique which joins the notorious Communist party-liner, (Congressman) Vito Marcantonio of New York, in voting time after time against measures that are for the security of this country."

To foster the idea that Mrs. Douglas was a "pinko" (Communist sympathizer), the Nixon forces referred to her as the "Pink Lady." The Nixon camp distributed 550,000 campaign leaflets—printed on bright pink paper—that purported to show a close association between the voting records of Mrs. Douglas and the controversial Congressman Marcantonio. Once more Nixon was accused of using unfair campaign tactics. Democrats charged that he was delivering below-the-belt blows in his use of the "soft-on-communism" issue.

Mrs. Douglas' own campaign was far from circumspect. On the one hand, she attributed fascist sympathies to Nixon and his followers—calling them "a backwash of young men in dark shirts" (dark shirts had been part of the uniform of European fascists). On the other hand, she charged that "on every key vote Nixon stood with party-liner Marcantonio against America in its fight to defeat communism."

Nixon won a sweeping victory, defeating Mrs. Douglas by 680,000 votes. He was rated across the country as one of the brightest young hopes of the Republican Party. He swiftly became the party's most sought-after public speaker. Despite the rigors of his duties as a freshman senator, he delivered up to a dozen important speeches a month in various parts of the nation—fighting speeches, lashing the Truman administration and declaring that a Republican victory in the 1952 presidential election was imperative.

Speculation filled the press on the question of who would be the candidates for President and Vice President in 1952. A movement developed among influential Republicans to nominate General Dwight D. Eisenhower for President. Eisenhower, the World War II military hero, had retired from active duty in 1948 to become president of Columbia University. He had later taken a leave of absence from Columbia to become Commander of the NATO forces in Europe. Although he had resisted past efforts to draw him into the political arena, he now cast aside this reluctance, ended the longtime mystery over his political preference, and entered the race for the Republican Party's presidential nomination.

Eisenhower faced formidable opposition for the nomination from Senator Robert A. Taft of Ohio. Nixon, a California delegate to the Republican National Convention, was pledged to vote for his state's favorite-son candidate, Governor Earl Warren. He actually favored Eisenhower's nomination and made his views known to the general's associates. Two of Eisenhower's most influential backers—Governor Dewey of New York and Herbert Brownell, Jr., who had managed Dewey's two presidential campaigns—concluded in advance of the convention that Nixon would be the best running mate if Eisenhower were nominated.

"Nixon seemed an almost ideal candidate for Vice President," Brownell later recalled. "He was young, geographically right, had experience in both the House and the Senate with a good voting record, and was an excellent speaker." Brownell said Nixon fit right into the plan to have Eisenhower, "who was experienced on the world scene, running with a young, aggressive fellow, who knew the domestic issues."

Brownell, Dewey and others recommended Nixon strongly to Eisenhower as a potential running mate. When Eisenhower made a list of five men who would be acceptable for the second spot on the ticket, Nixon's name was at the top.

At the convention in Chicago, Eisenhower won the presidential nomination on the first ballot. Immediately after his nomination, about two dozen leading Eisenhower supporters gathered in a hotel room to discuss a running mate. Various candidates were discussed and discarded. In the end, those present were unanimous in backing Nixon. Their views were relayed to Eisenhower, who concurred in the decision.

Nixon's name was placed before the convention by his fellow California Senator, William Knowland, who praised him as the man whose "bulldog determination enabled the government to hunt out and unravel the Alger Hiss case" and as "a young man who gives to the Republican ticket an appeal to the young men and young women of this nation." Nixon, age thirty-nine, with only six years of political experience, was nominated by acclamation.

Two weeks after the Republican convention, the Democrats met in Chicago to choose their ticket. President Truman had previously tried unsuccessfully to persuade Illinois Governor Adlai E. Stevenson (grandson and namesake of Grover Cleveland's second Vice President) to seek the presidential nomination. Stevenson sincerely did not want the nomination; he wanted to run for another term as governor. But a draft movement developed, swelled and ultimately carried Stevenson to the nomination. Chosen as his running mate was Senator John Sparkman of Alabama.

Meanwhile, Eisenhower and Nixon had met to discuss not only the campaign itself, but what kind of administration they would lead if elected. Eisenhower told his running mate that he envisioned the vice presidency as a significant office whose occupant should be more than a figurehead. He said he wanted his Vice President to be an active participant in the administration, with full knowledge of everything that was happening. Nixon could not have agreed more.

It was decided that Eisenhower—who enjoyed immense popularity among both Democratic and Republican voters—would seek to capitalize on this appeal by taking a lofty, nonpartisan approach. Nixon would be the one to slug it out toe-to-toe with the Democrats. Two chief issues were designated for special attention in the attacks on the Democrats—the "Communists-in-government" theme and the "mess in Washington." The "mess" referred to a series of scandals during the Truman administration, some of them involving men who had been political cronies of the President.

By mid-September Nixon was firing with both barrels on the issue of Washington corruption. And even Eisenhower, in something of a departure from his overall strategy, was speaking in tones of moral indignation about driving the "crooks and cronies" from power and bringing a Republican "Honest Deal" to Washington.

Nixon hammered at the same theme in a major attack on the Democrats. "What corruption means to all of us is that every time we pick up our paper, every day, we read about a scandal," Nixon said. "You know, as a matter of fact, this

(Truman) administration is going down in history as a scandal-a-day administration because you read about another bribe, you read about another tax fix, you read about another gangster getting favors from the government . . . and are sick and tired of it."

Amid all this harping by the Republicans about the misdeeds of the Democrats, a political bombshell burst in their own midst. Nixon, less than twenty-four hours after delivering his indignant "scandal-a-day" speech, suddenly found himself on the receiving end of scandal charges. It seemed that Nixon might even be forced off the ticket in mid-campaign. The resulting furor was the greatest ever to engulf a vice-presidential candidate.

The crisis was touched off by publication of an article in the New York *Post*, an ardently pro-Stevenson newspaper. "SE-CRET NIXON FUND," said a huge front-page headline. The article began: "The existence of a 'millionaire's club' devoted exclusively to the financial comfort of Senator Nixon, GOP vice-presidential candidate, was revealed today."

The story conveyed the impression that Nixon had been accepting enormous amounts of money from wealthy Californians, in return for which he presumably had been helping them get special favors from the government.

There was sufficient substance in the charges to cast serious doubt in the minds of top Republicans about the wisdom of keeping Nixon on the ticket.

These were the facts:

After Nixon's election to the Senate in 1950, several of his supporters suggested that he immediately start working toward the reelection campaign he was expected to wage six years later. This would involve making frequent trips from Washington to California to keep his political fences mended; traveling elsewhere to fulfill an ambitious speechmaking schedule; mailing copies of his speeches and other political literature to his constituents and supporters; and carrying on other related activities. All this would be costly. And Nixon, who was not a wealthy man, would be unable to pay for it from either his personal funds or his government salary and expense funds.

His supporters suggested that a fund be established with money collected from Nixon backers in California and that this fund be used to pay the political expenses. With Nixon's agreement Dana C. Smith, a Pasadena lawyer who had served as finance chairman of Nixon's Senate campaign, was named trustee of a special account at a Pasadena bank. Contributions were solicited from California business and professional people who had helped finance past Republican campaigns. No individual was permitted to give more than $500.

At the time of Nixon's vice-presidential campaign, the fund contained about $18,000. None of the money collected ever went directly to Nixon. When he incurred a political expense, he would have the bill sent to Smith for payment. Smith would then pay it from the trust account. Such payments were made solely for transportation, printing, mailing and office expenses. There was no evidence that Nixon had ever done special favors for contributors to the fund.

All of these facts notwithstanding, Nixon was in deep political trouble—deeper than he imagined at first. It is axiomatic in politics that denials rarely catch up with accusations. Even if the facts justified the legality and morality of the Nixon fund's existence, many voters might well be left with the impression that there was something crooked about the situation. Indeed, even some of those Republican leaders who were acquainted with the facts were not wholly satisfied with the propriety of such a fund. And among some of those who saw nothing wrong with the fund there was a feeling that the affair had destroyed Nixon's usefulness to the ticket.

If stories about the fund had appeared only in the New York *Post*, the problem might have been only a minor one for Nixon. However, almost immediately, other newspapers, television and radio stations had jumped on the story. In a matter of hours, the affair had become a national *cause célèbre*.

Nixon himself was initially unaware of the tremendous up-roar touched off by the story. He was on a whistle-stop tour of the West Coast at the time and was out of touch with events happening beyond his campaign train. At stops along his route he received fragmentary reports about the *Post* story—but shrugged them off as inconsequential. It came as a rude shock to him to learn he might well be forced off the ticket.

Within hours after the story broke, Democratic National Chairman Stephen Mitchell demanded that Eisenhower call for Nixon's resignation from the ticket or else eat his words about cleaning up the "mess in Washington." Other Demo-crats quickly chimed in with similar demands. Reporters on the Nixon train clamored for a statement about the fund. Nixon issued a brief statement outlining the facts and denying any wrongdoing. Having done this, he confidently assumed that a statement of continued support would soon be forth-coming from Eisenhower. But he was wrong.

A day went by without any word from Eisenhower. It was not until late afternoon of September 19, a day and a half after the crisis began, that Eisenhower made his first public statement on the affair. He said merely that "Dick Nixon is an honest man" and that "the facts will show that Nixon would not compromise with what is right."

Eisenhower still made no immediate effort to communicate with Nixon. This served to increase the anxiety of Nixon and his aides. They heard reports that messages to Eisenhower from politicians and citizens were running 50-50 on the ques-tion of whether Nixon should be dropped. An aura of gloom settled over the Nixon train.

On the night of September 19, Nixon learned that the fol-lowing day's editions of two of the nation's most respected newspapers—the Washington *Post* and the New York *Herald Tribune*—would carry editorials calling upon him to offer to resign from the ticket. The Washington *Post* editorial came as no shock, since that paper had frequently criticized him in the past. But the *Herald Tribune* was the most influential Republican paper in the East. Its top officials were extremely close to Eisenhower and some of his key advisers. Nixon assumed that the editorial represented the thinking of those closest to Eisenhower—perhaps even Eisenhower himself.

Nixon seriously began to consider withdrawing from the ticket. But Pat Nixon would not hear of such a thing. "You can't think of resigning," she told her husband. "If you do, Eisenhower will lose. He can put you off the ticket if he wants to, but if you, in the face of attack, do not fight back but simply crawl away, you will destroy yourself. . . ." Aides aboard the Nixon train agreed with this assessment.

After hearing this advice, Nixon sat alone in his train compartment for two hours, agonizing over the decision that confronted him. He knew his resignation would be taken as an admission of guilt that would kill his political career. Beyond that, he feared such a resignation might cost Eisenhower the election and tear the Republican Party asunder—in which case he would forever be blamed for the results. But perhaps even more important than these considerations was Nixon's personality. He was a fighter. It would have been out of character for him to walk away from the toughest battle of his life. Not surprisingly, he chose to stay and fight.

It was decided that the best way Nixon could wage his fight would be by taking his case directly to the voters, through a nationwide television broadcast.

Nixon still had not heard from the presidential candidate and was growing increasingly perturbed by Eisenhower's failure to consult with him. On September 20 Eisenhower called in newsmen aboard his train and candidly discussed the Nixon situation—with the proviso that they would not quote him directly in their stories. He made it plain that Nixon's place on the ticket was by no means assured. Eisenhower said he could not believe Nixon would do anything crooked, but that Nixon would have to prove this to the satisfaction of "fair-minded people." "Of what avail is it for us to carry on this crusade against this business of what has been going on in Washington if we ourselves aren't as clean as a hound's tooth?" Eisenhower said.

The substance of Eisenhower's remarks soon reached Nixon and his aides, who stewed all the more. Nixon was discussing the situation with his aides on September 21 in a hotel room in Portland, Oregon, when he was interrupted by a telephone call from St. Louis. At last, on the fourth day of the crisis, Eisenhower was on the line.

Eisenhower said:

> You know, this is an awfully hard thing for me to decide. I have come to the conclusion that you are the one who has to decide what to do. After all, you've got a big following in this country and, if the impression got around that you got off the ticket because I forced you to get off, it is going to be very bad. On the other hand, if I issue a statement now backing you up, in effect people will accuse me of condoning wrongdoing. I don't want to be in the position of condemning an innocent man. I think you ought to go on a nationwide television program and tell them everything there is to tell, everything you can remember since the day you entered public life. Tell them about any money you have ever received.

Nixon said:

> General, do you think after the television program that an announcement could then be made one way or the other? There comes a time in matters like this when you've either got to fish or cut bait. I will get off the ticket if you think my staying on it would be harmful. You let me know and I will get off and I will take the heat, but this thing has got to be decided at the earliest possible time. After the television program, if you think I should stay on or get off, I think you should say so either way. The great trouble here is the indecision.

But Eisenhower would not be hurried. "We'll have to wait three or four days after the television show to see what the effect of the program is," he insisted. A few minutes later Eisenhower ended the conversation by telling Nixon: "Well, Dick, go on the television show. Good luck and keep your chin up."

Nixon was notified that the Republican organization had pledged the necessary $75,000 to book a half hour of television and radio time for his appearance on September 23.

On September 22, the day before Nixon's TV appearance, the pro-Republican Chicago *Tribune* provided him with some ammunition for a counterattack by reporting that Democratic presidential candidate Adlai Stevenson had also had a fund at his disposal at one time. This fund had been collected from businessmen who had dealings with the Illinois state government while Stevenson was governor. Stevenson quickly confirmed the fund's existence, but explained that none of the money had been used for the benefit—political or personal—of Stevenson or any other elected official. Instead, it had been used to supplement the state salaries of Stevenson appointees who had left higher-paying jobs in the business world to become public servants. Stevenson said this enabled his administration to attract highly qualified men who otherwise would have been reluctant to take state jobs. He said these appointees never knew who had contributed the money used to supplement their salaries. Thus, he insisted, there was "no question of improper influence, because there was no connection between the contributors and the beneficiaries."

The heat remained on Nixon. By the day of his telecast, messages reaching Eisenhower were running three to one in favor of dropping Nixon from the ticket.

Eisenhower was campaigning in Ohio that day. The General was scheduled to address a rally in Cleveland shortly after the telecast. Arrangements were made to have Nixon's talk piped into the auditorium where the rally would take place. Thus, both Eisenhower and his audience would hear Nixon's address before the General began his own speech.

In Los Angeles, Nixon was still working on his speech when

a surprise telephone call came from former Governor Thomas Dewey of New York, a still-important figure in Republican politics. Dewey informed Nixon that all of Eisenhower's top advisers suggested he resign as nominee at the conclusion of his television appearance. Nixon was thunderstruck. He indicated that his remarks were already prepared. When Dewey persisted, demanding an answer, Nixon said:

"Just tell them that I haven't the slightest idea as to what I am going to do and, if they want to find out, they'd better listen to the broadcast. And tell them I know something about politics, too!" With that, he slammed down the phone. Little more than a half hour later, he was on his way to the TV studio. He was still not certain, as he rode across Los Angeles, how he would conclude his talk.

Then, suddenly, it was air time. A camera focused on Nixon, sitting behind a desk with five pages of handwritten notes before him. His wife sat nearby in an armchair. Nixon then said:

> My fellow Americans, I come before you tonight as a candidate for the vice presidency and as a man whose honesty and integrity has been questioned.
>
> I am sure that you have read the charge, and you have heard it, that I, Senator Nixon, took $18,000 from a group of my supporters. Now, was that wrong? . . . It isn't a question of whether it was legal or illegal, that isn't enough. The question is: was it morally wrong? I say that it was morally wrong —if any of that $18,000 went to Senator Nixon for my personal use. I say it was morally wrong if it was secretly given and secretly handled. And I say that it was morally wrong if any of the contributors got special favors for the contributions that they made.
>
> And now, to answer those questions, let me say this: Not one cent of the $18,000 or any other money of that type ever went to my personal use. Every penny of it was used to pay for political expenses that I did not think should be charged to the taxpayers of the United States. . . . Let me point out, and I want to make this particularly clear, that no contributor

to this fund, no contributor to any of my campaigns, has ever received any consideration that he would not have received as an ordinary constituent. . . .

Now what I am going to do—and incidentally this is unprecedented in the history of American politics—I am going at this time to give to this television and radio audience a complete financial history; everything I've earned; everything I've spent; everything I owe.

Nixon provided a full financial accounting—listing everything from his three-year-old automobile to his $4,000 life-insurance policy and from a $20,000 mortgage on his Washington home to a $3,500 debt he owed his parents. He then took a slap at the Democrats, whose scandals had included acceptance of questionable "gifts" such as mink coats.

"I should say this, that Pat doesn't have a mink coat," Nixon said. "But she does have a respectable Republican cloth coat, and I always tell her that she would look good in anything."

Recalling Roosevelt's famous speech referring to his dog, Fala, Nixon said:

One other thing I probably should tell you, because if I don't they will probably be saying this about me, too. We did get something, a gift, after the nomination. A man down in Texas heard Pat on the radio mention the fact that our two youngsters would like to have a dog. And, believe it or not, the day before we left on this campaign trip we got a message from Union Station in Baltimore, saying they had a package for us. We went down to get it. You know what it was? It was a little cocker spaniel dog, in a crate that he had sent all the way from Texas—black and white, spotted, and our little girl Tricia, the six-year-old, named it Checkers. And you know, the kids, like all kids, loved the dog, and I just want to say this right now—that, regardless of what they say about it, we are going to keep it.

(Not surprisingly, the references to the dog and to his wife's cloth coat were to become the best-remembered sections of

Nixon's speech. It was to be known as the "Pat and Checkers" speech.)

After delivering a few additional slaps at the Democrats and praising Eisenhower as "the only man who can save America at this time," Nixon at last came to the most eagerly awaited portion of his speech. "And now, finally, I know that you wonder whether or not I am going to stay on the Republican ticket or resign," he said.

> Let me say this: I don't believe that I ought to quit, because I am not a quitter. And, incidentally, Pat is not a quitter. After all, her name was Patricia Ryan and she was born on Saint Patrick's Day, and you know the Irish never quit.
>
> But the decision, my friends, is not mine. I would do nothing that would harm the possibilities of Dwight Eisenhower to become President of the United States. And for that reason I am submitting to the Republican National Committee tonight through this television broadcast the decision which it is theirs to make. Let them decide whether my position on the ticket will help or hurt. And I am going to ask you to help them decide. Wire and write the Republican National Committee whether you think I should stay on or whether I should get off. And, whatever their decision is, I will abide by it.

Nixon intended to say more, but ran out of time and was cut off the air in mid-sentence. Partly because of this untidy ending to his talk, Nixon felt as he went off the air that the telecast had been a failure. He picked up his notes from the desk, then threw them angrily to the floor. When an aide told him he had done "a terrific job," Nixon replied: "No, it was a flop . . . I couldn't get off in time."

For once, Nixon's usually keen political instincts were clouded by emotionalism. For, if his performance had been a "flop," it had been the most successful "flop" in American political history.

More than 60,000,000 persons, the largest audience ever to see a telecast up to that time, had tuned in for the address. And the audience response was the greatest ever accorded a radio or television speech. Thousands of persons left their homes that night and lined up outside Western Union offices. Telegrams flooded the Republican National Committee headquarters in Washington, Nixon's hotel in Los Angeles, Eisenhower's hotel in Cleveland and individual TV and radio stations across the country. Eventually, close to 2,000,000 telegrams and letters—bearing more than 3,000,000 names—were received. They ran 350 to 1 in favor of keeping Nixon on the ticket. And they contained enough financial contributions to more than pay for the $75,000 cost of the telecast.

Of course, the full extent of the response and the trend of public opinion was not discernible immediately following the telecast. Thus Eisenhower reacted cautiously at first.

Thirteen thousand persons, waiting in a Cleveland auditorium for Eisenhower's speech, listened to Nixon's talk and then burst into shouts of "We want Dick." When Eisenhower reached the platform, he delivered an off-the-cuff talk that spoke highly of Nixon's courage:

> I happen to be one of those people who, when I get into a fight, would rather have a courageous and honest man by my side than a whole boxcar of pussyfooters. I have seen brave men in tough situations. I have never seen anyone come through in better fashion than Senator Nixon did tonight.

However, Eisenhower said he felt a thirty-minute telecast was too brief to present a complete picture, so he was sending Nixon a telegram asking the senator to meet him the next day in Wheeling, West Virginia. After that meeting, he would reach his personal decision on the vice-presidential candidate and pass his recommendation on to the Republican National Committee.

In Los Angeles, Nixon at first received only fragmentary reports on Eisenhower's speech. The initial word he received was merely that Eisenhower had said he could not make a personal decision until he saw Nixon face to face.

Upon hearing this, Nixon—to use his own words—"really

blew my stack." He asked his aides: "What more can he (Eisenhower) possibly want from me?" He felt that, after the telecast, he had been entitled to a firm decision from Eisenhower. He told his aides there was nothing further he could do if Eisenhower still was not satisfied. He was going to resign. Nixon called in his secretary, and dictated a telegram of resignation, to be sent to the Republican National Committee. But Murray Chotiner, Nixon's chief political manager, tore the telegram to shreds. Nixon had clearly intended for it to be sent. It was only later, when he received the full text of Eisenhower's telegram, that he realized he would have committed a grave error by submitting his resignation.

After some delicate negotiations between the Eisenhower and Nixon camps, the vice-presidential candidate agreed to meet the General in Wheeling. In the meantime, Nixon was notified that the Republican National Committee had taken a quick poll—reaching 107 of its 138 members—and that they had all voted "enthusiastically" to keep him on the ticket.

When Nixon reached Wheeling he was surprised to find Eisenhower waiting for him at the airport—with a big smile and an outstretched hand.

"General, you didn't need to come out to the airport," Nixon said.

And then Eisenhower uttered the words that, for all practical purposes, put an end to Nixon's ordeal and to the crisis. "I certainly did, Dick," he said. "You're my boy."

Eisenhower had decided that no further consultation with Nixon was necessary after all. The two men rode together to a stadium, where Eisenhower made his decision official in a speech at a campaign rally. He announced that the Republican National Committee unanimously favored Nixon's retention on the ticket. He then read a letter expressing "implicit faith in his (Nixon's) integrity and honesty . . . from one who has known Richard longer than anyone else. His Mother." Finally, Eisenhower said he felt that Nixon had been vindicated and that he was proud to have him as a running mate.

It would be difficult to overestimate the importance of this crisis on the career of Richard Nixon or on the history of the vice presidency itself. For Nixon emerged from the crisis with far more political stature than he had entered with. And this additional stature influenced his conduct not only during the remainder of his campaign but also during the days of his vice presidency.

At the beginning of the campaign a poll had disclosed that only 45 per cent of the nation's voters knew the name of the Republican vice-presidential candidate. Now Nixon was a national topic of conversation. While it was true that some voters adopted attitudes of utter distaste for Nixon, many more suddenly developed feelings of sympathy and respect for a man who had previously left them cold. His new-found fame —some called it notoriety—was of tremendous help to Nixon in the campaign and the period that followed. Crowds far larger than those drawn by any previous vice-presidential candidate—and, in some cases, larger than those attracted by the 1952 presidential candidates—turned out to see him throughout the country.

Another effect of the furor was to focus a tremendous amount of public attention on the vice-presidential office.

Following the end of the fund crisis, the Eisenhower-Nixon campaign rolled smoothly toward victory. Eisenhower's tremendous popularity more than made up for his lack of political experience. Adlai Stevenson, although waging one of the most articulate presidential campaigns in history and endearing himself to millions of Americans, could not match the mass appeal of the war hero.

On election day Eisenhower and Nixon won by a landslide. They drew 33,824,351 popular votes to 27,314,987 for Stevenson and Sparkman. Their electoral-vote margin was even more marked, 442 to 89.

The election swept the Republicans into control of the executive branch for the first time in two decades. Nixon took the oath as Vice President on January 20, 1953, just eleven days after his fortieth birthday. He thus became the second youngest Vice President in history. (The youngest was John C. Breckinridge, who was thirty-six when inaugurated as James Buchanan's Vice President in 1857.)

Eisenhower, as promised, made Nixon an important member of his administration. And Nixon rarely passed up an opportunity to exert his influence on either the government or the Republican Party.

As a military man Eisenhower believed in a staff system of government that relied heavily on delegation of authority to subordinates. He appointed Sherman Adams, the former New Hampshire governor, as his top White House aide. Adams served as a chief of staff, with great power over the day-to-day operations of the President's office. But Nixon operated effectively as a true second-in-command to Eisenhower in other major areas—to an extent unmatched by any previous vice president.

He was the chief political operator of the administration. Although in politics only six years Nixon was considered one of the shrewdest political practitioners in the Republican Party. Eisenhower not only lacked experience in this field; he showed little taste for behind-the-scenes maneuvering. Many of his closest associates in government—both Cabinet appointees and other officials—came from the business world and had only scant experience in the political realm. Eisenhower assigned Nixon to take over many of the political tasks traditionally performed by Presidents. The Vice President was given responsibility for maintaining and building the strength of the Republican Party—by campaigning for party candidates, ironing out intra-party squabbles, speaking at fundraising functions and placing the administration's prestige behind state and local officeholders and hopefuls.

Eisenhower gave strong weight to Nixon's advice on both political and governmental affairs. Nixon participated in the decision-making process to a degree that far outstripped any of his predecessors. He was given unprecedented access to information and personnel from all branches of the government. Even the most secret military and intelligence data were made available to him. He received copies of the daily intelligence reports sent to the President from all parts of the world. And he was briefed regularly on military matters by Defense Department officials.

Of course, Nixon performed the traditional duties of the vice president as presiding officer of the Senate. In addition, he served as the chief liaison man between the President and the Congress. At the same time, he operated as a buffer between the conservative and moderate Republican members of the Senate and House.

Nixon also expanded greatly the role played by the vice president in both the Cabinet and the National Security Council. Eisenhower decided at the outset of his administration that both governmental bodies should meet regularly, even if he could not be present. In his absence, he said, Nixon should preside over the meetings. This was an important break with recent tradition and further enhanced the Vice President's prestige. In the past, when a president had been unable to attend Cabinet or National Security Council meetings, the secretary of state had usually presided.

Nixon, all told, presided over nineteen Cabinet meetings and twenty-six National Security Council meetings. Even when Eisenhower was present, the Vice President took a more active part in the meetings than his predecessors.

The Vice President was named chairman of the President's Committee on Government Contracts, assigned to combat racial discrimination in employment policies followed by some companies doing business with the government. The committee managed to curb substantially the discrimination practiced by government contractors. Nixon was also named chairman of the Cabinet Committee on Price Stability, an economic advisory group assigned to find ways of preventing inflation.

All these duties provided Nixon with his greatest satisfaction since entering public life. "I like [the vice presidency] much better than service in the House or Senate" he said. "In the vice presidency you have an opportunity to see the whole operation of the government and participate in its decisions."

From the start, Eisenhower considered Nixon a potential President—either through election or through succession in case of Eisenhower's own death or disability. Eisenhower was sixty-two when he became President, and although he had suffered no serious recent illnesses, he realized that his health could fail at any time. His delegation of a broad range of responsibility to Nixon was designed, at least in part, to prepare the Vice President for the possible assumption of the President's duties.

In September of 1955 Eisenhower was vacationing in Denver, Colorado, his wife's former home. Nixon was in Washington. On September 24 the Vice President noticed a newspaper story saying that the President was suffering from a slight case of indigestion. Nixon gave the story little thought, knowing that the President was subject to periodic stomach upsets of a mild nature. Nixon was relaxing at home when the phone rang. The caller was James C. Hagerty, Eisenhower's press secretary.

"Dick, are you sitting down?" Hagerty asked.

"No, what is it?" Nixon replied.

Hagerty told him to sit down, that he had some bad news. The news: Eisenhower had suffered a heart attack.

"My God!" Nixon exclaimed. Then he could not speak for several seconds. "Are they sure?" he asked finally.

"We are absolutely sure," Hagerty said. "It's going to be announced to the press in a half hour. . . . Let me know where you can be reached at all times."

Nixon was in a state of shock. He knew that, at any moment, he might become President. But what troubled him even more than that awesome prospect was the question of how best to fulfill his immediate responsibilities as a Vice President whose President might be unable to carry out the duties of his office.

Nixon was only the third Vice President in history compelled to deal with the problem of presidential disability. The other two, Chester Arthur and Thomas Riley Marshall, had held office in less complicated, less perilous times. But Nixon was living in the nuclear age. The man who controlled the United States government now could unleash weapons capable of destroying the world. Suppose a situation arose that made it imperative for the government to decide, on short notice, whether to use some of those weapons? And suppose Eisenhower was incapable of making the decision?

Nixon was well aware that there was considerable feeling that he was overly eager for power. He realized that he must do nothing to create the impression that he was usurping the President's prerogatives. He must provide whatever leadership was necessary, but he must do so unobtrusively.

As soon as he regained his composure he invited to his home one of his closest friends, Deputy Attorney General William P. Rogers. By the time Rogers arrived, the press had been informed of Eisenhower's heart attack and newsmen were on their way to the Vice President's house. Nixon and Rogers pulled the shades and discussed the crisis while Mrs. Nixon, in response to repeated ringing of the doorbell by the newsmen, told the press that the Vice President was not home.

At that time Nixon was unaware of how serious the President's heart attack had been. He knew only that there had been an attack and that the President, at last report, was alive. (Actually, the attack was classed as "moderate"—but any heart attack, particularly in a man almost sixty-five years of age, was a serious matter.)

The Vice President immediately called Denver and was

given a full report on Eisenhower's condition. The President was resting comfortably under an oxygen tent in Fitsimmons Army Hospital. Nixon was told that his chances for recovery appeared good but that it was too soon to know for certain. Eisenhower was under the care of his personal physician, Major General Howard Snyder, and other military doctors. At Nixon's request, one of the nation's most renowned heart specialists, Dr. Paul Dudley White of Massachusetts General Hospital, was brought into the case.

Nixon also spoke by phone with Secretary of State John Foster Dulles, Secretary of the Treasury George Humphrey and other officials. These discussions brought quick agreement that the best policy to be followed, at least on a temporary basis, was "business as usual" under a system of team leadership. Nixon ascertained that no urgent problems were awaiting decisions by Eisenhower. Department heads and other officials could just go on running their agencies on a day-to-day basis. If a major problem arose, it would be dealt with when the time came.

Though a team might be leading the country during this crisis, it was clear from the start to insiders that Nixon was leading the team. Diplomatically, subtly and modestly, the Vice President directed the emergency measures necessary to assure continuity of government. It was he who made the initial decision of consequence following Eisenhower's seizure. Four Cabinet members were scheduled to leave the next day for Ottawa to discuss economic and trade matters with Canadian officials. Nixon urged that the conference take place on schedule, to demonstrate that the government was continuing to function despite the President's condition. His decision was followed by the Cabinet members.

To calm rumor and ease the public's mind, Nixon talked with a few reporters.

> The only comment I can make is to express the concern that I share with all the American people for the early and complete recovery of the President. In comparison with this,

all other questions and problems are not worthy of discussion. . . . The President has set up the administration in such a way that it will continue its policies, which are well defined, during his temporary absence. The President has always made it clear that the business of government should go ahead. He set it up in such a way that it can go ahead despite the temporary absence of anyone.

Eisenhower sent word from Denver that he wanted the National Security Council and the Cabinet to continue meeting on schedule—with Nixon presiding. On Monday, September 26, Nixon went to the White House for a luncheon meeting with senior staff members and reviewed pending business. He was careful at this meeting, and in the days that followed, not to offend sensibilities. He avoided entering Eisenhower's personal office. When it was necessary for him to be at the White House, he used a conference room. Most of his work was done at his own office. And when meeting with Cabinet members he showed them the courtesy of going to their offices—although most of them thought it was their place to call on him.

On Wednesday, September 28, Nixon signed some official papers normally signed by the President. He signed his own name, "in behalf of the President." Later that day the Vice President conferred with various officials concerned with the country's security—including Central Intelligence Agency (CIA) Director Allen Dulles—in preparation for a National Security Council meeting scheduled the following day.

At the council meeting, attended by twenty-three top administration officials, Nixon presided over a two-and-a-half-hour discussion of the usual problems facing the administration and the special problems created by Eisenhower's illness. It was tentatively decided that Sherman Adams should go to Denver and serve as liaison man between the President and the officials in Washington. The Cabinet meeting, also presided over by Nixon, ratified this decision. Nixon opened the meeting with a silent prayer and read the latest medical report on the President. It was an optimistic report. Eisenhower had spent his first night outside the oxygen tent and had slept soundly for nine and a half hours.

Just before the meeting ended, Secretary of State Dulles, the senior Cabinet member, turned to Nixon and said: "Mr. Vice President, I realize that you have been under a very heavy burden during these past few days, and I know I express the opinion of everybody here that you have conducted yourself superbly. We are proud to be on this team and proud to be serving in this Cabinet under your leadership."

In Denver, Eisenhower gained strength with each passing day. A week after entering the hospital he signed two documents—chiefly to bolster the nation's confidence in his ultimate recovery. Several days later he publicly expressed his approval of Nixon's conduct during the crisis.

On October 8, two weeks after the President's heart attack, Nixon flew to Denver to visit him. Eisenhower, although pale and thin, was fully alert. He discussed his condition and some government problems. Nixon assured him there was no need to hurry back to work—that the administration team was carrying on.

It was not until November 11, seven weeks after entering the hospital, that Eisenhower returned to Washington. Ten days later he met with the National Security Council and the Cabinet for the first time since his seizure. His recuperation period was not yet over, but he was at least back to work on a part-time basis. The crisis was at an end.

Opinions vary on just how large a role Nixon played during the crisis. Some respected observers feel he served, in effect, as the government's leader during this period. Others feel that Sherman Adams served as "Acting President." The answer may lie somewhere between these two positions. Adams, even when Eisenhower was healthy, exercised great power within the administration—deciding what matters would be brought to the President's attention, approving certain actions that he felt were not sufficiently important to occupy the President's time and generally directing the White House staff. During Eisenhower's illness he enlarged his authority somewhat in order to present only the most important questions to the President. But it was Nixon who was functioning in a leadership capacity in Washington—maintaining unity within the administration, performing some of the duties normally belonging to the president and serving as the chief government spokesman in the capital.

Nixon had clearly played a much more important role than either Chester Arthur or Thomas Riley Marshall had taken during their respective President's illnesses. He thus had expanded once again the prestige of the vice presidency. He had also enhanced his own position.

But all was not rosy on the Nixon horizon. The presidential nominating conventions of 1956 were only a half year away. Even before Eisenhower's heart attack there had been a substantial question whether the President would seek reelection. Eisenhower had expressed his reluctance to run again. Just two weeks before his seizure he had told Republican National Chairman Leonard Hall: "What more do they want from me? I've given all of my adult life to the country. What more must I do?" He had then listed half a dozen men, including Nixon, whom he considered capable of carrying on as President. Following the heart attack many observers assumed Eisenhower would bow out after one term.

A flurry of speculation rose about his possible replacement as Republican presidential nominee. Nixon, among others, was mentioned. But there was a strong tide of sentiment against him. Some people felt he had not "grown" sufficiently in the vice presidency. Some still had a bad taste in their mouths as a result of the 1952 fund episode. Others complained that he had an abnormal desire for power. Still others resented his tough campaign techniques. Some just didn't like his personality.

Ultimately, after being assured by his doctors that he had recovered completely from the heart attack, Eisenhower consented to run for a second term. He did not announce the decision to the public immediately but let it be known to his intimates. Now the question became whether to keep Nixon on the ticket in 1956. Eisenhower was disturbed by the strong feelings against the Vice President by some influential political figures and by many ordinary citizens. He felt Nixon had done a good job as Vice President, but he was disappointed that his popularity had not risen higher.

Eisenhower first expressed this disappointment to Nixon in a meeting at the White House on December 26, 1955. He still considered Nixon presidential material but felt something had to be done to improve his public image. The President suggested that Nixon's career might best be advanced if he moved from the vice presidency to a Cabinet position. This was not an attempt to dump Nixon but a sincere effort by Eisenhower to give him more of a chance to "show his stuff." He offered to appoint Nixon to any Cabinet position he wanted during the second term, with the exception of Secretary of State and Attorney General.

Nixon considered the President's suggestion merely a trial balloon that did not require a firm answer. But he told Eisenhower to choose the vice-presidential candidate who could best help him—both in the campaign and the administration —without worrying about hurting Nixon's career or feelings. Eisenhower assured him he had no complaints about his performance as Vice President. "There has never been a job I have given you that you haven't done to perfection as far as I am concerned," the President said. "The thing that concerns me is that the public does not realize adequately the job you have done."

Despite his expressions of flexibility, Nixon did not want to move from the vice presidency to the Cabinet. He felt such a move would leave the clear impression that he had been dumped, and thus would diminish any hope he had of eventually being elected President. Moreover, he thought the vice presidency was giving him the most valuable experience possible in preparation for the Presidency.

The situation remained unresolved when Eisenhower announced on February 29, 1956, that he would run for reelection. The announcement, made at a press conference, immediately brought a question about whether Nixon would again be his running mate. Eisenhower hedged, saying he could not speak out on the subject of a running mate until being nominated at the Republican convention. The President's failure to give immediate, unequivocal support to Nixon was interpreted by some news analysts as an indication that he wanted another running mate.

A week later, at his next regular press conference, Eisenhower was asked again about Nixon. He replied: "I told him he would have to chart his own course and tell me what he would like to do." This really upset Nixon. He felt it was common knowledge in politics that a vice president cannot "chart his own course." Eisenhower's phraseology convinced him the President wanted another running mate. Nixon told a friend who worked for the Republican National Committee that he intended to announce he would not run for reelection. Word of his intention soon reached the national chairman, Leonard Hall, one of Nixon's closest political allies. Hall immediately sought Nixon out and argued that his withdrawal would split the party. Hall said Nixon had misunderstood Eisenhower's intention—that the President was not a political sophisticate and did not realize how his words would be interpreted.

At Hall's urging, Nixon agreed to delay a decision. Then something unexpected happened. The first Republican primary of the year, in New Hampshire, brought Nixon a surprising, unsolicited total of 22,936 write-in votes for Vice President. Since his name had not even been on the ballot, this boosted his political stock considerably.

At a press conference on April 27, a newsman asked Eisenhower whether Nixon had reported to him on the charting of his own course. The President replied: "He hasn't given me any authority to quote him, any answer that I would consider final and definite."

That afternoon the Vice President went to the White House. He told Eisenhower that he would be honored to run for reelection and that the only reason he had waited so long to say so was that he did not want to push himself onto the ticket. Eisenhower said he was delighted by Nixon's decision. He arranged a White House press conference at which Nixon announced his availability. A statement from the President, again using the word "delighted," was issued simultaneously. It appeared that the matter was settled.

On the night of June 7 Eisenhower was stricken with severe stomach cramps. When his condition did not improve, Eisenhower was taken on a stretcher from the White House to Walter Reed Hospital the afternoon of June 8.

The ailment was diagnosed as ileitis, an obstruction of the lower intestines. When it did not respond to medication, a team of physicians decided upon immediate surgery. By then it was 2:30 A.M. on June 9. Nixon had been informed of the President's new ailment the previous morning by White House Press Secretary James Hagerty. The surgery was successful and, although Eisenhower's condition was not nearly so serious as it had been at the time of his heart attack, it caused him much greater pain over a much greater length of time.

This time Eisenhower's period of inactivity was relatively brief. Within a few days he was doing a limited amount of work. And within six weeks he was in Panama for an important conference of Western Hemisphere heads of state. During the convalescence period Nixon once again carried out some of the President's duties and assumed a leadership position.

Eisenhower became more aware than ever of the problems inherent when a president is seriously ill. He brooded over the fact that, during the two hours he was under anesthesia, the country was without a chief executive and the armed forces were without a commander in chief. Had a national emergency developed during those two hours, he knew that no one would have had undisputed authority to act. But for the moment, the President contented himself with telling associates that he would resign if he ever felt his health would prevent him from carrying out his duties.

One result of the ileitis attack was to revive speculation about the 1956 Republican ticket. Hagerty told newsmen a month after the attack that Eisenhower and Nixon both still planned to seek reelection. Though some observers doubted whether the President's health would permit him to endure the rigors of another campaign and a second term, there was no serious talk about getting an alternate presidential candidate. But serious questions did arise about the wisdom of keeping Nixon on the ticket. In view of the possibility that Eisenhower might die or be forced to retire because of ill health during a second term, the vice-presidential nomination took on added importance. And there were still influential Republicans who felt Nixon had failed to measure up to presidential caliber. However, most of them were satisfied to grumble about Nixon, but had no intention of taking overt action to try to get him off the ticket.

Not so with Harold Stassen, the former Governor of Minnesota. Stassen had been among the first to urge Nixon to resign during the fund crisis and he now felt that Nixon must go. With a considerable national following, Stassen attempted to convince the President that there was much anti-Nixon feeling and that a neutral candidate such as Massachusetts Governor Christian Herter would be better for the ticket. Eisenhower withheld comment, stating that the Republican convention would determine the candidate for the vice presidency. Herter headquarters were established, but in the end, Stassen surrendered. Nixon had the party organization behind him. The Eisenhower-Nixon team successfully gained the nomination.

The Stassen episode illustrated once more that Nixon had serious image problems. And the Democrats were determined to exploit those problems in the election campaign.

Adlai Stevenson was again nominated by the Democrats to run against Eisenhower. This time he was no reluctant candidate. He had wanted the nomination and fought for it. Then he had stunned the convention with an unprecedented decision regarding a running mate. He had announced to the delegates that the choice of a vice-presidential candidate would be theirs alone; he would play no part in it. Stevenson said:

> The American people have the solemn obligation to consider with the utmost care who will be their President if the elected President is prevented by a Higher will from serving his full term. It is a sober reminder that seven out of thirty-four Presidents have served as the result of such an indirect selection. The responsibility of the Presidency has grown so great that the nation's attention has become focused as never before on the office of the vice presidency. The choice for that office has become almost as important as the choice for the presidency.

Stevenson's move focused new attention on the vice presidency. At the same time it was good politics. It enabled the Democrats to claim later that their vice-presidential candidate had been chosen in an open convention, while the Republican candidate had been forced onto the ticket over the objections of Stassen and others. The Democrats planned to aim many of their campaign attacks against Nixon rather than the popular Eisenhower. Stevenson's decision at the convention thus fit into the overall Democratic campaign strategy.

The three chief contenders for the vice-presidential nomination were Senators Estes Kefauver of Tennessee, John F. Kennedy of Massachusetts and Hubert H. Humphrey of Minnesota. Humphrey's candidacy soon waned, and a spirited contest for delegates developed between Kefauver and Kennedy. Kefauver won by a narrow margin. He went on to wage a vigorous, colorful campaign—often wearing the coonskin cap identified with his home state.

In the campaign, Stevenson drew attention to Eisenhower's poor health and lashed out at Nixon, calling him "this man of many masks." He warned that "every piece of scientific evidence that we have, every lesson of history and experience indicates that a Republican victory . . . would mean that Richard M. Nixon would probably be President of this country within the next four years."

The Vice President tried to cope with his image problems by presenting the voters with a "new Nixon." He and Eisenhower had agreed at the outset of the campaign that Nixon should take a "higher road" than in previous races. For the most part Nixon campaigned on the theme that the nation needed Eisenhower for another four years.

Just before the election the campaign was overshadowed by news from abroad. In Hungary, freedom fighters launched a revolution against their Communist rulers. And in the Middle East a crisis developed over the Suez Canal. British, French and Israeli military forces went into action against Egypt. Historically, such crises near election time have tended to help the party in power because of the "don't-change-horses-in-midstream" psychology. There is little doubt that Eisenhower and Nixon would have won the election handily in any case. But the crises abroad probably widened the victory margin. This time the Eisenhower-Nixon ticket won by an even bigger landslide than in 1952. The Republican popular-vote margin was 3,040,317 greater and the electoral-vote margin 15 greater.

Early in 1957 Eisenhower proposed a constitutional amendment that would permit the vice president, with the Cabinet advising, to decide when an ill president was unable to carry out his duties—provided the president was unable to make the decision himself. But Congress failed to act on the measure.

In November of 1957 the disability question arose again. Eisenhower's personal secretary, Mrs. Ann Whitman, burst into Sherman Adams' office with tears in her eyes on the afternoon of November 27. "He tried to tell me something but he couldn't express himself," Mrs. Whitman told Adams. Dr. Snyder was hurriedly called to the President's office. Eisenhower tried to talk to his physician but was unable to get any words out. At Snyder's insistence the President went to bed. The doctor thought Eisenhower had suffered a stroke but summoned specialists to confirm his diagnosis. Meanwhile, Eisenhower got out of bed and told Adams and Snyder that it was time for him to dress for a formal White House dinner in honor of the visiting King Mohammed V of Morocco.

Adams called Nixon and asked him to come to the White House. When the Vice President arrived, Adams explained in detail what had happened.

"How serious is his condition?" Nixon asked.

"We'll know more in the morning," Adams said. "This is a terribly, terribly difficult thing to handle. You may be President in the next twenty-four hours."

The President ultimately agreed to let Nixon attend the formal dinner as his representative. The dinner guests and newsmen were told that the President had suffered a chill. Meanwhile, the medical specialists confirmed Dr. Snyder's diagnosis. Eisenhower had indeed suffered a stroke. It was a mild one, however, that had impaired only his ability to speak. His reading, writing and reasoning powers were not involved.

Attorney General William Rogers made an informal judgment—as the nation's chief legal officer—that Eisenhower was capable of carrying out his duties and that it would not be necessary to delegate any additional powers to the Vice President. But the doctors warned that the stroke might be just the first in a series and ordered Eisenhower to rest for two months.

Eisenhower's stroke had come at a much more critical time than either his heart seizure or his ileitis attack. International tensions were high. Within three weeks Eisenhower was scheduled to attend a meeting of the heads of state of NATO. His presence had been counted on to rally the Allied forces—particularly the British and French, who had been complaining about the financial burdens of fulfilling their NATO troop commitments. The Soviet Union had just put its first Sputnik in orbit, taking a huge lead in the space race and casting doubts upon the United States' military and scientific establishment. On the home front, the first effects of a coming recession were being felt. And Eisenhower's new legislative program, budget and State of the Union message were coming up shortly.

When the true diagnosis was made public, numerous observers said it was time for him to retire. They feared that his reasoning power might be impaired. They recalled that the President had told a 1956 news conference: "I have said unless I felt absolutely up to performance of the duties of the President, the second I didn't, I would no longer be there in the job or I wouldn't be available for the job." But what if Eisenhower were incapable of knowing he was not "up to the performance of the job"?

A relatively large percentage of the American press joined the individuals calling upon the President to resign. Even the New York *Post*, which Nixon regarded as "the most anti-Nixon of all newspapers," said in an editorial: "The issue is whether the U.S. is to have Richard Nixon as President or no President. We choose Nixon."

Nixon moved to cut off this kind of talk by assuring a press conference that Eisenhower was fully capable of making important decisions and that there was no need for him to delegate any authority. But Nixon again took on some additional responsibilities. He participated in government meetings that would ordinarily have been attended by the President. He performed ceremonial duties. And he temporarily took over to some extent the role of the President as spokesman for the government.

In the immediate aftermath of the President's stroke, it was decided that Nixon should substitute for Eisenhower at the NATO meeting. Messages were sent to the other nations involved, and all agreed to meet with Nixon. As things worked out, Eisenhower made a surprisingly rapid recovery and was able to attend the NATO meeting. But even the formulation of the stopgap plan to send Nixon to the conference added to his personal prestige and that of the vice presidency.

Following his recovery from the stroke, Eisenhower once again tried to get Congress to act on the question of presidential disability. But, again, he got nowhere. He then decided to take steps of his own that did not require congressional approval. He drew up a letter, with the approval of Nixon and other officials, that set out procedures to be followed in case he again became disabled during the remainder of his term. The letter, whose key provisions were made public in March of 1958, said in part:

> The President and the Vice President have agreed that the following procedures are in accord with Article 2, Section 1, of the Constitution, dealing with presidential inability. They believe that these procedures, which are intended to apply to themselves only, are in no sense outside or contrary to the Constitution but are consistent with its present provisions and implement its clear intent.
>
> (1) In the event of inability the President would—if possible—so inform the Vice President, and the Vice President would serve as Acting President, exercising the powers and duties of the office until the inability had ended.
>
> (2) In the event of an inability which would prevent the President from so communicating with the Vice President, the Vice President, after such consultation as seems to him appropriate under the circumstances, would decide upon the devolution of the powers and duties of the office and would serve as Acting President until the inability had ended.
>
> (3) The President, in either event, would determine when the inability had ended and at that time would resume the full exercise of the powers and duties of the office.

This agreement was far from a satisfactory permanent solution to the question of presidential disability. But it was a practical temporary arrangement and set an important precedent on the road toward a permanent answer to the dilemma. In addition, it placed the vice presidency one more rung up the ladder away from obscurity. The terms of Eisenhower's letter were later to be adopted in almost identical language by his two immediate successors in the White House.

Nixon was in the news almost constantly during his second term. Much of the attention was generated by his role as the Vice President with the most extensive record of foreign travel up to that time. And controversy followed him most of the way.

In the spring of 1958 the Vice President and his wife launched a three-week good-will tour of eight Latin American countries. Violence and terrorism interrupted his trip through South America culminating in the incident in Caracas, Venezuela, which nearly resulted in the Vice President's death. Caught by surging mobs, Nixon barely made his way to the American Embassy; he learned later that Communist party members had plotted his assassination. When he returned to Washington, he was given a welcome by 15,000 people, including President Eisenhower.

In July, 1959, Nixon arrived in Moscow to open an American exhibition, part of a cultural exchange program. On meeting Premier Nikita Khrushchev, Nixon was subjected to a belligerent tirade opposing "capitalist aggression." The exchange which followed was known as the "kitchen debate" as it took place in the kitchen of an American model home in the exhibit. The thinly-veiled threats and counterthreats did little credit to either man, but the public skirmish, oddly, resulted in relaxed private talks. Nixon received a warm welcome from the Russian people during his tours and returned to the United States with the air of a conquering hero.

Within four months of his return from the Soviet Union, Nixon again made big news—this time on the domestic front. A one hundred and sixteen day strike had tied up the steel industry and some other segments of the economy before being halted temporarily by a federal-court injunction. The injunction was scheduled to run out on January 26, 1960, and it appeared that the strike would then be resumed. The effects of a prolonged strike on the economy could have been staggering. Eisenhower asked Nixon and Secretary of Labor James P. Mitchell to make discreet, behind-the-scenes efforts to settle the dispute.

Nixon and Mitchell met secretly with officials of the United Steel Workers and representatives of the steel industry. Through the efforts of Nixon and Mitchell a settlement was reached before the expiration of the injunction. Both union and industry leaders contended that Nixon had made a genuine contribution. This was the first steel-industry agreement since World War II that had not been followed by a price increase. United Steel Workers President David McDonald said following the settlement: "Vice President Nixon would make a good President." Though he also named some Democrats who would make good Presidents, this testimonial from a man whose union members traditionally voted Democratic was a solid boost for Nixon's presidential candidacy.

By most standards of probability Nixon should have had little chance to capture the Republican nomination for President in 1960. Not only had no vice president since Martin Van Buren been elected to succeed a living president; none had even been given the presidential nomination of a major party. Still, Nixon coasted to the nomination.

Among Nixon's major assets in his quest of the presidential nomination were: his record as the most effective Vice President in history and the man who had done the most to expand the significance of his office; his role as the Republican Party's most energetic campaigner during the previous eight years; and a shortage of serious competition for the nomination. Among his handicaps were: an initial hesitation by Eisenhower to give him an unqualified endorsement; a lingering fear among some other influential Republicans that he had still not "grown" to presidential caliber; and a feeling in some quarters that he had no real political philosophy, but merely took whatever position seemed most expedient at a given time.

Eisenhower's early doubt about the wisdom of giving Nixon the nomination, however, was the main obstacle to his candidacy. The President was reported by one of his speech writers, Emmet John Hughes, to have told him: "The fact is, of course, I've watched Dick a long time and he just hasn't grown. So I just haven't honestly been able to believe that he is presidential timber." Eisenhower later suggested privately the names of some other Republicans he felt would make better candidates—and Presidents—than Nixon. But no other potential candidate came to the fore. Thus, in the spring of 1960, the President declared he would support Nixon for the nomination. From that point Nixon was home free—although he did have to make some concessions to New York Governor Nelson A. Rockefeller to head off impending dissension at the Republican National Convention.

The convention gave him the nomination by a vote of 1,321 to 10 (the dissenting votes, all from Louisiana, were cast for Arizona Senator Barry Goldwater). Nixon, with the concurrence of party leaders, chose as his running mate Henry Cabot Lodge, the U. S. Ambassador to the Untied Nations, who had formerly served as a Senator from Massachusetts. Lodge was nominated unanimously.

Nixon now stood at the pinnacle of his career. He had beaten half of the jinx that had prevailed since Van Buren's time. But the other half would be more difficult. The closest presidential contest of the century was about to confront him.

CHAPTER FIFTEEN

The New Frontier—and Tragedy

THE DEMOCRATS approached the 1960 election with a seemingly inexhaustible supply of potential presidential candidates.

For openers, there were Senator John F. Kennedy of Massachusetts, a handsome millionaire war hero; Senate Majority Leader Lyndon B. Johnson of Texas, perhaps the most masterly manipulator of congressional power in history; Adlai Stevenson, who had grown in stature despite his two defeats at the hands of Eisenhower; Senator Hubert H. Humphrey of Minnesota, the darling of many of his party's liberals; and Senator Stuart Symington of Missouri, a former Secretary of the Air Force who was the favorite of former President Truman and was viewed as a possible compromise candidate. In the second rank of potential candidates were such dark horses as Michigan Governor G. Mennen (Soapy) Williams, New Jersey Governor Robert Meyner, Senator Estes Kefauver of Tennessee and California Governor Edmund G. (Pat) Brown.

The leading contenders took various routes in quest of the nomination. Kennedy set up the most effective national political organization ever designed to capture a presidential nomination. He had political agents, unswerving in loyalty and unmatched in prowess, functioning in every corner of the nation. Kennedy entered a number of important primaries. His principal opponent in the primaries was Humphrey, who lacked the political organization and funds to compete on an even basis. Johnson elected to stay out of the primaries, projecting the image of the responsible Senate leader who was "minding the store" in Washington while his rivals were advancing their own candidacies elsewhere. He was relying on his numerous congressional allies to swing the nomination to him at the convention. Stevenson and Symington stood in the wings, hoping for lightning to strike in case of a convention deadlock.

Kennedy's showing in the primaries, where he emerged as a winner seven times, made him the front runner for the nomination. In West Virginia he trounced Humphrey so badly that the Minnesota senator withdrew from the race for the nomination. One by one Kennedy overcame his supposed handicaps as a presidential contender. Some critics said he could never get elected because he was a Catholic and everyone knew what had happened to Al Smith in 1928. But Kennedy's primary victories—particularly in West Virginia, where anti-Catholic sentiment was supposed to be especially strong—rebutted these critics. Others said Kennedy was too young. But, at forty-three, he was only four years younger than Nixon, and he had displayed considerable maturity during the primary campaigns. Still others said he was too wealthy. But Johnson, Stevenson and Symington were hardly poor men, nor had a number of previous presidents been poor.

Thus, Kennedy entered the Democratic National Convention at Los Angeles in July with a hand full of aces. He had won the primaries. He had broad delegate support in states where he had not run in the primaries. He had a superb campaign organization. He had good looks, a beautiful wife, money, a Harvard degree, a hero's image and a reputation as an intellectual. (He had been awarded a Pulitzer Prize as author of the book *Profiles in Courage*.)

Lyndon Johnson set out to create a stop-Kennedy movement. He and his cohorts urged Hubert Humphrey to hold onto the delegate support pledged to him before his withdrawal from contention. They implored favorite-son candidates to stay in the race and prevent their delegates from swinging to Kennedy. And they tried to get Adlai Stevenson to be a more vigorous candidate, in the hope that he would draw delegates away from Kennedy.

But, for all his shrewdness, Johnson had one blind spot at the 1960 convention. He depended heavily on help from his congressional cronies in trying to stop Kennedy. And these cronies simply did not have the power. Control of the convention was in the hands of the various state organizations.

On the day before the balloting for the presidential nomination, Johnson was desperate. He challenged the Massachusetts senator to a debate before a joint caucus of the Texas and Massachusetts delegations. Kennedy arrived at the last moment to debate Johnson before hundreds of delegates and a vast television audience.

Johnson's strategy in the debate was to picture himself as a responsible, experienced leader and Kennedy as an immature, lackadaisical follower. He pointed out that he had answered all 50 quorum calls and all 45 roll calls during the Senate's six-day stretch of nonstop debates on the 1960 civil-rights bill. "Some senators" (Kennedy) had missed all the quorum calls and 34 of the roll calls, Johnson said. Kennedy shrugged off the criticism, replying that since Johnson had not said whom he meant by "some senators" he must have been "talking about someone else." He added:

> I want to commend him for . . . a wonderful record answering those quorum calls. . . . I was not present on all those occasions. I was not majority leader . . . So I come here today full of admiration for Senator Johnson, full of affection for him, strongly in support of him—for majority leader.

Following the debate, the consensus was that Kennedy had shown Johnson a thing or two rather than vice versa. He had appeared both competent and mature in handling the sallies of the veteran Texas senator.

Nothing could stop Kennedy now. He won the nomination on the first ballot, receiving 806 delegate votes (45 more than the minimum required for victory) to 409 for Johnson and

306 for all the other candidates combined. He realized he would need a vice-presidential candidate who could help him in areas where his support was weakest—notably in the South and Southwest.

One man who met this requirement, and Kennedy's other criteria for a vice-presidential candidate, was Lyndon Johnson. As a Texan with strong ties to many of the most powerful southern Democrats, he could be expected to help put a number of states below the Mason-Dixon line in the Democratic column. His long experience in Washington would help Kennedy push his programs through Congress if the Democrats won the election. Kennedy had said before the convention that, if he could not be nominated himself, he felt Johnson would be the best qualified nominee the Democrats could offer.

But would Johnson accept the vice-presidential nomination? The consensus in the Kennedy camp was that he would not. It was assumed Johnson felt he could exert greater influence as Majority Leader than as Vice President. He was a proud man who would probably cringe at the thought of running as number-two man on a ticket headed by a candidate ranked well below him on the Senate scale of prestige and power. Johnson's bitter attacks on Kennedy during the prenomination maneuvering might make it embarrassing for him to run with the Massachusetts senator. Finally, it was felt that acceptance of the vice-presidential nomination—in the event the Democrats lost the election—might damage any hopes he had of receiving the presidential nomination four years later.

Nonetheless, Kennedy decided that he should at least offer Johnson the vice-presidential nomination. Even if Johnson, as expected, refused to accept, the presidential nominee felt the offer would help his candidacy. It would restore friendly relations with one of the nation's most powerful Democrats, help unify the party, and improve Kennedy's prospects of carrying the South.

On the morning following his nomination Kennedy asked

his brother Robert, who was serving as campaign manager, to get someone to total up the electoral votes of the Northern industrial states plus Texas and any other Southern states that Johnson might help carry. Robert Kennedy assigned the job to two key campaign aides, Ken O'Donnell and Pierre Salinger. O'Donnell and Salinger were astonished. They had never dreamed that Kennedy would offer the vice-presidential nomination to Johnson. But when they finished their arithmetic they were equally surprised to discover that the electoral votes of the states involved could guarantee victory.

Meanwhile, Senator Kennedy phoned Johnson's hotel suite, two flights beneath his own, and asked if he could come down. Johnson offered to come upstairs, but Kennedy courteously insisted on being the one to pay the call. Johnson immediately concluded that he would be offered the second spot on the ticket.

The majority leader made a series of hurried telephone calls to long-time friends and confidants. What should he do if the vice-presidential nomination were offered? Typical of the responses he received was the initial advice from his close friend, Congressman Homer Thornberry of Texas. "Lyndon, I wouldn't touch it with a ten-foot pole," Thornberry said.

"But what will I tell Jack [Kennedy]?" Johnson asked.

"You know what to tell him better than I do, Lyndon. Tell him anything you want, but don't take it."

A few minutes later, Thornberry called Johnson back. "Lyndon, I've been thinking this over. I was wrong. You ought to take the vice presidency."

There was a long pause on Johnson's end of the line. Then he asked: "But, Homer, what'll I tell Sam?"

Sam was the legendary "Mr. Sam" Rayburn of Texas, Speaker of the House and Johnson's long-time mentor. The previous night he had tried to extract from Johnson a promise that he would not accept the vice presidency under any circumstances. Johnson had said the question was moot, since he had not been offered the nomination. But he had promised that, if an offer were made, he would check with Rayburn before accepting.

Now Johnson called Rayburn. The House Speaker reiterated his advice of the previous night. "You musn't do it." Rayburn said. "It would be a terrible thing to do."

At 10:05 A.M. Kennedy arrived at the Johnson suite. He said that many of the party's most prominent leaders thought Johnson should be on the ticket. They were concerned about the fact that in winning the nomination Kennedy had received only nine and a half delegate votes from the Southern states.

Johnson said that many of his friends were advising him not to take the vice-presidential spot if it were offered. Various other men expected to be offered the nomination and he did not want to stand in their way.

Kennedy said he had often expressed the view that Johnson was the best qualified man for the Presidency by virtue of his experience, but that he could not be nominated because he was a southerner. The presidential nominee said he felt that Johnson should be the one to succeed him if "anything happens to me."

Johnson asked for some time to think the matter over. Kennedy told him he would telephone him in a few hours. Kennedy returned to his own suite and told aides: "You just won't believe it. . . . He wants it!"

Now, whether he actually wanted Johnson on the ticket or had merely suggested the nomination as a conciliatory gesture, Kennedy had little choice but to proceed at least temporarily on the basis that he sincerely felt the Texan should be his running mate. To do otherwise would be to run the risk of bringing about an irreparable party split. He went to Speaker Rayburn, told him he wanted the party united behind the ticket and planned to give his Vice President significant assignments. He asked Rayburn to advise Johnson to accept the nomination. Other friends of both Kennedy and Johnson urged Rayburn to comply with Kennedy's request. They said that, without Johnson on the ticket, Kennedy would lose the election. That clinched the argument.

Rayburn went to Johnson's suite and advised him to take the nomination. "I'm a lot smarter man this morning than I was last night," he said.

But then the whole arrangement started coming apart at the seams. Kennedy knew that the choice of Johnson—a Southerner allied with the Texas oil interests and with various conservative members of Congress—would not sit well with the liberal wing of the party. But the degree of the liberals' outrage surprised even Kennedy. He was faced with the possibility of a revolt and an ugly fight on the convention floor over the vice-presidential nomination.

Kennedy sent his brother to the Texan's suite to try to get a reading on the attitude there. Robert Kennedy (called Bobby by his brother and others, but Bob by his subordinates) was ushered into a bedroom of the Johnson suite to talk with Sam Rayburn.

At this point a new character emerged as an important figure in the behind-the-scenes drama. He was Philip Graham, publisher of the Washington *Post* and *Newsweek* magazine. Graham was in a singular position. He was a close friend of both John Kennedy and Lyndon Johnson. Probably more than any other person attending the convention he was able—by virtue of their mutual trust in him—to bridge the gap between the two men.

Shortly after Robert Kennedy entered the Johnson suite, Graham arrived. Johnson immediately grabbed Graham's arm, pulled him into a bedroom and told him Kennedy was in the other room with Rayburn. He said he was certain that Bob Kennedy was offering the vice-presidential nomination to him and that a decision had to be made on whether to accept. Johnson's wife, Lady Bird, was also in the room. Johnson asked both his wife and Graham for advice. Graham, after first trying to evade answering, finally said he thought Johnson "had to take" the nomination. He later described Mrs. Johnson's attitude on the nomination at this point as "somewhere between negative and neutral."

Johnson, his wife and Graham were interrupted by Rayburn, who said that Robert Kennedy wanted to speak directly with the Texas senator. "No," Graham told Johnson. "You shouldn't see him. . . . Your position should be that you don't want it (the nomination), you won't negotiate for it, you'll only take it if Jack drafts you and you won't discuss it with anyone else." It was decided that Rayburn would pass this position on to Robert Kennedy and that Graham would pass it on to Senator Kennedy.

Graham got John Kennedy on the phone and explained Johnson's attitude. The presidential nominee said he was "in a general mess" because of liberal opposition to Johnson. Kennedy said he was in the midst of a meeting in which he was being urged to choose Senator Symington as his running mate. He asked Graham to call him back for a final decision "in three minutes."

Graham actually waited about ten minutes before calling Kennedy. In the meantime, Kennedy had concluded that the liberal revolt probably could be kept within reasonable bounds. "It's all set," he told Graham. "Tell Lyndon I want him and will have [Pennsylvania Governor David] Lawrence nominate him."

Graham relayed this message to Johnson. But the matter was still not settled. Considerable grumbling continued on various fronts—both among the die-hard liberals and members of the Kennedy and Johnson camps. Some of Kennedy's advisers were continuing to argue against Johnson's nomination. Perhaps Kennedy had underestimated the depth of the liberal feeling, they said. Perhaps there would be a floor fight, after all. Meanwhile, some of Johnson's friends were continuing to argue that he should not accept.

Robert Kennedy went back to the Johnson suite, this time succeeded in seeing the Senator and explained that his brother would understand if Johnson did not want to go through the unpleasantness of a possible floor fight. In case he decided to withdraw, Robert Kennedy said, his brother would like to name Johnson as Democratic national chairman. Johnson was stunned. Just a few minutes ago he had been told the nomination was all arranged. Now the candidate's brother seemed to be telling him otherwise.

"I want to be Vice President and, if the candidate will have me, I'll join with him in making a fight for it," Johnson said emotionally.

Kennedy replied: "He wants you to be Vice President if you want to be Vice President."

Kennedy then walked out of the room, leaving a concerned and angry Lyndon Johnson behind. Johnson ordered an aide to find Phil Graham and bring him to the room immediately. The senator loudly recounted the substance of the conversation. A half-dozen Johnson friends, including Sam Rayburn, were in the room. Rayburn said: "Phil, call Jack."

It took a few minutes to get a call through to Kennedy. Finally, Graham had the presidential nominee on the line.

"Jack, Bobby is down here and is telling the speaker and Lyndon that there is opposition and that Lyndon should withdraw," Graham said.

"Oh," Kennedy said calmly. "That's all right. Bobby's been out of touch and doesn't know what's been happening."

"Well, what do you want Lyndon to do?"

"I want him to make a statement right away; I've just finished making mine (announcing his choice of Johnson)."

"You'd better speak to Lyndon," Graham said, handing the telephone to Johnson. The majority leader spoke briefly to Kennedy. "Yes," he said. "Yes . . . yes . . . yes. . . . Okay."

It was settled at last. Lyndon Johnson would be the vice-presidential nominee.

Robert Kennedy was called back into the Johnson bedroom to get the message from his brother. He took the telephone, listened a moment and apparently did not like what he heard.

"Well, it's too late now," he said. He then put the receiver back on the hook with what Graham described as a "half slam."

Whether Robert Kennedy was upset by the final choice of Johnson or by the apparent crossing of signals between himself and his brother was one of several mysteries surrounding the events of this hectic period. Among the others were: Had Senator Kennedy really wanted Johnson on the ticket or had he just found himself too deeply committed to snatch the nomination away from the Texan? And had Robert Kennedy been acting on his own, or with his brother's approval, in suggesting that Johnson consider withdrawing?

But one thing is certain: The circumstances leading to the selection of the vice-presidential nominee had caused strained relations between Lyndon Johnson and the Kennedy brothers, particularly Robert.

The differences between Johnson and the Kennedys were set aside temporarily in the interest of a harmonious campaign. Johnson went to Kennedy's hotel suite, where he assured the nominee that he would become a full member of the Kennedy team and would work his heart out in the campaign.

Senator Kennedy, in announcing his decision before a battery of television cameras, warmly praised Johnson:

> I have said many times that, in these days of great challenge, Americans must have a Vice President capable of dealing with the grave problems confronting this nation and the free world. We need men of strength if we are to be strong and if we are to prevail and lead the world on the road to freedom. Lyndon Johnson has demonstrated on many occasions his brilliant qualifications for the leadership we require today.

Johnson watched Kennedy on television, then appeared before the cameras and read a statement of his own. He made clear his desire to be the running mate and his determination to wage a vigorous campaign.

That night, when the convention delegates met to vote on

the nomination, some liberals were still determined to put up a fight against Johnson. Governor Lawrence placed Johnson's name before the convention. Then House Majority Leader John W. McCormack, at Kennedy's request, made a move that caught the liberals by surprise. On behalf of the Massachusetts delegation, McCormack moved to close the nominations and take a voice vote on the nomination of Johnson. Florida Governor LeRoy Collins, the convention chairman, put the matter to a vote. The liberals shouted "no," but Collins ruled the the "ayes" had it. "Senator Lyndon B. Johnson has been nominated for the vice presidency of the United States by acclamation," Collins announced amid a chorus of boos from the liberals.

Kennedy's campaign strategy called for carrying the East, more than half of the South and at least two or three Midwest states. Johnson's main assignment was to drum up support in the South and to carry Texas.

This assignment was no easy one. Sentiment in many sections of the South was strongly against Kennedy. Despite the fact that Johnson was Texas' most prominent political figure, the state would hardly be a pushover for the Democrats. President Eisenhower had carried Texas in both 1952 and 1956. The state was a hotbed of extreme right-wing political activity.

Johnson campaigned vigorously and effectively across forty states in the North and South, but his main emphasis was on Texas and other southern states. Of the four national candidates—Kennedy, Nixon, Lodge and himself—he was the only one who had southern roots and talked the language of the southern courthouse square. He capitalized on his knowledge of southern politics and folklore, stumping both the major cities and the back country. He was welcomed by hundreds of thousands of southerners as one of their own. Nixon stumped in some of the South's major cities—but mainly skipped the smaller towns—and his campaign never seemed to take hold in most areas below the Mason-Dixon line.

Kennedy hammered constantly at the theme that the nation had been drifting aimlessly during the Eisenhower-Nixon years and that it was "time to get this country moving again." Nixon, on the defensive, ran chiefly on the Eisenhower record. He pitched his campaign on the "experience" theme. He was the man who had "stood up to Khrushchev," he said. He had been at Eisenhower's side. He had participated in making the major administration decisions. But a series of televised debates between the presidential candidates all but nullified the "experience" issue. The debates gave Kennedy exposure to millions of voters who previously had known much more about Nixon than about him. The concensus of experts was that Kennedy appeared more poised, perhaps even more knowledgeable than Nixon during the debates. He looked youthful, it was true, but not immature. And he appealed to the younger generation of voters.

When the ballots were counted, Kennedy and Johnson had won by the narrowest of margins—fewer than 120,000 popular votes out of almost 69,000,000 votes cast. Their electoral-vote margin was wider, 303 to 210.

The contribution of Lyndon Johnson to Kennedy's election cannot be emphasized too much. Kennedy's speech writer and biographer, Theodore C. Sorensen, wrote that Johnson "helped salvage several Southern states the Republicans had counted on capturing . . . and, had it not been for the return of Texas and Louisiana to the Democratic column from their 1956 Republican sojourn, and for the Carolinas' staying Democratic against a predicted Republican victory, Nixon would have won the election."

It was true that Johnson exercised less power during his years in the Kennedy administration than during those immediately before and after his assumption of the vice presidency. However, he continued the trend of expanding the scope of the nation's second highest office. During his years as Senate Majority Leader he had been regarded as a regional politician

—either as a Texan, a southerner or a southwesterner. Now he became, in fact as well as name, the Vice President of all the people.

"I am going to try to be the kind of Vice President that I would want if I were President," he said. And he fulfilled that promise. Kennedy recognized the difficulties Johnson was bound to encounter in growing accustomed to a subordinate's role. "Lyndon's job is the hardest one he could ever have," the President said. "And he is performing it like a man, m-a-n."

Kennedy, recognizing his Vice President's talent and energy, gave him a number of important executive assignments. He handed Johnson the job Vice President Nixon had previously held as chairman of the committee responsible for eliminating racial discrimination among government contractors. Since Johnson was from one of the states of the old Confederacy, his effective work in this position—as well as his general support of civil-rights programs—seemed all the more conspicuous. He played an important part in helping draft what was to become the highly significant Civil Rights Act of 1964. After racial demonstrations in the South had erupted into violence in 1963, the Vice President made one of his most eloquent speeches in a Memorial Day appearance at the Civil War battlefield in Gettysburg, Pennsylvania.

Referring to the aspirations of the demonstrators and the resistance of some white citizens to Negroes' demands for equal opportunities, Johnson declared: "The Negro says, 'Now.' Others say, 'Never.' The voice of responsible Americans—the voice of those who died here and the great man who spoke here—their voices say, 'Together.' There is no other way. Until Justice is blind to color, until education is unaware of race, until opportunity is unconcerned with the color of men's skins, emancipation will be a proclamation but not a fact. To the extent that the proclamation of emancipation is not fulfilled in fact, to that extent we shall have fallen short of assuring freedom to the free."

Among other executive positions to which Johnson was

named were the chairmanships of both the Aeronautics and Space Council and the Peace Corps National Advisory Council. The Space Council post, in particular, gave the Vice President a chance to demonstrate his executive capacity. Kennedy asked Johnson to prepare recommendations on the proper role of the United States in space exploration. Johnson, in turn, asked three leading corporation executives to help him draw up these recommendations. The executives made a thorough study of American space efforts and urged a great increase in appropriations. Johnson approved of their recommendations and passed them along to Kennedy. Largely on the basis of the recommendations, the President made a key decision in 1961 to try to put Americans on the moon "in this decade."

The Vice President continued to play an important supervisory role in the space program. In presiding over meetings of the Space Council, Johnson got a rare opportunity to demonstrate the kind of firm leadership he had exercised as Majority Leader. He made clear that the space program was his "baby" and poured more effort and enthusiasm into it than virtually any other vice-presidential assignment.

The triumphs of the American space program were also, to some extent, Johnson triumphs. But his part in the program led to friction between the Vice President and President Kennedy. The President clearly intended for Johnson to play a major role in the space field, but both he and some of his aides came to feel at times that the Vice President was grasping for too much of the program's power and glory.

On February 20, 1962, when astronaut John Glenn became the first American to orbit the earth, Johnson asked Kennedy's permission to fly to an island in the Carribbean and welcome Glenn upon his return to earth. Kennedy refused the request. Nine days later, when Glenn was due to be accorded the traditional hero's welcome with a ticker-tape parade in New York, Johnson told the President he wanted to be there. Again Kennedy refused. He felt that Glenn should be permitted to bask in the limelight alone. But the Vice President insisted.

Ultimately, Kennedy gave Johnson his way. Thus it was that John Glenn and Lyndon Johnson rode triumphantly up Broadway together in an open limousine.

These incidents helped to stir up the old antagonisms between members of the Johnson and Kennedy camps. Some reports of feuding between the two camps have been exaggerated. Often the backbiting and jealousy were more rampant among aides of Kennedy and Johnson than they were between the two men themselves. But it cannot be denied that there were periodic strains between the President and Vice President and, to a greater extent, between Johnson and Robert Kennedy. The President's brother had been appointed Attorney General. In addition, he served as a general trouble-shooter for the President on problems throughout the administration.

Neither Johnson nor Robert Kennedy ever really forgave the other for the hard feelings generated during the months and days leading up to selection of the 1960 presidential and vice-presidential candidates. Thus, when the two men's paths crossed during Kennedy's presidency, it was not surprising that sparks sometimes flew.

There were frequent arguments between the two men over the pace of the progress being made by Johnson's committee on equal employment opportunity. Robert Kennedy was the administration's overseer of all anti-discrimination programs during this critical period of the civil-rights revolution. Johnson used his renowned powers of persuasion—plus the threat of cancellation of government contracts—to get numerous corporations to sign agreements striking down racial barriers in hiring, promotion and use of plant facilities. Nonetheless, Robert Kennedy complained that the pace was too slow. He wanted more action, and he showed little tact in demanding it from Johnson. The Vice President was in the position of taking orders from the Attorney General. He did not like it, and he never forgot it.

It would be unwise to overstate the friction between Johnson and the Kennedy brothers. By and large their attitude—in public and private—was one of mutual respect and cooperation. They came from two seemingly different worlds—the Kennedys from wealthy Massachusetts stock and Johnson from humble early surroundings not too far removed from a frontier environment. (The Vice President's grandmother had once hidden in a flour barrel to escape marauding Indians.) They had different styles and different friends and different interests. But they recognized that each of them needed the other in order to reach common goals.

"If there's only one man left the President can trust, I want that man to be me," Johnson said. And President Kennedy told intimates: "Lyndon has been the most active Vice President in history. He's been in on all major decisions."

Johnson participated in the decision-making process at both the low point and the high point of the Kennedy administration. The low point was the decision to send a force of guerrilla fighters on the ill-fated mission to attack Communist Cuba in 1961. The mission ended in a fiasco at the Bay of Pigs. The high point was the decision to throw a naval blockade around Cuba in 1962 after it was discovered that Russian-built offensive missiles were in place on the island 90 miles off the Florida coast.

Johnson was a member of the special executive committee of the National Security Council (nicknamed EX-COMM) created by Kennedy to aid him during the missile crisis. This was one of the most critical periods in recent American history. There was no way of being sure that nuclear war might not erupt at any moment between the United States and the Soviet Union over the threat posed by the missiles in Cuba. On the night before the naval blockade was to begin, it was Johnson who served as EX-COMM's watch officer. While Kennedy and other members of EX-COMM slept, it was the Vice President who sat up all night with intelligence officers—going over top-secret reports and looking for danger signals. Obviously, Johnson would not have ordered any decisive action on his own authority. If quick action had been required, he would have awakened the President. But the fact that Johnson was the man assigned to serve as sentinel on this crucial night in our history was further evidence of both the heightened responsibility of the vice presidency and Kennedy's faith in his Vice President.

This faith was also demonstrated by Kennedy in his extensive use of Johnson as an emissary to foreign lands. What was most important about Johnson's foreign assignments was that, for the first time in American history, a Vice President was given actual bargaining power in his dealings with leaders of other nations. Kennedy gave him authority to negotiate on behalf of the government and make binding decisions, within specified limits. On a trip to South Vietnam, for instance, Johnson urged President Ngo Dinh Diem to build up his armed forces and institute social reforms. As expected, Diem complained that his people would not accept the taxes necessary to comply with Johnson's requests. The Vice President then made a concrete offer of increased American aid, which Diem accepted.

Johnson made eleven separate tours outside the United States during his vice presidency—more than any of his predecessors, even the well-traveled Richard Nixon. His first journey was to Senegal for the first anniversary of the African nation's independence. The visit called for fraternal elbow-rubbing with the country's black natives and gestures of respect for the equally black officials of other African nations. Knowing full well that news photographs showing him mingling with the African masses would not be welcomed by race-conscious white citizens in the American South, Johnson nonetheless spread so much good will in Senegal that one observer said he made the Russian envoys to the anniversary ceremonies look "like delegates from a White Citizens Council."

Next, Johnson toured Asia, visiting South Vietnam, India, Pakistan, the Philippines, Hong Kong, Formosa and Thailand. This tour was undertaken in the immediate aftermath of the

Bay of Pigs fiasco. His mission was to try to restore American prestige, to assure weak nations that the United States would stand with them against the Communists and to pledge U. S. aid in the battle against poverty, ignorance and disease. On this trip—as on virtually all those he made as Vice President —Johnson barnstormed as though he were campaigning for office back home. He kissed babies, hugged ragged natives and shook thousands of hands.

Such behavior delighted most of the foreign citizens he encountered and brought him great publicity at home, but it disturbed some officials of the State Department. They complained that the Vice President's folksiness was not in keeping with the niceties of diplomatic protocol. Johnson ridiculed such talk as the product of "stuffed-shirt" minds.

The most celebrated episode related to Johnson's foreign travels concerned a Pakistani camel driver named Bashir Ahmed. When the Vice President arrived in Pakistan's capital city, Karachi, his motorcade was surrounded by cheering throngs. He ordered his limousine stopped at several points along the route so he could wade into the crowds and shake hands with the citizens. At one point he came upon a small, poorly dressed man waiting to cross a street with a sack of straw. This man was Bashir Ahmed. Johnson shook Ahmed's hand and told him through an interpreter that it would be nice if the little camel driver could visit him in Texas someday. The Vice President promptly forgot the incident. But not Ahmed.

Shortly after his return to the United States Johnson learned—to his surprise—that his invitation had been accepted. Ahmed was coming to the United States and expected to be the Vice President's guest. The affair might have made Johnson look exceedingly foolish. But as things turned out, he reaped a publicity bonanza, and United States prestige in Pakistan received a needed shot in the arm. Ahmed proved to be a delightful guest in both Washington and Texas. His rapture at the wonders of American civilization bordered on the poetic.

When Johnson took him to his Texas ranch—and permitted him to sleep in a bed once occupied by Pakistani President Ayub Khan—the Cinderella story reached its zenith. Ahmed went home, loaded with gifts, and left in his wake a new appreciation in the United States of the unorthodox but effective diplomatic techniques of the Vice President.

Most of Johnson's trips abroad were extraordinarily well planned. At his own request he received written instructions from the President. Johnson was carefully briefed by State Department officials for weeks in advance of his scheduled departures. But his most spectacular foreign mission was undertaken on extremely short notice, without any advance preparation.

One night in August 1961 Johnson was visiting at the home of Speaker Sam Rayburn. They were interrupted by a telephone call from the White House. "Lyndon," the President asked, "are you available to go to Berlin?"

There was not a more explosive place in the world that night than Berlin. The Communists had just built a wall through the middle of the divided city—separating the Communist sector from the sectors defended by the western Allies. West Berliners regarded the failure of the Allies to prevent construction of the wall as an indication of weakness, perhaps even as the forerunner of abandonment of the entire city to the Communists. The United States was committed to protect West Berlin. This new move by the Communists, cutting off the free movement of Berliners between the eastern and western sectors, put the East and West once again dangerously close to war.

President Kennedy felt it was essential to send an emissary of the highest possible rank to Berlin to reassure the citizenry that the United States would keep its promises of protection and to serve notice to the Communists that the U. S. would not yield further ground. The obvious emissary was the Vice President. Twenty-six hours after receiving the call at Rayburn's home, he was winging toward Berlin.

On arrival in Germany, Johnson told cheering crowds that he had come "to express a conviction, to convey a pledge, to sound a warning and to reiterate a policy." In a speech before a special session of the West Berlin Parliament, he quoted from the Declaration of Independence and pledged "our lives, our fortunes and our sacred honor" to the defense of West Berlin. American troops were ordered to travel across Communist East Germany to reinforce the contingent already stationed in West Berlin. Despite Communist threats to block the American soldiers from crossing East Germany—an act that might have touched off nuclear warfare—the reinforcements rolled into Berlin on August 20. The Vice President, in a scene of high drama, greeted the first arrival. West Berliners, 300,000 strong, later cheered outside his window until he made an appearance.

The Berlin assignment put Johnson's prestige as Vice President at an all-time high. Newspapers around the world carried huge headlines quoting his words to the Berliners: "We will never abandon you." He was denounced by name over Radio Moscow and Radio Peking.

Nonetheless, over the next two years, there were persistent reports that Kennedy planned to dump Johnson from the ticket when he made his expected bid for reelection to the Presidency in 1964. Kennedy denied all such reports, repeatedly expressing his admiration for Johnson. "Anybody in this administration who thinks he will promote himself with me by biting at Lyndon Johnson has a very large hole in his head," the President said.

Kennedy and Johnson were already looking ahead to the 1964 election when they traveled to Texas in November of 1963. The state's electoral votes loomed large in their 1964 plans. A feud within the state's Democratic organization threatened to upset those plans. Kennedy, at Johnson's urging, agreed to make a two-day visit to Texas to try to heal the wounds within the party, raise campaign funds and boost the administration's stock with the voters.

What happened during that trip is so well known as to require no detailed description here. Suffice it to say that the assassin's bullets which snuffed out the life of John Fitzgerald Kennedy had a dual effect on Lyndon Baines Johnson. They filled him with the grief that engulfed the entire nation and, indeed, virtually all of the world—a grief that was particularly strong in Johnson because the tragedy had occurred in his native state. At the same time, no matter how he wished the circumstances had been different, those bullets placed him at the pinnacle of power that he had so long desired.

Johnson became the nation's eighth "accidental" President. He was the only one to inherit from his predecessor an extensive program of unfinished legislative business. For John F. Kennedy—for all his magnetism, intelligence and ability— had been unable to push a number of his so-called New Frontier programs through Congress.

Now, Johnson proposed to pass Kennedy's legislative program as a memorial to the martyred President. In the most important speech of his life, before a joint session of Congress five days after the assassination, he recalled Kennedy's eloquent inaugural address. Kennedy had said that all his hopes for the nation could not be fulfilled "in the first 100 days . . . nor in the first 1,000 days, nor in the life of this administration, nor even perhaps in our lifetime on this planet." But, he had implored, "Let us begin." Johnson now told the Congress and the nation: "Today, in this moment of new resolve, I would say to all my fellow Americans, 'Let us continue.'"

In this spirit, with the cooperation of a grieving Congress, Johnson proceeded to achieve passage of most of the previously stymied Kennedy legislation. And he added some important legislation of his own. When it was needed he exerted the type of political pressure for which he had been noted in his days as Senate Majority Leader.

The Civil Rights Bill of 1964, whose passage Johnson urged as the "most eloquent honor . . . [possible] to President Kennedy's memory," was enacted. A tax-reduction bill was passed. So was the Urban Transportation Act. So was a broad program of anti-poverty legislation. Most of the Kennedy legislative program, which probably would have faced continued rough going if he had lived, sailed through the Congress following his death.

For more than a year the nation was without a vice president. Next in line for the Presidency behind President Johnson was House Speaker John W. McCormack, seventy-one years of age, who had been elected Speaker following Rayburn's death. And behind McCormack was an even older man, Senate President Pro Tem Carl Hayden of Arizona, eighty-six.

Johnson recognized the necessity for an orderly arrangement assuring continuity of government in case he should become seriously ill or die. He had suffered a near-fatal heart attack in 1955. The time was not far off when Congress would finally act to solve the disability and succession problems. But this time had not yet arrived. As an interim step, Johnson continued the policy—established by President Eisenhower and perpetuated by Kennedy—of making arrangement for an acting president to serve in case the president became seriously disabled. In this case, in the absence of a vice president, it was Speaker McCormack who was designated to be Acting President if the necessity arose.

The unexpired term inherited by Johnson from Kennedy was only fourteen months long. It was a foregone conclusion that Johnson would seek at least one, and possibly two, presidential terms of his own. Even while carrying out Kennedy's legislative program, Johnson made it apparent that he intended to leave his own mark on the Presidency. He let it be known that he wanted, more than anything else, to be remembered as a great President.

To do so, of course, he would have to win the 1964 presidential election. And one of the most important decisions confronting him was the choice of a running mate. Johnson wanted not only to win the election; he wanted to win by such a landslide that it would be absolutely clear he had a mandate from the people for a Presidency of his own design. To win big he needed a running mate who would add strength to the ticket—or, at the very least, would not cost the ticket a substantial number of votes. Beyond that, he wanted someone who would fit the description of an ideal vice president that Johnson himself had given while serving under Kennedy. That is, if he had only one man left in his administration whom he could completely trust, he wanted that man to be his vice president.

Johnson would say of his search for a vice-presidential candidate that "In all my life I have never taken any decision more seriously." His search was to be the most intensive and costly ever conducted for a running mate.

CHAPTER SIXTEEN

The Great Society and the Future

FROM the standpoint of vote-pulling power, Lyndon Johnson's most effective running mate in the 1964 election probably would have been Robert F. Kennedy. The younger brother of the slain President, although opposed by many voters in the South because of his activity on behalf of the civil-rights movement, enjoyed broad support in almost every other section of the country. Moreover, his name on the ticket would have enabled Johnson to capitalize on the outpouring of idolatry and sympathy for the Kennedy family that had followed the assassination.

But Johnson did not want Robert Kennedy as his vice-presidential candidate. Although he had kept Kennedy in his Cabinet as Attorney General, Johnson had never forgotten nor forgiven the past humiliations inflicted upon him by the late President's brother. The two men worked cooperatively following the assassination, but their personal relationship remained distant. Thus Kennedy could not fit Johnson's description of an ideal running mate. And he had an even bigger strike against him. Johnson wanted to win the Presidency in his own right. How could he do that if he won the election only by resorting to use of the Kennedy name on the ticket?

The matter that came to be known in the White House as The Bobby Problem was a perplexing one. Johnson had to find some way to keep Bobby Kennedy off the ticket without incurring the wrath of the voters and/or influential members of the Democratic hierarchy. Kennedy wanted the vice-presidential nomination, but he knew that the decision rested with Johnson. When supporters in various states launched efforts to draft him as the running mate, Kennedy could offer them no public encouragement. When some of his backers organized a write-in campaign for him in the New Hampshire primary, he felt compelled to ask them privately to proceed with caution. It appeared at one point that Kennedy might receive more primary votes for Vice President in New Hampshire than Johnson would for President. That would never do, Kennedy realized, so he managed to trail the President in the primary while picking up a substantial write-in vote.

Throughout the spring and early summer of 1964, speculation about Johnson's running mate was a favorite topic in the press. Among those mentioned as possibilities were Kennedy, Adlai Stevenson, Defense Secretary Robert McNamara, Senators Hubert H. Humphrey and Eugene McCarthy (both of Minnesota), Peace Corps Director Sargent Shriver (Kennedy's brother-in-law), California Governor Edmond G. (Pat) Brown and New York Mayor Robert F. Wagner.

During this period the President ordered countless polls, costing many thousands of dollars, to assess the vote-pulling ability of various hopefuls. He talked endlessly to political figures in all parts of the country. But by late July, with the Democratic National Convention less than a month away, he had still not made a decision.

It was decided that two motion pictures would be shown to the delegates at the convention—one telling the life story of Lyndon Johnson and the other serving as a memorial tribute to John Kennedy. Johnson became extremely wary about the Kennedy film, fearing that it would stir up a wave of pro-Kennedy emotionalism that might sweep Robert Kennedy into the vice-presidential nomination. Consequently, the President ordered that no pictures of Robert Kennedy be included in the film and that the Kennedy film be shown after the balloting for a vice-presidential candidate.

Reports reached Johnson that Mrs. Jacqueline Kennedy,

widow of the slain President, might go before the convention to plead personally for the nomination of her brother-in-law for Vice President. The President decided it was time to act.

On July 27 the President telephoned Robert Kennedy and arranged for the Attorney General to meet with him at the White House on July 29. When Kennedy entered the President's office for the meeting, Johnson came right to the point. He said Kennedy probably would and should be President someday but that he had decided not to put him on the ticket in 1964. He offered Kennedy any Cabinet post he wanted, if and when incumbent Cabinet members resigned, or any foreign diplomatic position he desired.

Kennedy took the news calmly. He said he would support Johnson for the Presidency and offered his help in the campaign. The President asked him to serve as campaign manager, as he had done for his brother in 1960. But Kennedy said he did not want to resign yet as Attorney General—which he would have to do to become campaign manager. The meeting ended with Kennedy saying, as he walked out of the office, "I could have helped you, Mr. President."

Now only the press and the public had to be informed of the decision. Johnson waited a full day, hoping that Kennedy would announce his own withdrawal from contention. When that did not happen the President made his own announcement.

To announce baldly that the Attorney General alone had been ruled out as a running mate would have caused Johnson more trouble than necessary among Kennedy supporters. Instead, the President went before television cameras on the evening of July 30 and read a statement without precedent in American political history.

> With reference to the selection of the candidate for Vice President on the Democratic ticket, I have reached the conclusion that it would be inadvisable for me to recommend to the convention any member of my Cabinet or any of those who meet regularly with the Cabinet.

Johnson had thus ruled out of contention the entire Cabinet and two other potential vice-presidential candidates, Adlai Stevenson and Sargent Shriver. (Stevenson, who had been named Ambassador to the United Nations by President Kennedy and retained in that post by Johnson, met regularly with the Cabinet, as did Shriver.) The President claimed his reason for making this decision was that all these men were so indispensable in their current positions that he didn't want any of them moved to the Vice President's office. But the Attorney General himself quipped: "I'm sorry I took so many nice fellows over the side with me."

Adlai Stevenson picked up a telephone, called an old friend in Washington and said in a congratulatory tone: "Hubert, it's you."

Stevenson was only guessing that Senator Hubert Humphrey would be the eventual running mate. Humphrey, for his part, could hardly believe his ears when told what the President had said in his television appearance. A reporter had phoned with the news just before Stevenson's call. He told an aide that the reporter on the phone must be suffering from hallucinations. Then, when Stevenson called and said, "Hubert, it's you," Humphrey had trouble believing that as well.

True the President had given him some hints that he might ultimately become the vice-presidential nominee. Now the Stevenson call gave him a foretaste of what was to come. In the immediate aftermath of the President's telecast Humphrey was to become the focus of much of the speculation regarding the vice-presidential nomination. He avoided letting his hopes rise too high for he had been disappointed in the past.

A native of South Dakota who had moved to Minnesota, Hubert Horatio Humphrey had been a pharmacist and college teacher before entering politics. He came from a poor family and was a chief spokesman for the Midwest Populist position, a position that represented the interests of the poor working people, the small businessmen and the farmers.

After serving as the "boy wonder" Mayor of Minneapolis, Humphrey was elected to the Senate in 1948. Among his fellow freshman senators was Lyndon Johnson. Though they differed on a number of issues, on such questions as civil-rights legislation, the two became relatively close friends.

Humphrey soon became known around Washington as a sort of perpetual-motion machine. He was forever doing something, demanding something or just plain saying something. Much of the time he was saying something. He was considered the Capitol's champion free-style orator. It was said that he could deliver a two-hour speech on any subject known to man, with no advance preparation. Given a little encouragement, he could stretch it to three or four hours. But this is not to say he was in any sense regarded as a buffoon. He was a serious student of government, an eloquent pleader of unpopular causes and one of the hardest-working men in Washington.

It was Humphrey, even before he entered the Senate, who was considered chiefly responsible for the Dixiecrat rebellion at the 1948 Democratic National Convention. Humphrey forced adoption by the convention of a strong civil-rights plank in the party platform. The plank was repugnant to many Southerners. It was largely over this issue that the Dixiecrats bolted the Democratic Party and ran their own presidential candidate against President Truman. Because of this plank, Humphrey is credited with winning the Negro vote from that time on for the Democrats.

In the Senate, Humphrey became both a popular and an influential member. He grew to be the favorite national figure of many members of the Democratic Party's liberal wing. In 1956 he hoped to be chosen by Adlai Stevenson as the vice-presidential candidate but lost out to Senator Kefauver. In 1960 Humphrey made his valiant effort to challenge John Kennedy in the presidential primaries. Again he lost.

But he continued to add to his prestige through his work in the Senate, his tireless campaigning on behalf of Democratic candidates throughout the country and his other efforts. He reaped tremendous publicity by participating in an eight-hour discussion of international issues with Premier Khrushchev. He served ably on the Senate Foreign Relations Committee and as a United States delegate to the United Nations General Assembly. By 1964 he had risen to Democratic whip (assistant majority leader) of the Senate. He had been floor manager of the 1964 Civil Rights Act and had played a key role in achieving Senate passage of the partial nuclear test-ban treaty in 1963.

With this record Humphrey dared hope in the summer of 1964 that he would be the vice-presidential candidate. In March, President Johnson had told Humphrey that Humphrey was the kind of man he would like to have as a running mate. But the President had made it clear that this was no promise. Humphrey had replied at the time that he would not, on his own initiative, bring the matter up again. As he told friends, his attitude was "He (the President) knows me. I'm here."

This attitude prevailed until the time the President eliminated Bobby Kennedy and the other Cabinet members from the race. On the night Johnson made his television announcement Humphrey was visited by James Rowe, a mutual friend of the Minnesota senator and the President. Rowe brought a message—unofficial, but sent at the President's instigation. If Humphrey wanted to be Johnson's running mate, he would have to make it clear to the President that he intended to be a totally committed Johnson man as Vice President. Only then did Hubert Humphrey take the initiative in seeking the vice-presidential nomination. He phoned Johnson immediately, explained that he understood the meaning of the televised announcement and pledged that, if the President chose him, he would be 100-per-cent loyal to Johnson as Vice President. Johnson thanked him but made no commitment.

Polls taken for the President indicated Humphrey would be the most attractive vote-getter of the potential candidates who had not been eliminated by Johnson's statement of July 30. Statements of support for Humphrey were given to the President by important Democratic leaders. Bobby Kennedy and his closest associates lined up unanimously behind Humphrey.

The President began leaning noticeably toward Humphrey. He secretly had political aides check on virtually every facet of Humphrey's life to be certain there were no hidden skeletons that might later prove embarrassing. The investigation disclosed not a single skeleton.

Still, Johnson did not come right out and say that Humphrey was his choice. He let the word be spread that Humphrey faced stiff competition for the nomination from his fellow Minnesota senator, Eugene McCarthy.

The evidence indicates Johnson did so for two reasons. First, talk of such competition would heighten suspense and interest concerning a political convention that otherwise might be rather dull (since the identity of the presidential nominee was already known). Second, the President wanted to keep open his option to switch to McCarthy or some other vice-presidential candidate if the need arose.

When the convention opened in Atlantic City, New Jersey, Johnson was still playing a cat-and-mouse game over the nomination. He seemed to revel in the attention focused upon him as he pondered the question back at the White House. This attention emphasized that he was in absolute control of the convention and the party. To compound the drama, Johnson decided late in the game to let the name of Senate Majority Leader Mike Mansfield be added to those of Humphrey and McCarthy as potential candidates.

While the delegates were proceeding with the preliminary phases of the convention in Atlantic City, Johnson was releasing bits of information to the press corps in Washington. These dribs and drabs were given to the reporters in an extraordinary series of mobile press conferences as the President led panting newsmen on walking tours of the White House lawn. On Monday, August 24, Johnson said he had still not made up his mind about a running mate. But he did provide the press with some thoughts on what his vice president should be—a man capable of assuming the Presidency; a man who would be given more responsibility and prestige than any vice president in history; a man who would be a full working partner of the President; a man who would be responsible for matters concerning the space program, foreign affairs and civil rights.

Two days later the President disclosed that he was asking Humphrey to leave Atlantic City and fly to Washington to meet with him. The President wanted Humphrey to be aware of certain other conditions. His vice president must not argue publicly with the President; he must clear all speech texts with the White House; he must not lobby within the administration for any special groups or interests; and, while he could debate vigorously with the President or any other administration official before a decision was made, he must publicly support the administration on every policy.

By the time he received the message at the convention to fly to Washington, Humphrey was reasonably sure he would be the nominee. Just that morning Senator McCarthy had withdrawn from contention. Nonetheless, the suspense was getting to Humphrey. His tension was not helped any by the fact that Johnson had also invited Senator Thomas J. Dodd of Connecticut.

A new flurry of excitement erupted over Dodd's inclusion in the invitation. Was Johnson seriously considering him as a running mate? The President was being so mysterious that nobody could be sure. Evidently, Johnson was intent on squeezing every last ounce of suspense out of the decision.

When Humphrey and Dodd arrived in Washington, they were met at the airport by Jack Valenti, a presidential aide. He explained that the President wanted to avoid having their arrival coincide with Mrs. Johnson's televised arrival in Atlantic City. Thus, for almost an hour, the three men killed time by riding around the capital. When they finally arrived at the

White House, they waited outside in the car for about twenty minutes to be greeted by the President. Humphrey, exhausted, fell asleep. He was awakened by a tapping on the car window.

"Hubert, come on in," said the President of the United States.

Humphrey, Dodd and Johnson—surrounded by reporters and photographers—entered the White House. Dodd conferred privately first with the President. Then Humphrey was called into Johnson's office. The President put his arm around Humphrey and asked: "Hubert, how would you like to be my Vice President?"

The decision had been made. But Johnson and Humphrey proceeded to have perhaps the most frank and searching discussion of the vice presidency ever conducted between a presidential and vice-presidential candidate.

Johnson said he had done research on the vice presidency while serving in the office and had found not a single president who had gotten along with his vice president for very long. He and Humphrey had always got along well and he wanted them to continue to do so while heading the government. Humphrey agreed with this sentiment, as he did with everything Johnson said during the discussion. Johnson said he would want Humphrey to play a major role in such fields as agriculture, health, education and welfare—in addition to the previously discussed fields of civil rights, foreign affairs and space exploration. He would also want Humphrey to take a key role in maintaining the health of the Democratic Party—campaigning for party candidates, making speeches and helping raise campaign funds. To all this Humphrey readily agreed and pledged complete loyalty to the President.

All that was left was the formality of having the convention nominate Johnson for President and Humphrey for Vice President. Johnson broke precedent by going before the convention and, in effect, placing Humphrey's name in nomination. But it was clearly Johnson's convention and nobody seemed to mind. The delegates seemed delighted to have something un-usual liven up the convention. Both candidates were nomi-nated without opposition.

The campaign's outcome was never in doubt. The Republi-cans had nominated two representatives of their party's right wing, Senator Barry Goldwater of Arizona and Congressman William Miller of upstate New York. Some observers said this ticket, and the conservative platform that went with it, repre-sented the Republican Party's "gratification of the death wish." No concessions were made to the liberal or moderate sectors of the party. As a result, a number of influential Re-publicans refused to support the ticket.

By contrast the Democrats were united. Humphrey cam-paigned effectively throughout the country, even in areas of the South where he had been an unpopular figure. Goldwater aimed many of his most bitter attacks at the Minnesota sena-tor's liberal record, and delighted in referring to Humphrey as "Hubert Horatio" or just plain "Horatio."

The result was the worst debacle—and, conversely, the greatest triumph—in the history of presidential politics. The Johnson-Humphrey ticket was elected by a record margin of 16,951,220 votes out of 70,621,479 cast. More voters turned out than in any previous election. More voted for Johnson and Humphrey (43,126,218) than any ticket in history. And the victory percentage (61 per cent) was the greatest in history.

Lyndon Johnson had his landslide and his mandate. He also had, for the first time, a Vice President.

Hubert Humphrey became precisely the sort of Vice Presi-dent he had promised Lyndon Johnson he would be. He showed complete loyalty to the President and his programs. He put his vast energy and talent to work on a myriad of na-tional problems. No vice president in history, not even Rich-ard Nixon, was used by his President in such a broad variety of roles.

The perpetual-motion-machine Humphrey of Senate days was a pale shadow of the Humphrey who held the vice presi dency. Constantly on the go—delivering a speech here, persuading a senator there, mediating a dispute elsewhere—he never seemed to slow his pace. President Johnson kept his promise to give his Vice President more responsibility than anyone who had ever held the office.

In addition to presiding over the Senate and attending meetings of the Cabinet, the National Security Council and legislative leaders, Humphrey's multitude of duties included serving as chairman of the Space and Peace Corps Councils, coordinator of all federal activities in the civil-rights field, head of the National Advisory Council on anti-poverty programs, chairman of a Cabinet task force on youth and overseer of a program to encourage American and foreign tourists to "See the U.S.A." In addition, he was assigned by Johnson to take on such jobs as devising a new farm policy, serving as the administration liaison man with the nation's mayors and lobbying for Johnson programs on Capitol Hill.

Humphrey became probably the best-informed Vice President in history on the entire scope of government activities. As one White House aide put it in 1966: "If Hubert had to take over the government tonight, there would not be one slip because of lack of information on Humphrey's part. He is in on literally everything."

Humphrey was constantly reminded of the fact that he just might have to take over the government at any moment. The President mused frequently over the subject of his own mortality. In Humphrey's presence he said one day to a newsman: "You be good to your Vice President. He could be your President tomorrow morning." Not long afterward the Vice President was awakened by a Secret Service agent at 2 A.M. and told that the President had just been taken to a hospital. This illness turned out to be just a bad cold, but other ailments were more serious.

In October of 1965 Johnson underwent gall-bladder surgery. In November of 1966 he underwent surgery for removal of a nonmalignant polyp from his throat and for repair of a hernia in the scar left by the gall-bladder operation. On both occasions, under a continuation of the presidential disability agreement first put into effect by President Eisenhower and Vice President Nixon, Humphrey was authorized to exercise presidential powers if an emergency arose during Johnson's incapacitation.

No crisis arose during Johnson's operations. But the fact that Humphrey was in undisputed charge of the government even during these brief periods added another notch to the prestige of the vice presidency.

The Congress finally moved to try to clear up the vagueness in the Constitution concerning presidential disability and succession. Shortly after the assassination of President Kennedy the Senate subcommittee on constitutional amendments opened hearings on these questions. The subcommittee, headed by Senator Birch Bayh of Indiana, produced a draft amendment designed to close the gaps in the Constitution. But, after being passed by the Senate, the proposed amendment died in the House during the 1964 congressional session.

In 1965 the so-called "Bayh Amendment" was revived and received strong backing from President Johnson:

> While we are prepared for the possibility of a President's death, we are all but defenseless against the probability of a President's incapacity by injury, illness, senility or other affliction. A nation bearing the responsibilities we are privileged to bear for our own security—and the security of the free world— cannot justify the appalling gamble of entrusting its security to the immobilized hands or uncomprehending mind of a Commander in chief unable to command.

These were the key provisions of the proposed amendment:

If a president died, resigned or were removed from office, the vice president would become president. If the vice presidency became vacant through death, resignation, removal from office or succession of the vice president to the presidency, the president would appoint a vice president—subject to approval by a majority in each house of Congress. If a president felt incapable of carrying out his powers and duties, he would declare his inability in a letter to the president pro tem of the Senate and the speaker of the House. The vice president would then assume the powers and duties, but not the office, as acting president. The vice president could also declare a presidential inability, with the approval of a majority of the Cabinet or a majority of "such other body as Congress may by law provide," in the absence of a declaration by the president. In such a case, the vice president would become acting president. The president would assume his powers and duties again by declaring his ability to perform them in a letter to the Senate president pro tem and the House speaker. But the vice president—with the agreement of a majority of the Cabinet or some other advisory group designated by Congress —could declare that the inability still continued. In that case, Congress would decide the question. If Congress could not reach agreement by a two-thirds vote within three weeks, the president would automatically assume his powers and duties again.

The "Bayh Amendment," formally entitled the Twenty-fifth Amendment, was eventually passed by Congress on July 6, 1965. In order to become effective, it required ratification by the legislatures of three-fourths of the states. This was finally achieved on February 10, 1967, when Nevada became the thirty-eighth state to ratify. President Johnson said the nation no longer could afford to try to survive a leadership vacuum created by a presidential disability or a vacancy in the vice-presidential office. "In this crisis-ridden era, there is no margin for delay, no possible justification for a vacuum in national leadership," he said. "At last, through the Twenty-fifth Amendment, we have the means of responding to these crises of responsibility."

During the period in which the Twenty-fifth Admendment was under consideration by the state legislatures, it was a measure of Johnson's trust in his Vice President—and also a measure of the evolution of the vice presidency—that the

President chose to leave Humphrey in complete charge of the government during his brief periods of incapacitation.

Johnson declared on numerous occasions the respect he had for the job being done by Humphrey. On one occasion he said:

> The office of the Vice President is now held by a man who has long been in the forefront of America's mighty effort to lead the world toward lasting peace, a man who is valuable to our nation and invaluable to me. He knows more about more things than any man up at the Capitol.

Humphrey described Johnson as his "constituency of one." He once explained:

> The President has demonstrated a great deal of understanding and faith in me and has given me duties that go far beyond the historical pattern. Our relationships are good; they're warm. I am Vice President because he made me Vice President. There are no Humphrey policies, no Humphrey programs. I'm a close adviser and member of the team. There has been a slow but steady growth in the [vice-presidential] office. I think there's been a change particularly in the degree of responsibility the Vice President now has and the intensity and volume of work that falls on him, that flows from the President. Each Vice President has added something to the office, and I hope I have.

A brief look at some of the responsibilities that "flowed from the President" to Humphrey establishes clearly that he did, indeed, add something to the vice-presidential office. One could hardly pick up a newspaper without finding an article about Humphrey performing one duty or another that went beyond the scope of assignments given most previous vice presidents.

ITEM: When U Thant insisted in 1966 that he planned to leave his post as Secretary General of the United Nations, Humphrey was sent by the President to try to persuade him to accept another term. Johnson felt Thant's continued service was essential to the future progress of the UN. Thant eventually agreed to remain. Many other international statesmen made similar requests, but the fact that Johnson gave Humphrey this assignment underscored the Vice President's emerging role in world affairs.

ITEM: When racial violence threatened to erupt in Bogalusa, Louisiana, Humphrey helped bring about a truce between civil-rights leaders and city officials. The Vice President, after paying a visit to Louisiana at the President's request, was asked by Governor John J. McKeithen to try to head off threatened demonstrations by militant Negro groups. Humphrey persuaded the civil-rights groups to call off their demonstrations and submit their grievances to mediation.

ITEM: When Johnson visited war-torn Vietnam and other Asian countries late in 1966, Humphrey was assigned to stay at home and "mind the store." This assignment had more than the usual caretaker connotations, for the congressional elections were approaching. With Johnson out of the country, the major share of campaigning for Democratic candidates fell to Humphrey.

ITEM: Humphrey was dispatched on his own tour of Asia to confer with officials of nine nations on steps to improve economic, social and health conditions in the Far East. Johnson had previously laid down broad policy guidelines for these improvement programs, which were to be carried out with American aid. But it was left to Humphrey and other officials who accompanied him to work out the details and get the programs into operation.

ITEM: When Johnson's Vietnam policy was under sharp attack, particularly from the nation's liberals, Humphrey assumed major responsibility for trying to win support of the administration's views. This brought the Vice President bitter criticism from some of his former liberal friends, who opposed American involvement in the Vietnam war. But the Vice

President stood fast. "I'm not quite manageable on the Vietnam issue and a lot of my liberal friends resent it," he said. "But I don't think a liberal proves he's liberal by sitting around and blinking his eyes at acts of terror."

ITEM: Humphrey was assigned by Johnson to take charge of a program aimed at finding jobs for 500,000 unemployed teenagers. And it was Humphrey who supervised a program designed to prevent an additional 900,000 teen-agers from dropping out of school. These were only two of numerous duties given the Vice President in connection with the problems of the young and the poverty-stricken.

ITEM: Humphrey conferred at length in India with Soviet Premier Aleksei Kosygin on a broad range of cold-war issues. He returned with a keen analysis of the Russian leader for Johnson, who had not previously met Kosygin.

Humphrey and Johnson had occasional misunderstandings or strained relations. Once, Humphrey assured a group of labor leaders that the administration was going to ask for an increase in the minimum wage. Johnson commented sarcastically: "I see by the papers that I have a minimum-wage program." When former British Prime Minister Winston Churchill died, there was a stir in the press over the fact that Johnson did not send Humphrey to represent the United States at the funeral. Humphrey shrugged the matter off, but intimates said he was hurt by the affair. Johnson told the press: "I served as Vice President for three years, and it never occurred to me . . . that it was the duty and the function of the Vice President to be present at all official funerals." By and large, however, Johnson and Humphrey got along as well as any other President and Vice President in history.

Hardly a day went by that Johnson was not on the phone several times to Humphrey—to get his advice, to test ideas on him or to get inside information from Capitol Hill. Often the two men discussed government problems over breakfast. And it was not uncommon for Humphrey to cancel a long-scheduled appointment with someone else to rush to the White House in response to a hurry call from the President.

It is too early to reach a final assessment on Humphrey's contribution to the vice presidency. But it is already apparent that he succeeded in continuing the expansion of the scope of the office. How much of an expansion will result from his efforts must await a later judgment.

It is also too early to know what will be the future of Hubert Humphrey himself. From the time of Johnson and Humphrey's election in 1964 until early 1968, it was assumed by many political observers that both would stand for reelection. But then, in the spring of 1968, Johnson astounded the world by announcing that he would neither seek nor accept renomination.

Johnson had been under heavy fire from many quarters, including influential members of his own party, on such issues as the Vietnam war and the deepening crisis in American cities. His withdrawal statement, issued on March 31, conceded that there was sharp division in the country and appealed for unity.

"What we won when all of our people united just must not now be lost in suspicion and distrust and selfishness and politics among any of our people," Johnson said. "And believing this as I do I have concluded that I should not permit the presidency to become involved in the partisan divisions that are developing in this political year. With American sons in the fields far away, with America's future under challenge right here at home, with our hopes and the world's hopes for peace in the balance every day, I do not believe that I should devote an hour or a day of my time to any personal partisan causes or to any duties other than the awesome duties of this office—the presidency of your country. Accordingly, I shall not seek, and I will not accept, the nomination of my party for another term as your President."

The three leading contenders for the Democratic presidential nomination, following Johnson's withdrawal, were Humphrey, Robert F. Kennedy (who had been elected to the Senate from New York in 1964) and Senator Eugene Mc-

Carthy of Minnesota. Kennedy, after winning several of the primaries, was assassinated in Los Angeles on the night of his victory in the California primary. At the convention, which was marred by violence involving antiwar demonstrators in the streets of Chicago, Humphrey was nominated. Chosen as his running mate was Senator Edmund Muskie of Maine.

On the Republican side, former Vice President Richard M. Nixon easily won the presidential nomination. He picked as his vice-presidential candidate a man virtually unknown to most American voters, Maryland Governor Spiro T. Agnew. During the campaign, Agnew made several highly publicized blunders—including referring to a newsman of Japanese decent as a "fat Jap" and using the word "Polack" to describe Americans of Polish heritage. But he also proved to be a vigorous, hard-hitting campaigner. If his presence on the ticket did not add appreciably to the Republican strength, it did not hurt the party either.

The race was tight, with the Nixon-Agnew ticket staving off a strong Democratic surge as Election Day approached. The Republican victory achieved for Nixon his long-desired goal of capturing the presidency. Agnew entered the vice presidency as a man associated largely in the public mind with campaign blunders and jokes asserting that he was a political nonentity.

But Nixon made it clear early in the game that he wanted his Vice President to continue to expand the duties and prestige of the nation's second-highest office. Within three weeks of entering the White House, Nixon created a new Office of Intergovernmental Relations, with Agnew as its head. The office was assigned to supervise relations between the federal government and state and local governments. Agnew soon became a leading lobbyist within the administration for programs of particular interest to the nation's governors and mayors. Nixon also underscored his confidence in Agnew by leaving him in temporary charge of the government scarcely a month after taking office while the President made a diplomatic trip to Europe. No previous President had ever taken such a trip abroad so early in his administration, and although Agnew was not required to make any momentous decisions during this period, his role as minder of the Washington store added to his prestige at an opportune time.

Later, Agnew was assigned by Nixon to serve as the administration's chief spokesman at functions designed to maintain Republican Party strength during the years between national elections. Agnew became a star attraction at the party's fund-raising events. Some party officials said they found it easier to sell tickets for dinners at which Agnew was to speak than at those featuring Nixon. The Vice President's speeches were invariably pungent and controversial. In one, he attacked the nation's news media for what he contended was biased coverage. The speech created a furor, with some spokesmen for the news media claiming that Agnew favored news censorship. In other speeches, Agnew lashed out at antiwar demonstrators, Democratic politicians, ardent racial integrationists and other targets destined to make him a favorite of conservative voters. He also made highly publicized and effective trips abroad on behalf of the administration.

By early 1970 a Gallup Poll disclosed that, at least among those surveyed, Agnew was the third most admired man in America—trailing only President Nixon and evangelist Billy Graham. No previous Vice President had ever placed so high in the ratings. Some observers, including former presidential candidate Barry Goldwater, predicted that Agnew would be the Republican presidential nominee in 1976. Some Republican strategists even argued that he would be a stronger presidential candidate in 1972 than Nixon.

Although he continued to be the butt of jokes, Agnew was far from the unknown he had been when nominated for the vice presidency. His name was a household word, and his activities—controversial as some of them were—focused great attention on the office of Vice President. It seemed clear that, once again, a man chosen for the nation's second-highest office was destined to keep the vice presidency from fading into obscurity.

GREAT AMERICANS AND THEIR AWARDS   255

Epilogue

WHEN Thomas Jefferson was elected Vice President, he said he looked upon the office as one that would make few demands on either his time or his energy. "It will give me philosophical evenings in the winter and rural days in the summer. The second office of the government is honorable and easy."

Jefferson would hardly recognize the vice presidency today. The present occupant of the office is far too busy for philosophical evenings or leisurely rural days. He works an average of fourteen hours a day all year round. His speechmaking alone takes more time than some previous vice presidents devoted to all their official activities. Spiro Agnew and Hubert Humphrey each got between 800 and 1,000 letters and about 250 telephone calls every week inviting them to deliver speeches in various parts of the country—not to mention letters and calls on other subjects. Humphrey sometimes traveled farther in one week on official business than many previous vice presidents traveled in an entire year. During one typical period of a few days in 1966, Humphrey went from Washington, D. C., to the United Nations in New York, then to New Jersey, Indiana, Minnesota, California, Oregon, Washington and Montana. He had an Air Force jet at his disposal for long-distance trips, and government limousines for short hauls.

In Washington he and Agnew kept staffs of forty-five busy in three different offices—one at the Capitol, one in the Senate

Office Building and one at the Executive Office Building near the White House. Agnew is paid $62,500 a year in salary, plus $10,000 for expenses (compared with the $5,000 total paid the first Vice President, John Adams). Agnew, or some other future Vice President, will one day live in an official mansion. In 1966 Congress authorized expenditure of $750,000 for such a mansion (nicknamed the "Veepee Tepee" by Washington wags). Although President Johnson ruled out immediate expenditure of these funds on the ground that the Vietnam war and domestic programs required spending cutbacks in nonessential fields, it seems certain that the government will eventually provide its vice presidents with an official residence.

The obvious question concerning the vice presidency today is: Where does it go from here? The equally obvious answer seems to be that the office is bound to continue increasing in prestige and responsibility. Vice Presidents of the caliber of Richard Nixon, Lyndon Johnson, Hubert Humphrey and Spiro Agnew are unlikely to be followed by men of much lesser stature. Responsibilities assigned to vice presidents during the middle of the twentieth century are unlikely to be snatched away in the twenty-first century. If anything, future vice presidents will probably be given even more important duties than those of the present day.

Numerous suggestions have been made in recent years for increasing the functions of the vice president by law. Some qualified observers have recommended the addition of a second vice president, so that one man could carry on the traditional functions of the office and the other could serve as the president's chief administrative aide. Former President Herbert Hoover proposed before a Senate subcommittee in 1956 that Congress create by statute the office of Administrative Vice President. Richard Nixon suggested in his 1960 presidential campaign the naming of the vice president as "first offi-

cer" of the executive branch, with responsibility for coordinat-
ing all activities dealing with international affairs.

Congress has been reluctant to take the lead in assigning
additional duties to the vice president. There is still a possibility that future presidents and vice presidents may come to
disagree widely on basic policy matters. In such cases, a president would be severely handicapped if compelled by law to
give his vice president jurisdiction over programs on which
they differed. It is still theoretically possible, under the Constitution, for a president and a vice president from different
parties to be elected simultaneously. If the Electoral College
fails to give any presidential candidate a majority, the House
of Representatives is empowered to elect a president from
among the men receiving the three highest totals in the Electoral College. In such a case the Senate would choose a vice
president from the top two vice-presidential candidates in the
Electoral College. If the House were controlled by one party
and the Senate by another, or if other unusual political circumstances prevailed, the nation might once again be headed
by a president and a vice president from differing parties.
Factionalism within parties might, as well, provide serious
difficulties were a rural conservative to be paired with an urban
liberal.

The wisest course of action would seem to be to continue
permitting each president to decide how he can best use the
particular talents of his vice president. Under this system, we
have seen the vice presidency rise from a position of relative
obscurity to one of high responsibility. There is every reason to
believe this trend will continue—and perhaps even be accelerated—in the future.

No system can guarantee that able men will always be
elected to the vice presidency or that the maximum use will be
made of each vice president's abilities. But that is also true of
the presidency. Nothing in life, much less in politics, is
certain.

However, if the recent trend continues, it does seem almost certain that no future vice president need worry about being seriously compared with the hapless Vice President of the Broadway Stage, Alexander Throttlebottom. For Throttlebottom, and his real-life models, seem to be gone forever.

⊷⊱⊰⊶

Bibliography

ANY CONTEMPORARY writer who deals with the vice presidency owes a great debt to DONALD YOUNG, author of *American Roulette: The History and Dilemma of the Vice Presidency* (New York, 1965). Of all the books written on the vice presidency in the past, Mr. Young's is the most readable and authoritative.

Other general works related to the subject, which may be of interest to readers of this book, include:

DISALLE, MICHAEL, *Second Choice*. New York, 1966.

HARWOOD, MICHAEL, *In the Shadow of Presidents: The American Vice Presidency and Succession System*. Philadelphia and New York, 1966. (For readers aged 12 to 16.)

HATCH, LOUIS C., and SHOUP, EARL L., *A History of the Vice Presidency of the United States*. New York, 1934.

LEVIN, PETER R., *Seven By Chance: The Accidental Presidents*. New York, 1948.

SILVA, RUTH C., *Presidential Succession*. Ann Arbor, Michigan, 1951.

TOMPKINS, DOROTHY C., *The Office of Vice President: A Selected Bibliography*. Berkeley, California, 1957.

WILLIAMS, IRVING G., *The Rise of the Vice Presidency*. Washington, 1956.

Books dealing with the broad scope of American political life, which proved most helpful in preparation of this work, include:

BROGAN, D. W., *Politics in America*. Garden City, New York, 1960.

DAVID, PAUL T.; GOLDMAN, RALPH M.; and BAIN, RICHARD C.; *The*

Politics of National Party Conventions. Revised ed. New York, 1964.

DUMOND, DWIGHT LOWELL, *America in Our Time.* New York, 1947.

HARLOW, RALPH VOLNEY, *The United States: From Wilderness to World Power.* New York, 1949.

HOFSTADTER, RICHARD, *The American Political Tradition.* New York, 1948.

ROSSITER, CLINTON, *The American Presidency.* Revised ed. New York, 1960.

STONE, IRVING, *They Also Ran.* Revised ed. New York, 1964.

TUGWELL, REXFORD G., *How They Became President: Thirty-five Ways to the White House.* New York, 1964.

Following, in the chronological order in which they were used for reference purposes in the preparation of this book, are works concerning individuals whose careers are of special interest:

ADAMS, JOHN, *Diary and Autobiography of John Adams.* Cambridge, 1961.

———, *The Works of John Adams.* Boston, 1850–1856.

SMITH, PAGE, *John Adams.* Garden City, New York, 1962.

MALONE, DUMAS, *Jefferson the Virginian.* Boston, 1948.

———, *Jefferson and the Rights of Man.* Boston, 1951.

———, *Jefferson and the Ordeal of Liberty.* Boston, 1962.

PARTON, JAMES, *The Life and Times of Aaron Burr.* New York, 1858.

WANDELL, SAMUEL H., and MINNIGERODE, MEADE, *Aaron Burr.* New York, 1925.

AUSTIN, JAMES T., *The Life of Elbridge Gerry.* Boston, 1829.

TOMPKINS, DANIEL D., *Public Papers of Daniel D. Tompkins.* New York, 1902.

CALHOUN, JOHN C., *The Life of John C. Calhoun.* New York, 1843.

COIT, MARGARET L., *John C. Calhoun.* Boston, 1950.

WILTSE, CHARLES M., *John C. Calhoun, Nullifier.* Indianapolis, 1949.

BUTLER, WILLIAM ALLEN, *Martin Van Buren.* New York, 1862.

LYNCH, DENIS TILDEN, *An Epoch and a Man: Martin Van Buren and His Times.* New York 1929.

VAN BUREN, MARTIN, *The Autobiography of Martin Van Buren.* Washington, 1920.

MEYER, LELAND W., *The Life and Times of Colonel Richard M. Johnson of Kentucky.* New York, 1932.

CHITWOOD, OLIVER P., *John Tyler: Champion of the Old South.* New York, 1939.

SEAGER, ROBERT T., II, *And Tyler Too.* New York, 1963.

GRIFFIS, WILLIAM E., *Millard Fillmore.* Ithaca, New York, 1915.

RAYBACK, ROBERT J., *Millard Fillmore.* Buffalo, New York, 1959.

JACKSON, WALTER M., *Alabama's First U.S. Vice President: William Rufus King.* Decatur, Alabama, 1952.

STILLWELL, LUCILLE, *John Cabell Breckinridge.* Caldwell, Indiana, 1936.

HAMLIN, CHARLES E., *The Life and Times of Hannibal Hamlin.* Cambridge, 1899.

LOMASK, MILTON, *Andrew Johnson: President on Trial.* New York, 1960.

STRYKER, LLOYD P., *Andrew Johnson: A Study in Courage.* New York, 1929.

SMITH, WILLARD H., *Schuyler Colfax.* Indianapolis, 1952.

MANN, JONATHAN, *The Life of Henry Wilson.* Boston, 1872.

NASON, ELIAS, and RUSSELL, THOMAS, *The Life and Public Services of Henry Wilson.* Boston, 1876.

BARNUM, AUGUSTIN, *The Lives of Grover Cleveland and Thomas A. Hendricks.* Hartford, 1884.

STEVENSON, ADLAI E., *Something of Men I Have Known.* Chicago, 1909.

MAGIE, DAVID, *Life of Garret A. Hobart.* New York, 1910.

BUTT, ARCHIBALD W., *Taft and Roosevelt.* Garden City, New York, 1930.

PRINGLE, HENRY F., *Theodore Roosevelt: A Biography.* New York, 1931.

MARSHALL, THOMAS R., *Recollections of Thomas R. Marshall.* Indianapolis, 1925.

ROLLINS, ALFRED B., JR., *Woodrow Wilson and the New America.* New York, 1965.

SMITH, GENE, *When the Cheering Stopped: The Last Years of Woodrow Wilson*. New York, 1964.

THOMAS, CHARLES M., *Thomas Riley Marshall*. Oxford, Ohio, 1939.

COOLIDGE, CALVIN, *The Autobiography of Calvin Coolidge*. New York, 1929.

———, *Have Faith in Massachusetts*. Boston, 1919.

LATHEM, EDWARD, *Meet Calvin Coolidge*. Brattleboro, Vermont, 1960.

DAWES, CHARLES GATES, *Notes as Vice President*. Boston, 1935.

TIMMONS, BASCOM N., *Portrait of an American: Charles G. Dawes*. New York, 1953.

———, *Garner of Texas, A Personal History*. New York, 1948.

JAMES, MARQUIS, *Mr. Garner of Texas*. Indianapolis, 1939.

SCHLESINGER, ARTHUR M., JR., *The Crisis of the Old Order*. Boston, 1957.

———, *The Coming of the New Deal*. Boston, 1958.

———, *The Politics of Upheaval*. Boston, 1960.

MACDONALD, DWIGHT, *Henry Wallace: The Man and the Myth*. New York, 1947.

GUNTHER, JOHN, *Roosevelt in Retrospect*. New York, 1950.

ALLEN, GEORGE E., *Presidents Who Have Known Me*. New York, 1950.

TRUMAN, HARRY S, *Memoirs*. Garden City, New York, 1955–1956.

BARKLEY, ALBEN B., *That Reminds Me*. Garden City, New York, 1954.

BARKLEY, JANE R., *I Married the Veep*. New York, 1958.

ADAMS, SHERMAN, *Firsthand Report*. New York, 1961.

DE TOLEDANO, RALPH, *Nixon*. New York, 1956.

EISENHOWER, DWIGHT D., *Mandate for Change: 1953–1956*. Garden City, New York, 1963.

HUGHES, EMMET JOHN, *The Ordeal of Power*. New York, 1962.

MAZO, EARL, *Richard Nixon: A Political and Personal Portrait*. New York, 1959.

NIXON, RICHARD M., *Six Crises*. Garden City, New York, 1962.

ROVERE, RICHARD H., *Affairs of State: The Eisenhower Years*. New York, 1956.

WHITE, THEODORE H., *The Making of the President 1960*. New York, 1961.

MOONEY, BOOTH, *The Lyndon Johnson Story*. New York, 1956.

NEWLON, CLARK, *L.B.J., The Man from Johnson City*. New York, 1964.

WHITE, WILLIAM S., *The Professional: Lyndon B. Johnson*. Boston, 1964.

ZEIGER, HENRY A., *Lyndon B. Johnson: Man and President*. New York, 1963.

EVANS, ROWLAND, and NOVAK, ROBERT, *Lyndon B. Johnson: The Exercise of Power*. New York, 1966.

WHITE, THEODORE H., *The Making of the President 1964*. New York, 1965.

BAKER, LEONARD, *The Johnson Eclipse: A President's Vice Presidency*. New York, 1966.

AMRINE, MICHAEL, *This Is Humphrey*. Garden City, New York, 1960.

Index